Reimagining the Promised Land

Reimagining the Promised Land

Israel and America in Post-war Hollywood Cinema

Rodney Wallis

BLOOMSBURY ACADEMIC
NEW YORK • LONDON • OXFORD • NEW DELHI • SYDNEY

BLOOMSBURY ACADEMIC
Bloomsbury Publishing Inc
1385 Broadway, New York, NY 10018, USA
29 Earlsfort Terrace, Dublin 2, Ireland

BLOOMSBURY, BLOOMSBURY ACADEMIC and the Diana logo
are trademarks of Bloomsbury Publishing Plc

First published in the United States of America 2020
This paperback edition published 2022

Copyright © Rodney Wallis, 2020

For legal purposes the Acknowledgments on p. vii constitute
an extension of this copyright page.

Photograph © Mary Evans Picture Library

All rights reserved. No part of this publication may be reproduced or
transmitted in any form or by any means, electronic or mechanical,
including photocopying, recording, or any information storage or retrieval
system, without prior permission in writing from the publishers.

Bloomsbury Publishing Inc does not have any control over, or responsibility for,
any third-party websites referred to or in this book. All internet addresses given
in this book were correct at the time of going to press. The author and publisher
regret any inconvenience caused if addresses have changed or sites have
ceased to exist, but can accept no responsibility for any such changes.

Library of Congress Cataloging-in-Publication Data
Names: Wallis, Rodney, author.
Title: Reimagining the promised land : Israel and America in post-war
Hollywood cinema / Rodney Wallis.
Description: New York : Bloomsbury Academic, [2020] | Includes
bibliographical references and index.
Identifiers: LCCN 2020009210 | ISBN 9781501350825 (hardback) | ISBN
9781501350849 (pdf) | ISBN 9781501350832 (ebook)
Subjects: LCSH: Israel–In motion pictures. | National characteristics,
American, in motion pictures. | Motion pictures–United
States–History–20th century.
Classification: LCC PN1995.9.I72 W35 2020 | DDC 791.43/652924–dc23
LC record available at https://lccn.loc.gov/2020009210

ISBN: HB: 978-1-5013-5082-5
PB: 978-1-5013-7385-5
ePDF: 978-1-5013-5084-9
eBook: 978-1-5013-5083-2

Typeset by Integra Software Services Pvt. Ltd.,

To find out more about our authors and books visit www.bloomsbury.com
and sign up for our newsletters.

An immense thank you to Jodi Brooks for her years of guidance, patience, and encouragement. Extra special thanks to Jenn Mak, without whom nothing is possible.

Contents

List of Figures		viii
Introduction: The United States and Israel: Parallel promised lands		1
1	'God's Chosen People': America as Israel in the fifties' Cold War epic	13
2	A new frontier: The birth of Israel as frontier myth in *Exodus* (1960)	49
3	The age of interventionism: American heroism in *Cast a Giant Shadow* (1966)	75
4	Rise and fall: Israel and America in counterterrorist cinema, 1977–86	101
5	The 'War on Terror' in *Munich* (2005)	137
Conclusion		161
Notes		174
Bibliography		206
Index		225

List of Figures

1.1	Moses (Charlton Heston) strikes a pose reminiscent of the Statue of Liberty	23
1.2	Moses as Christ figure	25
1.3	Judah (Charlton Heston) wears the crown of thorns	29
1.4	The light catches Judah's Star of David	29
1.5	Pontius Pilate (Frank Thring) gives the 'Roman salute.'	31
1.6	The physically imposing Moses in three-quarter shot	35
1.7	The effeminized Rameses (Yul Brynner)	37
1.8	Judah as Christ figure	39
1.9	The 'starving' Messala (Stephen Boyd) lovingly stares into the eyes of his boyhood friend	42
2.1	Ari Ben Canaan (Paul Newman) and Kitty Fremont (Eva Marie Saint) look over the Promised Land of the Jezreel Valley in *Exodus*	59
2.2	Julie Maragon (Jean Simmons) and James McKay (Gregory Peck) look over the Promised Land of the American West in *The Big Country* (William Wyler, 1958)	59
2.3	Ari Ben Canaan makes his grand entrance out of the Mediterranean	61
2.4	Major Caldwell (Peter Lawford) unwittingly looks into the eyes of a Jew	64
2.5	Kitty with Karen (Jill Haworth), her young Israeli clone	65
3.1	Mickey Marcus (Kirk Douglas) stands over the Israeli Prime Minister Jacob Zion (Luther Adler)	85
3.2	Marcus plays the role of the heroic American 'advisor.'	86
3.3	Kirk Douglas stands over Yul Brynner	88
4.1	The distinctly non-Arab Dahlia Iyad (Marthe Keller)	105
4.2	A tortured Lander confesses to his (and America's) crimes	114
4.3	Kabakov (Robert Shaw) encounters the bathing Dahlia	121
4.4	Muzi (Michael V. Gazzo) sucks on Kabakov's revolver	124
5.1	A Black September member looks down from the balcony attached to the Israelis' room in the Olympic village	141

5.2 The Mossad hitmen on a steam-soaked platform in *Munich* 144
5.3 Palestinians cheering the Munich massacre 149
5.4 The opening credits of *Munich*, with 'New York' positioned conspicuously near the centre of the frame 154
5.5 The closing shot of *Munich*, against the backdrop of the then intact World Trade Center towers 157

Introduction

The United States and Israel: Parallel promised lands

Film historian Robert Burgoyne argues that 'In its range and coverage of the field of national imaginings, the Hollywood cinema is in many ways an unparalleled expression of national culture, one that has molded the self-image of the nation in pervasive and explicit ways.'[1] Crucially, Burgoyne argues that Hollywood's fostering of an idealized notion of American national identity is achieved not purely through the projection of the positive and organic traits that reinforce the notion of the United States' supposed 'exceptionalism,' but through the deployment of 'oppositional logic' that explicitly contrasts Americanism with an undesirable image of the feared and hated Other. Burgoyne refers to this form of identity construction as 'identity from across,' as an idealized notion of American identity emerges out of an inherent opposition to everything that it is ostensibly not.[2]

Hollywood's deployment of oppositional logic in its construction of American identity dates back to the earliest days of American film production. Throughout the first few decades of the twentieth century, the Western would emerge as 'the first truly cinematic genre and the first distinctively American contribution to the new art form.'[3] Early cinematic Westerns essentially perpetuated the traditions established by early frontier mythology, in which, to quote cultural historian Richard Slotkin, the Indians' presence remained 'necessary to the revelation of the heroic stature of the Anglo-American hero. The Indian is his foil, the opponent against whom he exercises and develops his heroic powers as a representative of civilization.'[4] As a result, one of the defining tropes of early American cinema was its frequent deployment of the image of the Native American as a savage racial Other against which Euro-American civilization was unequivocally valorized. Ultimately, Hollywood's invocation of frontier mythology in its construction of American national identity would transcend the Western genre; for instance,

Slotkin has detailed how overtly nationalist genres such as the wartime combat film repeatedly constructed Asiatic enemies as demonic racial aliens in a manner that distinctly echoed the language of the traditional Hollywood Western.[5]

Hollywood's deployment of oppositional logic in its construction of an idealized conception of Americanism goes beyond the invocation of frontier mythology. Political scientist Michael Rogin, who has written extensively on the centrality of what he terms the 'demonological impulse' to the construction of American political identity, positions the silent epic *The Birth of a Nation* (D.W. Griffith, 1915) – a film which in both title and content purports to tell the story of the birth of the modern American nation – as a landmark exemplar of oppositional logic at play, through its presentation of Anglo-Saxon 'purity' being under attack from barbarous liberated slaves.[6] Oppositional logic would continue to play a key role in Hollywood's construction of American identity throughout the Cold War years (*c.* 1947–91). Tony Shaw has extensively detailed how, during this period, Hollywood frequently constructed an idealized conception of American heroism by juxtaposing American characters who were imbued with innocence, intelligence and copious reserves of courage, against Communists who, whether homegrown, as in *My Son John* (Leo McCarey, 1952), or of Russian origin, as in *Rambo: First Blood Part II* (George P. Cosmatos, 1985), were cowardly, mentally unstable and inhumane.[7]

In more recent times, scholars such as Lina Khatib[8] and Tim Jon Semmerling[9] have argued that contemporary Hollywood cinema has mobilized the image of the Arab as a demonological Other against which is constructed idealized Western identity. Both Khatib and Semmerling position this mobilization as the latest evolutionary step in what Edward Said famously termed 'Orientalism,' which is best understood as the projection of negative attributes onto the Orient and its inhabitants by Western cultural products.[10] According to Said, Orientalist representations principally serve to engender the identity of the West, which Said contends is presented as 'rational, developed, humane, superior,' by constructing it as the binary opposite of the Orient, which is presented as 'aberrant, undeveloped, inferior.'[11] Thus, the Orientalist representations identified by Khatib and Semmerling can be seen as exemplifying Hollywood's tendency to construct identity through an oppositional logic.

The aforementioned scholarship attests to the abundance of literature which examines the ways in which Hollywood constructs American national identity, to quote Burgoyne, 'from across.'[12] However, there has been a notable absence of scholarship that looks at the ways in which Hollywood constructs national identity through sameness and similarity; that is, through the mobilization of images of nations with whom the United States is seen as being politically and/or culturally aligned. Such a process warrants close analysis, as it enables us to achieve a greater understanding of how Hollywood effectively perpetuates dominant myths and ideologies. This book will attempt to fill this lacuna by closely examining how the state of Israel has been imagined and invoked by Hollywood throughout the second half of the twentieth century, and how these representations have consistently functioned to articulate an idealized conception of American political identity. Hollywood's various imaginings of Israel constitute a particularly interesting case study, for Israel is not merely a key ally of the United States; rather, it is a widely accepted truism that the United States of America and the state of Israel are indelibly bound in a manner rarely seen throughout the history of international relations.

The unique relationship between the United States and Israel dates back to the earliest stages of European settlement on the American continent. The Puritans who settled in New England in the early seventeenth century imagined their reformation struggle against the traditional Church as mirroring the persecution of the Jews as told in the Old Testament, while at the same time mythologizing their journey across the Atlantic as a re-enactment of the Hebrew Exodus. As the successors to the children of Israel, the pilgrims' new world of America constituted a new Promised Land for a new 'Chosen People.'[13] As most famously articulated by John Winthrop in his sermon 'A Modell of Christian Charity,' delivered on board the ship *Arabella* while en route to the Massachusetts Bay Colony in 1630, the Puritans, in covenant with God, would establish in America a 'City Upon a Hill' based on moral law that would serve as a model for all the other nations of the world.[14] In the words of historian Eran Shalev, 'This image of an American people chosen for a special destiny was to remain a mainstay of American self-fashioning and negotiation of nationhood for years.'[15]

The notion of a synonymity between Americans and ancient Hebrews would persevere in the colonies up until the establishment of the American nation. Historian Michael B. Oren asserts that 'The colonists' image of themselves as a New Israel attained special poignancy during the War of Independence. Casting King George III in the role of pharaoh and the Atlantic acting as the Red Sea, patriot writers likened George Washington to Moses, and John Adams to Joshua leading the people to freedom.'[16] For further enlightenment on the linking of Jewish and American destinies, one can look to the events surrounding the Declaration of Independence on 4 July 1776. Soon after the adoption of the

Declaration a special committee consisting of Benjamin Franklin, Thomas Jefferson and John Adams – three of the Declaration's five principal authors – was assigned the task of designing a seal for the new nation. Franklin's proposal consisted of the image of 'Moses standing on the Shore, and extending his Hand over the Sea, thereby the same to overwhelm Pharaoh who is sitting in an open Chariot, a Crown on his Head and a Sword in his Hand. Rays from a Pillar of Fire in the Clouds reaching to Moses, to express that he acts by Command of the Deity.'[17] This image would be accompanied by the motto, 'Rebellion to Tyrants is Obedience to God.'[18] Similarly, Thomas Jefferson proposed that one side of the seal feature the children of Israel struggling in the wilderness, led by a cloud and a pillar of fire.[19] While neither suggestion was ultimately adopted, they nevertheless demonstrate the founding fathers' fondness for Jewish mythology, and also, by extension, the historical centrality of the ancient Hebrews to modern America's self-imagining.

The American affinity for Jewish mythology ultimately translated into strong support for the Zionist struggle to establish a national home for the Jews in Palestine. Surveys consistently indicated that Americans were generally in favour of Zionism, particularly in the wake of the Holocaust.[20] Moreover, in the earliest stages of the Zionist campaign for a Jewish state, the US government remained a source of significant and crucial support. In 1944 a resolution was introduced into both the House and the Senate that read, 'Resolved that the United States shall use its good offices and take appropriate measures to the end that the doors of Palestine shall be opened for free entry of Jews in that country, and that there shall be full opportunity for colonization so that the Jewish people may ultimately reconstitute Palestine as a free and democratic Jewish commonwealth.'[21] The Zionist movement would enjoy even greater support from the United States following the death of Franklin Roosevelt and the ascendency of Harry Truman to the presidency. As detailed by Adel Safty, Truman, motivated by a constellation of factors, issued a statement on 4 October 1946 that lent major support to the Zionist programme of partition that assigned 75 per cent of the total area of Palestine to the Jews. This was followed by the application of major pressure from Truman's office on the recently established United Nations to recommend partition. When the issue went to a vote in late 1947, Truman's office pressured several sovereign nations to vote in the affirmative for partition, with the president's advisors allegedly 'threatening hell' if the campaign were to fail.[22] The significance of the United States' influence in the establishment of the state of Israel is attested by the words of Israel's then chief rabbi, who in 1949 told Truman, 'God put you in your mother's womb so that you would be the instrument to bring about the rebirth of Israel after two thousand years.'[23]

The following decade would see a souring of diplomatic relations between the United States and Israel. In the words of historian Douglas Little, 'by the mid-1950s the relationship between the United States and Israel resembled a power struggle between a domineering stepparent and a rebellious stepchild.'[24] The definitive event of this tempestuous period in the US–Israel relationship was the Suez Crisis, which erupted in November 1956. The President of Egypt, Gamal Abdel Nasser, nationalized the Suez Canal Company, and subsequently refused to allow Israeli shipping to pass through the canal. In response, Israel launched a surprise attack on the Sinai Peninsula, with the backing of Britain and France. The US President Dwight D. Eisenhower refused to support the tripartite aggression for a myriad of reasons, foremost among them the desire to safeguard Western access to cheap oil.[25] The United States applied significant pressure on Israel to withdraw from Sinai, which they eventually did in March of 1957. According to Little, 'Although the United States and Israel had avoided an open breach, their bitter clash during early 1957 revealed a level of reciprocal mistrust and diplomatic estrangement that would once have seemed unthinkable but that now seemed unavoidable.'[26]

However, in spite of the US government's opposition to Israeli actions over Suez, American public opinion of Israel remained generally positive. Eytan Gilboa details how polls conducted throughout the crisis and immediately afterwards revealed that 'Israel was seen more as a victim than as an aggressor in the Suez-Sinai crisis.'[27] The widespread sympathy among Americans for Israel throughout the crisis can be seen as, at least in part, a reflection of the greater emphasis placed on the United States' 'Judeo-Christian' heritage, a notion which gained currency largely due to the rise of Christian fundamentalism that marked American life in the 1950s. During this time, the ideal of an inherent kinship between Jewish and Christian 'values' began to take hold in American society. As sociologist Will Herberg explained in his popular 1955 book *Protestant-Catholic-Jew: An Essay in American Religious Sociology*, the three religions referenced in his book's title were 'three diverse, but equally legitimate, equally American, expressions of an over-all American religion, standing for essentially the same "moral ideas" and "spiritual values".'[28] The degree to which the alignment of Jewish and Christian identities in post-war American life impacted relations between the United States and Israel is reflected by President

Lyndon Johnson, who, in toasting Israeli President Zalman Shazar at the White House in 1966, remarked that 'Our Republic, like yours, was nurtured by the philosophy of the ancient Hebrew teachers who taught mankind the principles of morality, of social justice, and of universal peace. This is our heritage, and it is yours.'[29]

At a time when the world was reduced to a polarity in which the 'righteous' West, led by the United States, faced off against the 'atheist tyranny' of the Soviet Union, the supposed kinship between Christians and Jews ensured that Israel would be seen by the United States as a key ally in the Cold War struggle. The alliance would take on even greater significance in the wake of Israel's crushing defeat of its Arab neighbours in the Six Day War of 1967, with Israel subsequently being seen by Washington as the United States' lone reliable friend in a region considered to be of immense strategic importance. Over the ensuing half century, the United States would provide Israel with crucial military support amid a seemingly endless cycle of wars with its Arab neighbours, unyielding diplomatic support amid increasing international consternation regarding Israel's treatment of the displaced Palestinians living within its borders, and seemingly limitless economic support in the form of tremendous amounts of financial aid. The enduring symbiosis between the United States and Israel has come to be known as the 'special relationship,' and it is one that has continued to persevere in spite of ever-changing tides of both American and Israeli politics.

Hitherto, there has been very little attention paid to the ways in which this relationship has played out in Hollywood cinema. A number of studies have examined Hollywood's various representations of the state of Israel; however, they have largely appeared within broader examinations of cinematic representations of the figure of the Jew in both Hollywood and international cinema. Significant studies of cinematic representations of the figure of the Jew include Lester D. Friedman's, *Hollywood's Image of the Jew* (1982), Patricia Erens' *The Jew in American Cinema* (1984), Omer Bartov's *The 'Jew' in Cinema: From the Golem to Don't Touch My Holocaust* (2005), and Nathan Abrams' *The New Jew in Film: Exploring Jewishness and Judaism in Contemporary Cinema* (2012).[30] In these studies the authors present Hollywood's respective imaginings of Israel as symbolic of shifting attitudes towards Jews within the United States, and in turn reflecting the development of the special relationship between the United States and Israel.

This book argues that Hollywood's disparate representations of Israel serve not as a reflection of the special relationship, but rather as an inversion. By this I mean that whereas the special relationship is largely predicated on the United States' essentially unconditional support for Israel, in Hollywood cinema Israel has frequently functioned as an ideological pillar against which is propped up idealized notions of American identity. Ultimately, I will demonstrate that throughout the history of Hollywood Israel has consistently served as a key source of self-imagining for the United States of America.

Methodology and chapter overview

This study unfolds chronologically, beginning with an examination of two films produced within the first decade of Israel's existence as a modern nation state. This chronological approach allows for developments in the cinematic representation of Israel to be seen alongside developments in the social and political life of the United States. Chapter 1 focuses on *The Ten Commandments* (Cecil B. DeMille, 1956) and *Ben-Hur* (William Wyler, 1959), two immensely successful, big-budget epics from the 1950s that centre not on the then recently established state of Israel, but instead the ancient Hebrews' fight for national liberation.[31] Scholars such as Maria Wyke,[32] Martin Winkler,[33] and Sumiko Higashi[34] have identified the postwar cycle of epic cinema that frequently depicted the fundamental clash between freedom and oppression as allegorizing the contemporaneous Cold War conflict between the United States and the Soviet Union. Building on this scholarship, this opening chapter focuses on the ways in which *The Ten Commandments* and *Ben-Hur* deploy the temporal and geographic setting of Biblical Palestine in their respective valorizations of the United States' Cold War identity. Of primary focus is how each film explicitly constructs ancient Hebrews as modern-day Americans, while simultaneously presenting the Hebrews' enslavers – be they Egyptian Pharaohs or Roman elites – as stand-ins for contemporaneous totalitarianisms. As this chapter demonstrates, the product of such constructions is the reaffirmation of the Puritan notion of the American continent as a divinely ordained Promised Land and Americans as 'God's Chosen People.' Moreover, significant cultural capital is afforded to the alignment of American and Jewish identities within the American cultural imaginary.

My analytical approach to both *The Ten Commandments* and *Ben-Hur* is guided by an interest in the relationship between each cinematic text and its respective source material. *The Ten Commandments* draws on the Exodus story from the Bible – the most widely read book in the history of Western civilization. *Ben-Hur* is based on Lew Wallace's novel of the same name, published in 1883.[35] Wallace's *Ben-Hur* was the bestselling American novel from the time of its publication, until the publication of Margaret Mitchell's *Gone with the Wind* in 1936.[36] Both films were also remakes of highly successful films produced during Hollywood's silent era.[37] In my analysis I elucidate how these cinematic texts each engage with the historical moment of their production and exhibition by identifying how they diverge from their source material through invention, excision and distortion, in turn enabling a better understanding of each film's ideological intentions. Many of the films discussed in this study are similarly based on popular source material, and thus this methodological approach prevails throughout. The significance of this opening chapter lies in its serving as a foundation for better understanding Hollywood's subsequent deployments of Israel, which, as will be demonstrated, consistently position the Jewish state as either an ally of or a stand-in for the United States of America.

Chapter 2 focuses on *Exodus* (Otto Preminger, 1960), the first major cinematic treatment of the birth of the Jewish state. *Exodus* was based on an immensely successful novel of the same name by Leon Uris, which was released in 1958.[38] By the time of the film's release the book had been on the bestseller list for 80 weeks, selling over four million copies.[39] Its influence was so profound that, in the words of historian Edward Tivnan, the story of *Exodus* ultimately became 'the primary source of knowledge about Jews and Israel that most Americans had.'[40] Produced so soon after the publication of the book, the collection of filmmaking and acting talent behind the film version of *Exodus* was appropriately prestigious – director Otto Preminger was a two-time Oscar nominee for Best Director, the script was penned by the legendary writer Dalton Trumbo, and the cast featured such iconic Hollywood performers as Paul Newman, Eva Marie Saint, Lee J. Cobb and Sal Mineo. Released on 15 December 1960, *Exodus* claimed the number one spot at the box office during Christmas of that same year, and would go on to be one of the top five box office hits of 1961.[41]

Chapter 2 asserts that *Exodus* positions Israel as a stand-in for the United States by presenting the birth of the Jewish state in language traditionally associated with the United States' frontier mythology. The most significant manifestation of the popular expression of this frontier mythology has undoubtedly been the Hollywood Western. *Exodus* stages the establishment of Israel in the form of a Hollywood Western through the mobilization of images that serve to evoke a number of the genre's central tenets. These images include the fetishization of the Israeli landscape and the positioning of white settlers as its rightful claimant, an Israeli Sabra protagonist (Paul Newman) who is modelled on the cowboy heroes of American frontier myth, his American lover (Eva Marie Saint) who mirrors the 'pure young woman' of so many classic Westerns, and the region's Arab population as marauding barbarians impeding the moving train of Western 'progress.' The mobilization of these generic motifs ultimately succeeds in presenting the outbreak of hostilities between Arabs and Israelis as a savage race war akin to that of the frontier conflict that was so central to the United States' development into nationhood. Furthermore, through a detailed genre analysis, *Exodus* will be positioned in relation to the vicissitudes of the Western genre. As a result, it will be elucidated how, by celebrating Israeli nationhood and presenting its establishment in the manner that mirrors the settling of the American frontier, *Exodus* espouses traditional conceptions of frontier mythology at a time when Westerns were moving away from such narrativizations, and were instead proffering challenges to the America's traditional historical narrative.

Chapter 3 focuses on the film *Cast a Giant Shadow* (Melville Shavelson, 1966), which was based on a bestselling book that detailed the life of Jewish-American soldier Mickey Marcus.[42] *Cast a Giant Shadow* was produced by and featured John Wayne, while also featuring major stars such as Kirk Douglas, Frank Sinatra, Angie Dickinson, Yul Brynner and Senta Berger. After *Exodus*, *Cast a Giant Shadow* is undoubtedly the most notable Hollywood film to centre on the founding of Israel. Though not particularly successful at the box office,[43] *Cast a Giant Shadow* constitutes an interesting case study by virtue of it being produced by Batjac (John Wayne's production company), and due to its presentation of Israel as being not only allied with the United States, but in desperate need of American intervention.

Chapter 3 argues that *Cast a Giant Shadow* is less concerned with the peculiarities of the nascent stages of the Arab–Israeli conflict and instead functions as an unabashed endorsement of American military interventionism in foreign conflicts at a time in which the United States was dramatically escalating its military presence in Vietnam. The film is positioned as the second instalment in an unofficial trilogy of overtly propagandistic pro-interventionist cinema produced by Batjac in the 1960s, alongside *The Alamo*, (1960), Wayne's directing debut, as well as the notoriously jingoistic pro-Vietnam War film *The Green Berets* (1968), which was also directed by Wayne and was released two years after *Cast a Giant*

Shadow. My analysis of this largely overlooked entry in the Wayne oeuvre ultimately reveals how Israel served to enable Wayne, to paraphrase the critic Eric Bentley, to effectively put his art at the service of his political beliefs.[44] By extension, it will be illuminated further how the state of Israel has been deployed by Hollywood for the purpose of articulating the United States' own national identity.

Chapter 4 focuses on two films that deploy the then new ideal of a militant Israel as a model of right-wing wish fulfilment for the post-Vietnam United States. The first of these is *Black Sunday* (John Frankenheimer, 1977). Based on a bestselling novel of the same name by Thomas Harris published in 1975,[45] *Black Sunday* tells the story of a heroic Israeli Mossad agent (Robert Shaw) who thwarts a Palestinian terror attack on the Super Bowl. The second film discussed in this chapter is *The Delta Force* (Menahem Golan, 1986), which depicts Lebanese terrorists hijacking a plane full of Americans before being defeated by a United States Special Forces unit working alongside the Israeli military. The chapter contains a detailed breakdown of the United States' experience in Vietnam, as well as an overview of the emergence of Israel as a respected military power in the wake of the so-called Six Day War in 1967, and the dramatic success of their counterterror operations in Entebbe, Uganda, in 1976. Using this historical contextualization as a foundation, I examine the various ways in which *Black Sunday* articulates American post-war anxieties pertaining to the alleged 'softening' of the United States in the wake of defeat in Vietnam and concomitant rise of second-wave feminism. In addition, I detail the film's presentation of its ruthless Israeli protagonist as an idealized model of action. This is followed by an examination of *The Delta Force*, which is positioned as both a highly politicized imitation of George P. Cosmatos's iconic Reaganite action film *Rambo: First Blood Part II* (1985), and as overtly drawing on the real-life counterterrorism operations of the state of Israel. Through my analysis of each film, I will elucidate the precise manner in which Israel serves as a model of action for post-Vietnam America.

Chapter 5 focuses on Steven Spielberg's *Munich* (2005). Based on the bestselling non-fiction book *Vengeance* (1984) by George Jonas, which recounts the Israeli government's covert campaign of targeted assassinations of Palestinian militants whom they linked to the massacre of Israeli athletes at the 1972 Munich Olympics by members of the Arab terrorist group Black September,[46] *Munich* explores the crisis of conscience experienced by the Israeli agents employed to carry out the vengeful mission. For many commentators who sit to the right of the political spectrum, the film was seen as drawing a moral equivalence between terrorism and counterterrorism, and was thus, by extension, inherently and vociferously 'anti-Israel.' However, I argue that such commentary misses the point of *Munich*, and that the film is not particularly concerned with historicizing the Mossad and its execution of a campaign of vengeance against the militants deemed responsible for the massacre in Munich, but is instead a commentary on the United States' so-called 'War on Terror' launched in response to the attacks of 11 September 2001. Furthermore, I position the film as a typically Spielbergian commentary in that it is, above all else, an attempt to satisfy mass desires by championing a strong and aggressive response to terrorism, while simultaneously enabling more liberal members of its audience to feel pangs of conscience through the explicit depiction of a Western government solemnly compromising its supposed values in the fight against terror. In so doing I demonstrate how *Munich* can be understood as carrying on a long tradition of Hollywood deploying the image of Israel as a means of articulating America's collective anxieties and its national political identity.

In the Conclusion, I examine the ramifications of this historical deployment of the image of Israel by Hollywood for the United States, Israel, and also the Arabs who are subsequently presented as a demonic racial Other against both Americans and Israelis.

This study does not set out to identify or to comprehensively examine every film produced within the Hollywood system that represents or invokes the state of Israel. The aforementioned films have been selected as case studies because each serves as a manifestation of my claim that throughout post-war Hollywood Israel has predominantly served as a means through which Hollywood has articulated American identity. What lends my argument particular validity is that, having taken into account the prominence of each film's original source material, the stature of the filmmakers and actors responsible for each film, and the box office revenues generated by each film, the films selected for analysis undoubtedly constitute the most significant of Hollywood's imaginings of the Jewish state.

In identifying the mobilization of Israel as a means of constructing American national identity across the most significant of Hollywood's imaginings of the Jewish state, I will demonstrate that the repeated deployment of Israel for this purpose is no mere coincidence, but the defining element of said imaginings. Here it is pertinent to acknowledge that the films examined throughout this study span a range of genres (the historical/Biblical epic, the war/adventure film, the thriller/ disaster film, the action film), while also representing a range of production scales (few films in the history of Hollywood can match the grandiosity of *The Ten Commandments* and *Ben-Hur*, while *The Delta Force* is a classic example of

B-grade schlock cinema). In identifying how Israel functions to create a particular notion of American nationhood across such an eclectic mixture of films, it can be seen how certain ideologies pervade the Hollywood system.

As products of the time and place of their production and exhibition, mediated texts provide perhaps the most lucid view of the past. A society reveals itself through the stories it tells, and throughout the annals of American cinema it has been the stories that Hollywood has told about Others that have proven to be among the most revelatory. The stories 'about' Israel produced by Hollywood throughout the post-war period discussed in this book attest to the centrality of the Other in American culture's construction of its own national identity. However, whereas the Native American, the African American and the Arab have, at different times, each functioned as a demonological Other against which American identity is constructed in opposition, cinematic images of Israel have consistently framed the Jewish state as being in alignment with or as a parallel of the United States. It is a wholly unique manner of imagining that demonstrates the surreptitious means through which Hollywood has historically constructed, and subsequently exported, dominant notions of American national identity.

1

'God's Chosen People': America as Israel in the fifties' Cold War epic

The establishment of the modern state of Israel in 1948 would not serve as the basis of a major Hollywood film until 1960 with the release of *Exodus*, directed by Otto Preminger. However, Israel was nevertheless existent in Hollywood cinema throughout the twelve years that immediately followed the birth of the Jewish state, appearing most prominently in its pre-historical form as a setting for a number of the Biblical/historical epics that pervaded the era. *The Ten Commandments* (Cecil B. DeMille, 1956) and *Ben-Hur* (William Wyler, 1959) are undoubtedly the two most significant examples of the epic genre's deployment of the land of pre-historical Israel. *The Ten Commandments*, a semi-remake of a silent film of the same name directed by DeMille in 1923, was less a film and more of a cultural phenomenon. By the time it was withdrawn from distribution in 1960, *The Ten Commandments* had supplanted *Gone with the Wind* (Victor Fleming, 1939) to claim the number one position on *Variety*'s list of All-Time Rentals Champs.[1] As of late 2015, the film remains among the top-ten all-time grossing Hollywood films after adjusting for inflation.[2] In *Masked Men: Masculinity and the Movies in the Fifties* (1997), Steven Cohan describes the significance of *The Ten Commandments* in the following terms:

> During this period no film epitomized the gigantism of the fifties blockbuster better than *The Ten Commandments*, with its all-star cast, thousands of extras (including the Egyptian army), foreign locations, budget escalations, Academy Award winning special effects, and a final running time of three hours, 39 minutes. The film's enormous popularity was unmatched even by the other big successful films of this period, to the point where its continuous exhibition during the second half of the decade gave it the aura of a major cultural event in its own right, experienced by the entire nation and transcending the circumstances of ordinary moviegoing.[3]

Three years after the release of *The Ten Commandments*, *Ben-Hur* would go on to achieve even greater success. The film grossed $74.7 million domestically and $72.2 million internationally during its initial release, becoming the highest grossing film of 1959 and the second highest grossing film up to that point, behind only *Gone with the Wind*. *Ben-Hur*'s commercial success was matched by resounding critical acclaim; the film was nominated for twelve Academy Awards and won a then unprecedented eleven, including Best Picture. Due to the combination of its overwhelming success and its immense scale and production cost (with a budget of $15,175,000 it was, at the time, the most expensive film ever made),⁴ *Ben-Hur* has achieved a unique cultural resonance, ultimately becoming a paradigmatic term signifying colossal size and extravagance.⁵

By the mid-1960s the popularity of Biblical/historical epic had largely dissipated. However, the genre has remained a popular subject for film scholars, for whom it constitutes a form of cultural expression that served to project an idealized notion of American Cold War identity. Speaking of the era's New Testament epics, Maria Wyke argues:

> The United States takes on the sanctity of the Holy Land and receives the endorsement of God for all its past and present fights for freedom against tyrannical regimes (imperial Britain, Fascist Italy, Nazi Germany, or the Communist Soviet Union). In such narratives, a hyperbolically tyrannical Rome stands for the decadent European Other forever destined to be defeated by the vigorous Christian principles of democratic America.⁶

Martin Winkler, in his discussion of epic films set in ancient Rome, similarly asserts, 'The struggles of the protagonists ... against their oppressors develop in purely American terms. Their fights become quests for political independence and spiritual freedom or both; as such they are analogous to actual American history and to Americans' perception of themselves as champions of liberty.'⁷ Likewise, in her commentary on *The Ten Commandments*, Sumiko Higashi contends that the era's Biblical epics 'were constructed as public history that foregrounded the rise and fall of empires in a linear development culminating with the founding of America.'⁸

Building on such scholarship, this chapter argues that *The Ten Commandments* and *Ben-Hur* each project an idealized conception of Cold War identity by explicitly constructing ancient Hebrews as modern-day Americans, while simultaneously presenting the Hebrews' enslavers – be they Egyptian Pharaohs or Roman elites – as stand-ins for contemporaneous totalitarianisms. Here it is crucial to acknowledge that the conflation of American and Hebrew identities in each film should not be understood as a conscious attempt to valorize the then recently established state of Israel. Instead, this conflation functions as a reaffirmation of the Puritan notion of Americans as 'God's Chosen People,' and the American continent as a divinely ordained Promised Land. This opening phase of post-war Hollywood's deployment of Israel is particularly significant, as it establishes a relationship of parallelism between the United States and Israel that would go on to inform subsequent representations of Israel. Moreover, this phase of Hollywood cinema contributed significant capital to what was the burgeoning alignment of American and Jewish identities within the American cultural imaginary, ultimately making the ground fertile for the blossoming of the special relationship in subsequent decades.

The Ten Commandments as Cold War sermon

According to Rick Altman, the functionality of genre cinema is highly dependent on 'the interpretive community to which its members belong,' with text morphing into message, 'only in the context of a specific audience in a specific interpretive community.'[9] As such, prior to discussing the manner in which a particular film from the Biblical/historical epic cycle of the 1950s operated at an allegorical level, it is important to first establish the cultural context of the milieu.

The end of the Second World War ushered in a dramatic reconfiguration of the global geopolitical landscape. The destruction of Western Europe and the defeat of Japan created a power vacuum that would ultimately be filled by two nations governed by diametrically opposed ideologies – the liberal democracy of the United States and the socialist Soviet Union. In March 1947 the president of the United States, Harry Truman, prompted by increasing concerns that the unstable post-war governments of Greece and Turkey would fall prey to Soviet encroachment following British withdrawal from the Mediterranean, delivered an address to Congress in which he framed the contemporary world as being defined by a far-reaching struggle between two alternate ways of life – 'free,' represented and upheld by the United States, and 'totalitarian,' which was represented by the Soviet Union. Truman asserted, 'it must be the policy of the United States to support free peoples who are resisting attempted subjugation.'[10] This speech articulated what would ultimately be known as the Truman Doctrine, which amounted to a renunciation of the United States' traditional policy of isolationism, and the explicit privileging of the containment of Communism at the subordination of all other geopolitical concerns. According to historian Melvyn P. Leffler, Truman enjoyed the overwhelming support of both the general public and the American media, with his decision to aggressively resist the Soviet Union 'deemed no less significant than the Monroe Doctrine and the decision to oppose Hitler'.[11] The articulation of the Truman Doctrine constituted the US government's official launching of the Cold War, and its virulent opposition to Communism would go on to serve as the cornerstone of the United States' international and domestic policy for the next forty years.

With the launching of the Cold War and the subsequent emergence of the ever-present threat of Mutually Assured Destruction, religious adherence and the notion of Americanness would achieve a new level of synonymity. In what Douglas T. Miller and Marion Nowak attribute to 'insecurity brought on by hydrogen bombs and atomic spies,' the nation underwent a profound religious revival, with the church serving as 'the mainstay of traditional values.'[12] Bible sales spiked, with *The Revised Standard Version of the Holy Bible* rated as the non-fiction bestseller in 1952, 1953 and 1954,[13] while surveys consistently found that between 95 and 97 per cent of Americans professed a belief in God, with official church membership ranging between 57 and 69 per cent of the population.[14]

In what was a bold affirmation of Americans as 'God's Chosen People,' in 1954 the United States became a nation – according to its newly modified Pledge of Allegiance –'under God.' In 1956 – the year *The Ten Commandments* was released – the Senate confirmed 'In God We Trust' as the national motto. The conflation of faith and democracy in the early part of the fifties played a key role in the nascent Cold War being painted in religious terms, with 'good' America playing the role of the defender of the faith against the spectre of 'evil' atheistic Communism. In 1951 former Second World War general and future president Dwight D. Eisenhower intoned, 'It is only through religion that we can lick this thing called Communism.'[15] Two years later President Eisenhower proclaimed, 'Recognition of the Supreme Being is the first, the most basic expression of Americanism. Without God, there could be no American form of government, nor an American way of life.'[16] John Foster Dulles, Secretary of State from 1953 to 1959 and the son of a Presbyterian minister, publicly claimed that 'there is no way to solve the great perplexing international problems except by bringing to bear on them the force of Christianity.'[17] Dulles' sentiments were apparently shared by much of the population, as evidenced by a Gallup poll taken in 1958 that revealed that 80 per cent of the American electorate 'would refuse to vote for an atheist for President under *any* circumstances.'[18] In addition, the Federal Bureau of Investigation chief J. Edgar Hoover, a notorious anti-Communist and the one man whose power and influence arguably eclipsed that of each of the six presidents he served, also made frequent inferences to the power of Christianity to help win the fight against Communism. Hoover's bestselling anti-Communist tract *Masters of Deceit*, published in 1958, asserted that, 'all we need is faith, real faith …. The truly revolutionary force of history is not material power but the spirit of religion.'[19] This was the context in which Hollywood's cycle of Biblical/ historical epic films achieved profound cultural resonance.

While the Cold War would never escalate into a large-scale conflagration between the United States and the Soviet Union, it was nevertheless, to quote Tony Shaw, 'a *total* conflict requiring contributions from all sectors of American life.'[20] As Shaw details throughout *Hollywood's Cold War* (2007), the Cold War was 'a propaganda contest par excellence,' in which the combatants deployed 'words and images, using psychological warfare laced with ideological slogans on an unparalleled scale, as a substitute for guns and bombs.'[21] As America's pre-eminent cultural medium, Hollywood cinema was naturally a primary source of propagandist artillery. This was a situation openly and proudly affirmed by the industry itself; in 1951 Eric Johnston, head of the MPAA (Motion Picture Association of America), announced in the *Film Daily Year Book* that Hollywood was on the front line in the Cold War, describing the role as one 'that we can fill with credit and distinction as we have with every call in the past, … with ingenuity, with a large dash of daring and a large helping of the sauce of wholesome showmanship.'[22] Hollywood's participation in this heretofore unseen propaganda contest was particularly pronounced from the late 1940s until the end of the 1950s, a period which marked the peak of Cold War tensions. Shaw and Denise Youngblood identify approximately seventy explicitly anti-Communist films produced by Hollywood between 1948 and 1953.[23] Meanwhile, films that consciously sold the ideal of 'people's capitalism,' which showed that 'the fruits of American free enterprise could be enjoyed by all, not just the rich,' pervaded the remainder of the decade.[24]

Throughout this period Cecil B. DeMille emerged as one of Hollywood's leading Cold War warriors. In 1953 DeMille asserted that Hollywood filmmakers 'have two missions – to fight subversion in our own industry and to make the pictures we produce effective carriers of the American ideals we are pledged to preserve.'[25] This imploration came in the wake of a decade of virulent anti-

Communist campaigning. In 1944 DeMille served as one of the founding members of the Motion Picture Alliance for the Preservation of American Ideals (MPA). The MPA's statement of principles articulated a resentment of 'the growing impression that this industry is made of, and dominated by, Communists, radicals, and crackpots,' and it pledged 'to fight, with every means at our organized command, any effort of any group or individual, to divert the loyalty of the screen from the free America that gave it birth.'[26] One year later DeMille established the Foundation for Political Freedom. This organization regularly sent information to the House Un-American Activities Committee (HUAC), the investigative committee of the United States House of Representatives that rigorously investigated suspected threats of Communist subversion or propaganda, and which was responsible for implementing the Hollywood blacklist that effectively ended the careers of hundreds of artists.[27] In 1950 DeMille spearheaded a campaign demanding all members of the Screen Directors Guild to take a loyalty oath, which carried with it the implicit threat that those who refused would be blacklisted.[28]

DeMille's 1956 version of *The Ten Commandments* would constitute his most notable cinematic contribution to Hollywood's propaganda campaign against the Soviet Union. The film tells the story of the Hebrews' liberation from slavery in Egypt as told in the Book of Exodus, while also including other invented material such as a backstory in which Moses (Charlton Heston) is the favoured son of the Pharaoh Sethi (Cedric Hardwicke), a consequent rivalry with the eventual pharaoh Rameses (Yul Brynner), and a love interest for Moses in the form of the Egyptian princess Nefretiri (Anne Baxter). Its narrativization of the struggle between freedom and oppression constitutes a classic example of how the epic form reproduced the rhetoric of the Cold War. DeMille himself created a frame of reference that assured the film would be read as a commentary on the conflict. The film begins unusually with DeMille appearing alone on a stage in the fashion of a public service announcement film, sternly intoning to his audience:

> The theme of this picture is whether men ought to be ruled by God's law or whether they are to be ruled by the whims of a dictator like Rameses. Are men the property of the state or are they free souls under God? This same battle continues throughout the world today.

DeMille's valorization of living according to 'God's law' is a clear reference to the contemporary image of the United States as a divinely blessed nation under

God. In asking, 'Are men the property of the state or are they free souls under God?' DeMille is overtly alluding to the widely held conception of the Soviet Union as a modern-day slave state. Here DeMille echoes the official Cold War doctrine of his government, which in 1950 asserted in the National Security Council report 68 (NSC-68), 'There is a basic conflict between the idea of freedom under a government of laws, and the idea of slavery under the grim oligarchy of the Kremlin … [which] seeks to impose its absolute authority over the rest of the world.'[29]

Having invited audiences to read the villains of the film as stand-ins for modern-day totalitarianisms, the film proceeds to encourage audiences to read it as a Cold War sermon in a myriad of other ways. In an age in which, to quote Stanley Corkin, 'definitions of us and them [were] absolutely drawn in politics and popular culture,'[30] the Russian heritage of Yul Brynner (born in Vladivostok in what is now Russia), who plays Rameses, functions as an overt allusion to the film's anti-Soviet subtext.[31] In addition, DeMille's construction of the Pharaonic kingdom is imbued with inferences to Nazi Germany. For instance, as noted by Steven Cohan, the monolithic architecture of the Egyptian capital recalls Albert Speer's grandiloquent monuments to the Third Reich, while the various members of the House of Pharaoh are frequently attended to by blond Aryan-looking muscle men.[32] Cohan also points to the scenes depicting the Hebrew slave camps as mirroring images taken from the Nazi concentration camps,[33] which began to enter the United States' collective consciousness through newsreel footage that documented the liberation of the camps by Allied forces in 1945.[34]

On the surface, the film's invocation of Nazi Germany would appear to problematize the positioning of *The Ten Commandments* as an overt Cold War allegory. However, in the collective consciousness of post-war America, the Russians were not the Nazis' despised enemy with whom the Wehrmacht fought to the death in the rubble of Stalingrad and Berlin, but rather their equally malevolent successors. 'Americans both before and after the Second World War,' argue Les K. Adler and Thomas G. Paterson, 'casually and deliberately articulated distorted similarities between Nazi and Soviet ideologies, German and Communist foreign policies, authoritarian controls and practices, and Hitler and Stalin.'[35] In 1947 J. Edgar Hoover authored an article that was published in *American Magazine* that referred to Soviet Communism as 'Red Fascism.'[36] Throughout this period American politicians commonly referred to Soviet labour camps, which were known of in America before even the 1917 Bolshevik revolution, in language that drew comparisons with Nazi concentration camps.³⁷ President Harry Truman himself remarked in a press conference held in May 1947, just two months after the declaration of the Truman Doctrine, 'There isn't any difference in totalitarian states, I don't care what you call them – you call them Nazi, Communist or Fascist, or Franco, or anything else – they are all alike.'³⁸

The United States' post-war alignment of Soviets and Nazis is reflected by the disparate ways in which Hollywood represented the Soviet Union both during and after the war. Siegfried Kracauer breaks down Hollywood's wartime treatment of Soviet Russia in the following terms: 'In the war, when Stalin joined the Allies, Hollywood permitted no one to outdo it in glowing accounts of Russian heroism. *Mission to Moscow, Miss V. from Moscow, The North Star, Three Russian Girls, Song of Russia* – a veritable springtide of pro-Russian films – flooded the movie houses in 1943 and 1944.'³⁹ However, in the war's aftermath, 'Gone are the brave Russian women fighters, the happy villagers, and the democratic allures of the rulers. In their places sombre bureaucrats, counterparts of the Nazis, spread an atmosphere of oppression.'⁴⁰ Kracauer's observation demonstrates how post-war America ignored the key distinctions between Nazism and Communism, and instead collapsed the two ideologies into a singular mono-totalitarianism. This post-war conflation of Nazism and Communism was central to the construction of the United States' Cold War identity. Not only did it ensure that Americans would understand the Soviet Union as a demonic ideological Other, but it also served to undermine the immeasurable contribution made by the Russians to the defeat of the Nazis, in turn advancing the popular narrative that it was the Americans who were the true heroes of the Second World War.

The Ten Commandments' promotional materials buttressed the narrative's overt allegorization of the Cold War conflict. A souvenir programme declared that the conflict dramatized by the film was 'as modern as the headlines in the morning newspaper. Whether man shall be ruled by the whims of a dictator, or whether men are free souls under God's Law.'⁴¹ Another programme carried with it the imprimatur of 'democracy's "great saviour,"' the recently retired British Prime Minister Winston Churchill, who compared the Pharaoh's 'massive machinery of oppression' to those of unnamed modern forces 'engaged in mortal combat for the future of mankind.'⁴² Other material invoked symbols and terminology intended to associate the film's narrative with the United States' own self-proclaimed national ideals. One such souvenir programme featured Charlton Heston as Moses standing before the Liberty Bell; inscribed on the bell is Moses's proclamation in Leviticus: 'Proclaim liberty throughout the land unto all the inhabitants thereof.' Also reproduced in the programme was the seal of the United States encircled by a quote by Oliver Cromwell: 'Rebellion to tyrants is obedience to God,' in what is a reflection of the inextricable linkage of liberty and religiosity in 1950s' America.[43]

The critical response to *The Ten Commandments* supported both the studio's and DeMille's efforts to frame the film as an overt Cold War parable by explicitly linking the film's narrative to contemporaneous political concerns. A critic for the *Los Angeles Examiner* concluded that the lesson of the film 'could apply right now to the case of the Hungarians vs. the Russians,' in what was a reference to the Soviet army's brutal crushing of the anti-Communist revolution in Hungary that had taken place only weeks prior to the film's premiere.[44] James Powers in the *Hollywood Reporter* contended, 'This is the theme of this great picture, liberty under God, the sanctity of the individual and his struggle for freedom from oppression created [sic] tyrannical state and the men who see no higher authority than that with which they invest themselves.'[45] The film's overt allegorization of the Cold War conflict was not lost on those foreign governments who were at odds with its ideological message; by the end of 1958 *The Ten Commandments* was banned in all of Eastern Europe and also in China.[46]

In *The Ten Commandments* DeMille's positioning of the Exodus legend as a Cold War parable is enabled not merely through the alignment of the Egyptian villains with modern-day totalitarianisms. DeMille also Americanizes the Hebrew deliverer Moses through the deployment of a series of aesthetic and narrative devices. Even as a member of the authoritarian Egyptian royal dynasty, DeMille's Moses is the quintessential self-made success story of American folklore. Unlike Rameses, who owes his immense wealth and power to having won the lottery of life, Moses, through his own skill and initiative, has achieved great success as a builder of colossal monuments, and is thus presented as being worthy of both his royal status and the love of his surrogate father. Moses's aptitude as a master builder is most clearly demonstrated in the spectacular depiction of the raising of the obelisk in the building of a new city in tribute to the Pharaoh Sethi. Moses, who perpetually dominates the frame, gives the order to proceed with the operation despite the reservations of his overseer Baka (Vincent Price) who bemoans the lack of sand, and thus he is shown to be the figure most responsible for the monument's erection. Accompanying the action is a chorus of cheers and the triumphant blasting of horns on the soundtrack, resulting in a glorious celebration of Moses's can-do spirit. Through both its ambition and its accomplishment, the scene exemplifies Tony Shaw's claim that the film unabashedly sanctifies 'America's capitalist-based creativity.'[47] The scene also presents the highly proficient and successful capitalist as innately humanitarian. Moses ensures that his workers are rested and well fed, displaying a compassion that is completely absent in the authoritarian Rameses. This comes after a scene in which Moses helps to rescue a Hebrew slave woman (his mother, although it is unbeknownst to him at the time) from being crushed by a massive stone during the building of Sethi's colossal city. Much to the chagrin of Rameses' pitiless administrators, Moses declares that 'blood makes poor mortar' in what is a virulent denunciation of the slave state's inhuman bureaucracy. Moses is further Americanized when the Hebrews begin their journey through the desert and the film's narration (voiced by DeMille) equates him to an eagle, a historical symbol of the United States, intoning that, 'He bore them out of Egypt as an eagle bears its young up on its wings.'

The film's final shot provides the exclamation point on Moses's inherent Americanness. With the Jews having successfully reached the Promised Land of Israel Moses cries out, 'Go! Proclaim liberty throughout all the lands!' invoking a phrase from Leviticus 25:10 that is also inscribed on the Liberty Bell in Philadelphia, Pennsylvania – an iconic symbol of the American struggle for independence from its British overlords. Pertinently, as pointed out by critic Michael Wood, Moses makes his proclamation while striking a pose reminiscent of the Statue of Liberty – a move that unequivocally serves to position Moses as a metonym for the United States of America.[48] Moreover, as Marc Vernet asserts, the land upon which Moses stands throughout the final sequence explicitly recalls the rugged terrain of the Old West as depicted throughout the films of John Ford and Howard Hawks.[49] The film's denouement thus aligns the Jews' return to ancient Israel with the relocation of European immigrants from the Old World to the Promised Land of America. In so doing it confirms that in this version of the Exodus narrative, the Promised Land is not Eretz Israel, but the 'New Israel' of America.

Another way in which *The Ten Commandments* encourages American audiences to identify with Moses and his people is through its de-ethnicization of the ancient Hebrews. To quote Lester D. Friedman, DeMille's religious epics make 'no attempt to understand the Jews' religious and cultural heritage.'[50] Traditional Jewish practices are shown only in instances where they directly impact the drama, as in the scene depicting the first Passover in which lamb's

Figure 1.1 Moses (Charlton Heston) strikes a pose reminiscent of the Statue of Liberty.

blood is placed on the doors of the Israelites to protect them from the Angel of Death who has come to claim the lives of the Egyptians' firstborn. Bruce Babington and Peter William Evans similarly argue that the film's representation of the Torah is 'purged of ethnic particularity and tend[s] to the universal.'[51] As Babington and Evans note, 'all that Moses imposes on the Israelites are the ten strictures taken over by Christianity,' which 'are de-ethnicized literally in the replacement of Hebrew script on the tablets by an invented writing' (and which are spoken by the voice of God in modern American English).[52] The film thus serves as a cinematic reiteration of the notion that the Ten Commandments constitute the fundamental basis for American Law, a claim publicly espoused by then President Harry Truman in 1951.[53]

The overt linking of Judaism and Christianity in *The Ten Commandments* positions the film as one of the more notable examples of what Michelle Mart terms 'the Christianization of the Jews.'[54] Prior to the 1950s anti-Semitism was a fundamental tenet of American life, 'from the anti-Jewish violence perpetrated by the Ku Klux Klan, to popular culture stereotypes of Jews as greedy and dirty, to the segregation of Jews from white neighborhoods and limits on Jewish admission to certain universities.'[55] However, in the 1950s, the combination of the pervasive spirit of anti-Communism, the nation's concomitant religious revival and the subsequent privileging of ecumenism, as well as the creation of the state of Israel, resulted in a situation in which 'many Americans – the majority of whom were Protestant – came to identify with a broader "heritage" or "civilization" that included Jewish religion and history.'[56] This coming together of Judaism and Christianity ultimately gave rise to the notion of the United States and Israel sharing a Judeo-Christian heritage, which served to further affirm the status of each as 'God's Chosen People.' Mart points to Biblical epics such as *The Ten Commandments*, as well as films like *Samson & Delilah* (Cecil B. DeMille, 1949), *The Prodigal* (Richard Thorpe, 1955) and *The Story of Ruth* (Henry Koster, 1960) as being among the foremost contributors to this phenomenon.[57]

The most notable example of *The Ten Commandments* contributing to the Christianization of the Jews comes in the form of its explicit rendering of Moses into a Christ figure. In the beginning of the film an Egyptian High Priest prophesies that a deliverer will be born who will eventually lead the Jews out of bondage, prompting the Pharaoh Sethi to order the death of all male Hebrew children. In an attempt to save her son, Moses's mother casts the baby Moses adrift in the Nile where he is eventually found by the Egyptian princess Bithiah (Nina Foch) and subsequently raised as a member of the Egyptian royal family. However, the film's prophesying of the impending arrival of a deliverer conflicts with the account in the Book of Exodus, where Pharaoh's edict instead stems from the fear that the children of Israel are becoming too plentiful in Egypt and will soon pose a threat to the established order.[58] Instead, the order to kill all male Hebrew children as a form of pre-emptive strike against the arrival of a deliverer instead recalls the Massacre of the Innocents as depicted in the New Testament's Gospel of Matthew, in which Herod the Great, alarmed by the prophesy of the birth of a child who will one day become King of the Jews, orders the execution of all male children in Bethlehem.[59]

Having alluded to the birth of Christ in his depiction of Moses's entry into the house of Pharaoh, DeMille repeatedly invites audiences to conflate the two saviours throughout the rest of the film. For instance, after Moses kills the Egyptian Baka, he is arrested after having been betrayed by the Judas-like Hebrew Dathan (Edward G. Robinson). Moses is subsequently brought before the Pharaoh Sethi in shackles; notably, this scene is absent from the Book of Exodus, which instead simply states that after killing an Egyptian a fearful Moses fled to the desert.[60] In this wholly invented scene Moses appears before his inquisitors clad in a loincloth, flanked by soldiers whose outfits recall that of Hollywood screen Romans, and chained to a crossbar in a manner that explicitly invokes the Crucifixion.

Figure 1.2 Moses as Christ figure.

As argued by Melanie Wright, Moses's proclamation to the Pharaonic court, 'I am the son of Amram and Yochebel, Hebrew slaves,' recalls Jesus's enigmatic responses at his trial as it is depicted in the Gospel of Luke.[61] Sethi is unable to condemn the man he once considered a son and hands him over to his legitimate offspring, Rameses. By washing his hands of the matter, Sethi becomes the Pontius Pilate to Moses's Jesus Christ. Moses is subsequently banished to the desert with only a modicum of rations. Before leaving Moses to what he expects will be his death, Rameses mocks him as 'King of the Slaves,' which, in the context of Pharaonic Egypt, equates to 'King of the Jews' – the same moniker that the New Testament claims was deridingly applied to Jesus Christ by his executioners. Later in the film, the visual representation of the first Passover positions Moses at the centre of a long table flanked by his followers at each side, creating an image that replicates the iconography of Christ's Last Supper. In a reflection of the religious fervour pervading the nation during this time, a contemporary review of the film published in *Variety* declares that with this scene the film 'hits the peak of beauty,' describing it as 'stirring and, in contrast with production generally, marked by simplicity and deep feeling.'[62] Also, as observed by Mart, when Moses encounters the burning bush it is described in language directly out of the Book of John: 'and the Word was God …. He is not flesh but Spirit, the Light of Eternal Mind …. His light is in every man.'[63] It is notable that in this scene it is Charlton Heston who provides the voice of God, as DeMille wanted the voice to plausibly resemble that of Heston's character's father; thus, Moses is receiving the word of God while literally being the son of God. It is also important to note that it is only in the final three minutes of the film that the audience sees Moses as the centenarian of Jewish legend, and even then his advanced age is only indicated by the length of his beard, with only a token effort made to make his face and hands look like those belonging to a man of 120 years of age. The enduring image of Moses to emerge from the film – bearded, carrying a staff, on the penumbra of middle age – is thus one that resembles traditional representations of Jesus. In the words of Alan Nadel, 'beneath his Hebrew robes he is Jesus in disguise.'[64] In sum, DeMille does not present the story as a central chapter of ancient Jewish mythology. Instead, the Exodus narrative is presented as one that is fundamentally Christian – the religion that lay at the heart of the United States' national character throughout the 1950s.

Freedom vs. oppression in *Ben-Hur*

The ancient Hebrews' struggle for liberty would again serve as the narrative framework for the articulation of American political identity in William Wyler's *Ben-Hur*. Released just three years after *The Ten Commandments*, *Ben-Hur* in many ways functions as an unofficial sequel to DeMille's retelling of the Exodus. The film's hero Judah Ben-Hur is, like Moses, a Hebrew prince played by Charlton Heston who leads a struggle for Jewish liberation. *Ben-Hur* also repeats *The Ten Commandments*' utilization of the ancient world to construct an equally grandiose Biblically infused narrativization of the struggle between freedom and oppression that echoed the contemporaneous political rhetoric of the Cold War, while similarly proffering a cinematic manifestation of the coming together of Judaic tradition and Christian belief in 1950s' America.

Where DeMille's film depicts the Hebrews' liberation from slavery in ancient Egypt, Wyler's film depicts the subjugation under which the Jews were still suffering thousands of years after their return to the land of Canaan, this time under the heel of the omnipotent Roman Empire during the reign of the Emperor Tiberius (AD 14–37). Crucially, the proto-nationalist struggle that underpins the narrative is far more pronounced than in the Lew Wallace novel upon which the film is based. In the film Judah expresses opposition to Rome from the opening scenes, imploring his childhood friend Messala (Stephen Boyd), now a commanding officer in the Roman army, to 'Withdraw your legions. Give us our freedom.' Conversely, in the novel, Judah, while fundamentally disagreeing with the notion of Roman exceptionalism, does not express vehement opposition to Rome and its presence in Judea; at one point Judah even expresses a desire to relocate to Rome and train to be a soldier. In the novel Judah challenges Rome's authority in order to avenge the wrongful imprisonment of his mother and sister who, following Judah's accidental dislodging of a roof tile that falls and nearly kills the Roman governor of Judea, are ordered to be arrested along with Judah by Messala, who opportunistically exploits the incident to enrich himself by confiscating the family's fortune and property. In the film it is instead Judah's sister who dislodges the tile, with Messala seizing the opportunity to make a public example of the powerful Judah as punishment for his resistance to Roman rule. This subtle alteration positions the film version of Judah as being diametrically opposed to authoritarian colonial power, thus enabling the film to play out the clash between freedom and oppression that mirrored popular conceptions of the Cold War conflict.

As in *The Ten Commandments*, the ancient Hebrews of *Ben-Hur* are first and foremost the spiritual antecedents of modern Christian Americans, and thus the film can be seen as similarly engaging in the Christianization of the Jews. The film begins with a six-minute musical overture against a close-up of a fresco of Michelangelo's *The Creation of Adam*. Voice of God narration intones that the story takes place 'In the year of our Lord.' The scene that follows depicts the Jewish denizens of Jerusalem lining up to be counted by their Roman overlords, reinforcing the historical permanence of Jewish oppression that is also at the heart of *The Ten Commandments*. The remainder of the film's prologue depicts the birth of Jesus, with the scene coming to an end with the iconic image of a star shining brightly above the manger. The scene then transitions into a shot of the film's title card – featuring the name of the eponymous Jewish hero – which has the effect of indelibly linking Judah Ben-Hur with the divine birth of Christ.

This opening sequence introduces one of the film's central motifs, namely the intersection of Judah's life with that of Christ's at key moments from the Gospels. The first such intersection of the Judah and Christ narratives occurs when Judah is marched through the desert as part of a Roman chain gang. Here it is pertinent to note that because Judah's arrest is positioned as a consequence of his refusal to aid the Roman subjugation of his people, Judah himself can be read as a Christlike martyr who is victimized by Roman authorities out of fear for the untapped revolutionary power that he represents. In this scene Judah, who is by now close to death, is denied water that is being served to the rest of the prisoners. He subsequently collapses into a wretched heap, uttering the words 'Help me, God.' A figure seen only from behind, later revealed to be Jesus, suddenly appears and provides Judah with desperately needed refreshment, essentially raising him from the dead (and in the process affirming the kinship of Jews and Christians by virtue of their worshiping the same deity).

Judah's next encounter with Christ occurs after Judah visits his mother and sister who have contracted leprosy following their arrest and imprisonment, and have since been condemned to a leper colony. Upon departing the colony Judah stumbles across a crowd, making its way to witness the Sermon on the Mount. Judah's coincidental witnessing of this formative event in the early development of Christianity underscores the central role played by the power of destiny in the unfolding of the narrative; indeed, it is an incident as seemingly innocuous as a loose tile falling from Judah's roof that facilitates his and his family's imprisonment. For example, throughout his time on the Roman slave ship Judah repeatedly (and correctly) intones his belief that his God will save him. Later, having been fortunate enough to escape from the prison hulk, Judah makes his return to Jerusalem. While sleeping under a tree Judah is stumbled across by the magi Balthasar (Finlay Currie) who mistakes him for Christ – a scene that is completely absent from the novel. Judah's meeting of Balthasar facilitates Judah's eventual friendship with the Arab Sheik Ilderim (Hugh Griffith), who is a close friend of Balthasar. This encounter ultimately results in Judah riding the Sheik's horses in the chariot race that ends in the death of Judah's rival Messala. In a line of dialogue that effectively encapsulates the centrality of destiny to the film's narrative, Sheik Ilderim poses the question, 'You are a Jew, but you rode in the great circus?' Judah replies, 'Yes, but by strange choice, by stranger fortune.' The integral role of destiny to the unfolding of the narrative serves to position Judah as somehow being 'chosen' by God, in turn affirming his messianic status, while also aligning him with the film's American audience.

The film's positioning of Judah as a messianic Christ figure is reiterated when, upon winning the chariot race, Judah is greeted by Pontius Pilate (Frank Thring), the Roman prefect of Judea who presided over the trial of Jesus. Against the deafening cheers of the crowd, Pilate remarks to Judah, 'you are the people's one true god,' and proceeds to place a laurel wreath on Judah's head. Trickles of blood stream down Judah's face from wounds he sustained during the race, the image evoking that of Christ after he has been adorned with the crown of thorns.

Figure 1.3 Judah (Charlton Heston) wears the crown of thorns.

Figure 1.4 The light catches Judah's Star of David.

The following scene depicts Judah making one last visit to the dying Messala, who is on his deathbed after being mortally wounded during the race. As Judah stands over Messala's mangled body, the Star of David worn around the neck of the recently deified Judah catches the light, creating a powerful image that effectively symbolizes the film's dovetailing of Christianity and Judaism.

Judah's third and final encounter with Christ comes during the film's denouement, in which the forsaken Christ trudges towards the site of his crucifixion. Judah attempts to give Christ a drink of water, reciprocating the kindness shown earlier by Christ in Judah's hour of need. The depiction of the crucifixion serves as the exclamation point on the film's Christianization of the Jews. Immediately following the erection of the cross, the Judean skies thunderously roar and shoot bolts of lightning before pouring with rain. Shots of the dying Christ and rivers of water mixed with his blood washing over Jerusalem are juxtaposed with the image of Judah's mother and sister both literally 'seeing the light' as flashes of lightning illuminate their faces. Judah's mother and sister are each then shown as being miraculously cured of leprosy. This is followed by the film's final scene in which Judah, after solemnly touching the mezuzah that sits outside his door and embracing his ameliorated mother and sister, remarks, 'I felt His voice take the sword out of my hand.' This contrasts with the novel in which Judah becomes an ardent follower of Christ long before his crucifixion. In a clear denunciation of the 'eye for an eye' rhetoric of the Old Testament Judah, as if baptized by the pouring rains that accompanied Christ's death, now embraces the philosophy of 'turning the other cheek' preached by Christ. The film ends with the shot of an empty cross standing on a hill, signifying Christ's eventual resurrection. The film thus parallels Christ's elevation from mortal man to divinity with Judah's own religious conversion. In so doing, *Ben-Hur* mirrors *The Ten Commandments* and its positioning of Judaism as the spiritual antecedent to the Christian religion residing at the heart of American Cold War identity, thus conveying the ideal of contemporary Americans as 'God's Chosen People,' while also making the ground fertile for what will eventually be known as the special relationship between the United States and the state of Israel based on the ideal of mutually shared values, culture and history.

Another way in which *Ben-Hur* echoes *The Ten Commandments* is through its employment of the spectre of Nazism as the ultimate symbol of authoritarian malevolence. The film's Nazification of Rome begins in its opening scene wherein hordes of Hebrews are shown lining up to be counted and subsequently taxed by their Roman overlords. Here the film recalls the image of powerless Jews having their details meticulously recorded by the notoriously pedantic Nazi bureaucracy before being herded into cattle cars and shipped to extermination camps. Moreover, the Roman tribune Messala is established early on as being redolent of the Nazi ideologues. Messala speaks of Rome being 'chosen' to dominate the globe, a term which positions the Romans as the ancient world's 'master race.' In imploring Judah to use his influence to quell any Jewish opposition to Roman rule, Messala insists, 'rebellion is futile and can only end in one way – extinction for your people,' evoking the near total annihilation of the Jewish race by Nazi Germany a mere fifteen years prior to the film's release. Messala also casually speaks of his recent experiences in Libya, revealing a callous inhumanity and the brutality of the Roman army, stating, 'Then we marched on their capital – barbaric city, but fascinating – or was, till we destroyed it. Now it's nothing but ashes.' As noted by Martin Winkler, Messala's recollections conjure images of the scorched-earth tactics deployed by the Nazis during the Second World War.[65]

Prior to the final severing of all threads of friendship between Judah and Messala, Judah excoriates his erstwhile friend for speaking of the Emperor 'as if he were God.' Messala's reverential riposte – 'He *is* God, the only God. He is power, real power on earth' – recalls the phenomenon of the so-called 'Hitler Myth' that overwhelmed Germany throughout the 1930s and early 1940s, and which consequently elevated Hitler to the status of a demigod, demanding complete and unwavering submission.[66] Furthermore, in the lead up to the famous chariot race sequence, Pontius Pilate salutes Caesar and the enormous crowd proceeds to morph into a sea of raised arm 'Roman salutes,' in a scene that evokes the Nazi rallies depicted in infamous propaganda films such as Leni Riefenstahl's *Triumph of the Will* (1935). Here it is worth noting that in his examination of the history of the Roman salute in Western cultural texts, Martin Winkler argues that 'Not a single Roman work of art – sculpture, coinage, or painting – displays a salute of the kind that is found in Fascism, Nazism, and related ideologies.'[67] According to Winkler, it is primarily through the utilization of Nazi typography in films set in the age of ancient Rome, such as *Ben-Hur* and *Quo Vadis* (Mervyn LeRoy, 1951), that the term 'Roman salute' first entered and ultimately became accepted as part of the cultural lexicon.

Ben-Hur's more pronounced invocation of Nazism in its construction of authoritarian villainy is best understood as a consequence of the political leanings and personal history of the film's director William Wyler. One of Hollywood's

Figure 1.5 Pontius Pilate (Frank Thring) gives the 'Roman salute.'

most prominent liberals during the post-war years, Wyler vigorously opposed the McCarthyite witch-hunt that plagued Hollywood.[68] Sarah Kozloff details how at a Directors Guild of America meeting held on 22 October 1950, Cecil B. DeMille suggested that Wyler was affiliated with Communist front groups, to which Wyler responded, 'I am sick and tired of having people question my loyalty to my country. The next time I hear somebody do it, I am going to kick hell out of him. I don't care how old he is or how big.'[69]

Devoid of DeMille's rabid anti-Communist attitude, Wyler instead deployed Nazi Germany as the model for his caustic construction of Rome. It is appropriate to understand Wyler's mobilization of the image of the Third Reich as being directly informed by his personal experience as a European Jew. Wyler was born in 1902 into a Jewish family in the city of Mulhouse in Alsace-Lorraine, a territory contested by the French and German armies during the first month of the First World War, which would go on to be held by Germany until the war's end in 1918. Mulhouse was also the hometown of Alfred Dreyfus, the Jewish French army captain wrongly accused of pro-German treason in what would eventually be known as 'The Dreyfus Affair' – France's most infamous episode of anti-Semitism. According to Kozloff, the enduring scandal and the continuing conflict between Dreyfus's relatives in Mulhouse and their anti-Semitic opponents made a strong impact on the young Wyler.[70]

In the years leading up to and encompassing the Second World War, Wyler, having since immigrated to the United States, devoted significant energies towards extricating Jewish family and friends from the ever-expanding threat posed by Nazi Germany. Kozloff details Wyler being involved in trying to rescue at least twenty-five people, which demanded the petitioning of the State Department for a visa application and Wyler personally having to guarantee to sponsor each immigrant financially. In two other cases, Wyler attempted to send monthly stipends to Jews being held in Vichy concentration camps, with the hope that the money could be used to bribe the guards.[71] It can thus be seen how Wyler's appropriation of Nazism in his construction of a malevolent Rome is a reflection of his own personal conception of the ultimate form of totalitarian evil. Through this understanding of Wyler's personal history, we achieve a clearer vision of how *Ben-Hur* serves to condemn modern-day authoritarian states.

The Nazification of Rome not only privileges reading the film as a Cold War allegory, but it also encourages American audiences to identify with the film's Jewish protagonists. As argued by Winkler, Romans, as the killers of Christ, 'are "bad guys" in the fiction and popular culture of Christian societies almost by necessity.'⁷² By equal necessity, the Romans, as the destroyers of the Second Temple in AD 70 that precipitated the Jewish expulsion from the Holy Land, are the natural enemies of Zionist-infused Judaism, as reflected by the rhetoric of early Zionist leaders such as Max Nordau.⁷³ Accordingly, in *Ben-Hur* Judah and his people are depicted as feeling the crack of Rome's whip long before his conversion to Christianity, with the film's prologue clearly establishing that Rome's oppression of the Jews was well and truly institutionalized prior to the arrival of Christ.

Here it is instructive to note that the film is completely devoid of any allusion to the Jews being responsible for the death of Christ, a traditional means of vilifying Jews for two millennia. This contrasts significantly with the novel which has Judah identifying Christ's enemies as 'rabbis and teachers' who say that 'he is guilty of a great crime' in preaching 'a new dispensation.'⁷⁴ Also, in its depiction of the Passion of the Christ the novel echoes the New Testament narrative by describing the Hebrews of Jerusalem as having 'loaded him with curses,' while giving 'their sympathies to the thieves.'⁷⁵ Conversely, the film presents the Jewish mob as largely sympathetic to Christ's plight, with Judah's mother and sister imploring the cruel Roman centurions to show mercy as Jesus struggles along the Via Dolorosa. The film also excises the novel's detailing of Pontius Pilate washing his hands of the matter following the Jews' demanding of Jesus's execution. Instead, the film positions the Jews as sharing Christ's victimhood at the hands of the Romans, who are constructed as precursors to the murderous twentieth-century regime responsible for the near total annihilation of the Jewish race (and who would ultimately be defeated by a military alliance in which the United States played a primary role). Jews and Christians, already united by virtue of each being 'God's Chosen People,' are thus also aligned according to the logic of 'the enemy of my enemy is my friend.' Consequently, the film engenders a Jew/American and Roman/Nazi binary that mirrors the Manichaean dichotomy of the Cold War world, whilst simultaneously reflecting and affirming the era's Christianization of the Jews.

Tough Hebrews

In *American Tough: The Tough-Guy Tradition and American Character* (1972) Rupert Wilkinson asserts that, whereas men in other countries 'used their culture's notions of toughness and strength to define their masculinity vis-à-vis women,' Americans, from an early point in their history, 'as a whole used the same notions to define their national identity.'[76] Wilkinson goes on to claim that 'Historically, the American concern with toughness has three main sources: a plain man, anticourtier tradition that goes back to Tudor and Stuart England; a complex of frontier myths and images; and the tension in a business society between striving and self-indulgence.'[77] Emerging from these diverse but interconnected sources, argues Wilkinson, is an American national identity that is inextricably bound with notions of individual toughness and hyper-masculinity.

Wilkinson's contention that toughness has been historically central to notions of American identity is supported by Michelle Mart's claim that the development of the 'tough Jew' archetype in American literature of the 1960s played a key role in Jews ultimately becoming 'insiders' in American culture. According to Mart, in presenting Jews as both pioneers and warriors, the tough Jew exemplified 'characteristics of ideal masculinity' with which Americans could easily identify.[78] Paul Breines, whose book *Tough Jews: Political Fantasies and the Moral Dilemma of American Jewry* (1990) popularized the term, defines the tough Jew, rather simply, as 'Jews who fight, who are violent in the public political sphere,' and who in turn present a counter to the traditional conception of the Jew as 'the frail and meek object of anti-Semitic initiatives.'[79] Breines identifies Ari Ben Canaan from the 1958 Leon Uris novel *Exodus* (the basis for the 1960 Otto Preminger film of the same name, which will be discussed in detail in the following chapter) as the 'the virtual prototype of the American image of the Israeli tough Jew.'[80] However, the characterization of Moses by the blonde, blue-eyed, ruggedly handsome all-American Charlton Heston in *The Ten Commandments* constitutes an even earlier example of Breines' tough Jew archetype, further affirming the Americanization of the Hebrew Exodus narrative.[81] In contrast to the familiar image of Moses as a long-bearded elder cultivated by classic European artworks such as Michelangelo's sculpture of the horned Moses and Rembrandt's painting of Moses smashing the tablets of God's Law, Heston's Moses, at least throughout the film's first two hours, is young and athletic, and flaunts not only the physique but also the minimalistic wardrobe of a modern-day professional wrestler, prompting *Time* magazine to sneeringly describe the movie as a 'Sexodus.'[82] In the words of *New York Times* critic Vincent Canby, Heston suggested 'both the rugged American frontiersman of myth as well as God who creates Adam in Michelangelo's Sistine Chapel fresco.'[83] The impressive physicality of Heston's

Moses is amplified by DeMille's preference for medium and three-quarter shots. As Steven Cohan notes in his discussion of the film:

> Throughout the nearly four-hour running time of *The Ten Commandments*, and in contrast to other epics of the period, DeMille seldom uses tight close-ups of his stars (there are only two or three medium close-ups of Heston, for instance, in the entire film), but instead films them in medium or three-quarter shots. The director's avoidance of close-ups keeps attention riveted upon the bodies of the actors; cuts to medium shots then sustain that perspective by featuring the torso as part of the (relatively) more intimate and individuated view of a particular performer.[84]

In correspondence with Moses's imposing physique, he is also presented as being a supreme warrior. Following his banishment from the House of Pharaoh, Moses easily fights off a pair of thuggish Amalekites who attack the daughters of the Bedouin Jethro. The sequence positions Moses as being analogous to the American tough guy, whom Wilkinson defines as one 'who can take care of himself,' and who is 'not afraid to face down rivals and aggressors.'[85] Earlier in the film, when the king and queen of Ethiopia are brought before the Pharaoh Sethi after having been conquered by Moses and subsequently brought into Egypt's empire, Moses is presented as being able to elicit the submission of his enemies, and is thus 'violent in the public political sphere.'[86] Here it is instructive to note that Moses insists that Ethiopia has

Figure 1.6 The physically imposing Moses in three-quarter shot.

been brought into the empire 'as a friend'. In so doing, Moses articulates what Charles Hilliard has termed the Cold War rhetoric of 'benevolent supremacy', which sought to ideologically distance the United States from the declining imperial powers of Europe and also the emerging totalitarianism of the Soviet Union, and instead position the nation as a militarily proficient defender of liberty and personal freedoms across the post-colonial world.[87] In addition to demonstrating his virtuosity as a warrior, this scene underscores Moses's hyper-masculinity through its depiction of the queen of Ethiopia palpably lusting after Moses. This arouses the jealous ire of the Egyptian princess Nefretiri, a tension that is established through a series of shots comprising close-ups of Nefretiri and medium shots of Moses standing before Sethi that, while not approximating Nefretiri's perceptual point of view, nonetheless convey with unequivocal lucidity that Moses is the subject of Nefretiri's lascivious gaze. This sequence serves to eroticize Moses/Heston for the audience's spectatorial pleasure, while also encouraging white heterosexual American males to narcissistically identify with the character. In presenting Moses as a virile lothario who is irresistible to women the film serves to further underscore the innate Americanness of the character by virtue of his ability to, in the words of Mart, 'exemplify characteristics of ideal masculinity'.[88]

The construction of Moses as a rugged hyper-masculine figure is reinforced through the film's emasculation of Moses's nemesis Rameses. Whereas for much of the first half of the film Moses displays a conspicuously hirsute chest, the physically smaller Rameses is shown to be completely devoid of body hair, with the notable exception of a long ponytail that he occasionally wears. Rameses is also frequently adorned in epicene accouterments such as a skirt and ornate jewellery.

Having been feminized aesthetically, Rameses is also emasculated in the figurative sense. He is unable to please his woman, Nefretiri and thus it is implied that he lacks the virility of the Americanized Moses. Nefretiri both loves and lusts after Moses, and when she is finally convinced that she can never possess him she deploys her acerbic tongue to verbally emasculate Rameses at every opportunity. Rameses is also incapable of protecting his young son from the curse of the Angel of Death as foretold by Moses, and he is forced to watch his child recede hopelessly into death. As conveyed by the cloak of darkness that pervades this scene, Rameses is a broken man resigned to the veracity of Moses's omnipotent God, on bended knee helplessly praying to, in the words of Nefretiri, 'nothing but a piece of stone with the head of a bird'.

Figure 1.7 The effeminized Rameses (Yul Brynner).

The film's feminized construction of Rameses not only serves to emphasize the masculinity of Moses, but as Cohan argues, it signifies Rameses' racial difference from the normative Moses.[89] Central to Rameses' racial Otherness is the casting of Yul Brynner. Cohan contends that Brynner's distinctive shaved head 'gave him a look that jarred with American notions about the relation between a full head of hair and virility.'[90] Meanwhile, his Russian ethnicity, coupled with press stories that indicated that he was also of Mongolian and Romany descent, engendered a 'mythical Eurasian heritage [that] ensured that his unorthodox physical appearance connoted not the intellectualism of the American egghead, but the exoticism of the foreigner.'[91] Here it is pertinent to note that American audiences knew Brynner almost exclusively as the king of Siam from the Rodgers and Hammerstein musical *The King and I*, a role that he had played to great acclaim on Broadway since 1951 as well as in a highly successful film version released only months prior to *The Ten Commandments*. As Leo Braudy argues, 'the continuity of an actor's image can supply complex filling for the gaps in his immediate characterization,'[92] and for many audiences Brynner's characterization of Rameses would have been implicitly framed by his image as the peculiar Siamese king. Rameses, as projected by the ethnically Russian and superficially Asiatic Brynner, emerges as a conflation of ethnic Otherness and sexual ambiguity in much the same way as the characters played by the iconic sex symbol Rudolph Valentino in the films of the 1920s; as argued by Miriam Hansen, the Valentino persona was one that, while adored by many American women, was fundamentally rejected by many 'masculinist' American men.[93]

Cohan also asserts that the film's construction of Rameses ensures that the racial Otherness of ancient Egypt is read specifically as Asian rather than African, and thus it has 'the significant effect of aligning Rameses to the West's representation of the East as a site of colonial domination.'[94] In so doing *The Ten Commandments* can be seen as engaging in the practice of what Edward Said terms 'Orientalism.'[95] According to Said, a fundamental tenet of Orientalism is the feminization of the East by Western cultural products, which serves to establish a lucid racial hierarchy that primes the Oriental for subjugation and tacitly justifies Western colonization of the region.[96] Crucially, Said argues that the positioning of the Oriental as a strange, inherently inferior cultural Other principally serves to formulate not the identity of the East, but that of the West; Said contends that the West is presented as 'rational, developed, humane, superior' by virtue of its construction as the binary opposite of the Orient, which is constructed as 'aberrant, undeveloped, inferior.'[97] Orientalism is thus best understood as a representational practice that serves to engender identity through the deployment of oppositional logic. In this instance the Orientalist construction of Rameses functions to highlight the inherent hyper-masculinity – and, by extension, the inherent Americanness – of Moses.

Like Moses, Judah Ben-Hur is a hyper-masculine precursor to the tough Jew archetype. As such, he is a stark contrast to the earlier incarnations of the character. The protagonist of Wallace's novel is a sensitive boy of seventeen whose features are defined by 'softness' and 'beauty.'[98] Meanwhile the 1925 silent film version directed by Fred Niblo cast as Judah the 26-year-old Mexican actor Ramon Novarro, who has been positioned by film historians such as Miriam Hansen as an ersatz Rudolph Valentino – the archetypal example of exoticized androgyny in 1920s' Hollywood.[99]

Wyler's casting of the 35-year-old barrel-chested Charlton Heston as Judah thus constitutes a significant departure from the traditionally epicene characterizations of Judah, as well as Hollywood's traditional mode of representing Jews, which had often conformed to the frail and meek object of anti-Semitic initiatives highlighted by Breines. Indeed, Heston's Judah constitutes an even tougher, more physically imposing Jew than does Heston's Moses. Whereas in Wallace's novel Judah's mother emphasizes the importance of being a great orator and philosopher, the film unequivocally privileges the

Figure 1.8 Judah as Christ figure.

warrior aspect of Judah's character.[100] The first appearance of Judah clearly establishes his athletic prowess. Challenged by Messala to a friendly spear-throwing contest Judah accurately hits the centre of a wooden beam, dislodging Messala's spear and, in the process, establishing his inherent physical superiority over his Roman overlords. Later in the film Judah, after being unfairly arrested and imprisoned, easily overpowers three centurions who visit him in his cell, which helps to position Judah as one whom, like Moses, 'can take care of himself.'[101] Judah is eventually neutralized only after being blindsided and sustaining a blow to the head from a large set of metal keys. In a reiteration of the film's construction of Judah as a messianic figure a bar is placed through his arms behind his back, forcing him into a position that not only evokes the image of Christ on the cross, but which also recalls the position Heston assumes in *The Ten Commandments* in the scene where Moses appears before Sethi on the charge of killing the Egyptian Baka.

Even while restrained Judah again overwhelms three Roman guards. He manages to escape and apparently kills another guard before arming himself with a spear and breaking into Messala's private room, where he confronts his erstwhile friend over the prevarications that have led to the imprisonment of his family. Later, having been sentenced to hard labour in the galleys of a slave ship, Judah remarks that he has worked for over three years on a number of ships, yet in contrast with the majority of his fellow condemned he appears to be unbroken, both physically and mentally. Judah embodies Wilkinson's claim that the American tough guy is one who 'can take it,' who 'can cope with many kinds of stress,' and who possesses a will that 'takes over from physique, driving a sick or exhausted body to the limits of endurance.'[102] Clearly impressed with Judah's muscular physique and tenacious fighting spirit, the ship's consul Arrius (Jack

Hawkins) offers Judah the opportunity to train as a gladiator and charioteer, to which Judah refuses. However, in what is a further underscoring of the role played by destiny in the unfolding of the narrative, Arrius, without offering any hint of justification, orders that Judah remain unchained in the galleys, enabling him to easily escape when the ship is later attacked by Macedonian pirates while his fellow slaves are left to drown. This is in stark contrast to the novel in which it is established that Arrius is not merely impressed by Judah, but in fact knew and even 'loved' Judah's late father Ithanas, and is also said to be moved by Judah's pleas for innocence in an exchange that is completely absent from the film.[103] Once liberated, Judah easily overpowers a Roman guard in much the same way as when he was first arrested, ultimately choking him to death. Judah then overcomes an armed pirate and jumps into the ocean to save Arrius, which sets up the next stage of the narrative in which Judah makes his way back to Jerusalem and confronts Messala as the surrogate son of a wealthy and powerful Roman.

Judah's return to Jerusalem ultimately leads to what is undoubtedly the film's most iconic sequence and also its most vociferous expression of Judah's immense toughness and athletic prowess – the nine-minute chariot race. To this day the sequence stands as one of the pinnacles of cinematic spectacle; as Michael Wood argues, 'The hero of *Ben-Hur* is not Ben-Hur, who only won the chariot race, but William Wyler, the director, the man responsible for providing the chariot race for us.'[104] In a reiteration of both the omnipotence of the Judeo-Christian God and Judah's being guided by providence, prior to the race Judah is shown solemnly praying to God, while his rival Messala flippantly hails Jupiter and asks that he guide him to victory. Judah proceeds to win the race against seemingly insurmountable odds; the wheels of Messala's chariot are mounted with spikes that Messala uses to destroy Judah's chariot, and when this fails to effectively repel Judah, Messala begins to thrash him with his whip. However, Messala's nefarious tactics prove to be his downfall. Judah eventually manages to wrestle the whip out of Messala's hands in an incredible display of strength and dexterity that exemplifies Wilkinson's claim that the American tough guy is 'dynamic' and possesses a style 'that celebrates action, impact, and the power of speed.'[105] Messala is subsequently dislodged from his chariot, resulting in him being trampled by rampaging horses and leaving him mortally wounded. Judah's killing of the Roman villain effectively symbolizes the eventual decline of Roman power and the concomitant rise of Christianity across Europe around AD 300–500 – a historic toppling of a slave state that, in accordance with contemporaneous Cold War rhetoric, can be seen as foretelling the United States' inevitable defeat of the Soviet Union.

The Ten Commandments' projection of Moses as a typically American hyper-masculine hero in direct opposition to the effeminacy of Rameses is somewhat mirrored by the relationship between Judah and Messala in *Ben-Hur*. While Messala is not palpably effeminate, his character is nonetheless underpinned by an atypical sexual orientation. As Vito Russo details in *The Celluloid Closet: Homosexuality in the Movies* (1981), it is Messala's unrequited love for Judah that is at the root of the antagonism that develops between the two characters. Russo quotes Gore Vidal, one of the film's screenwriters, who claimed credit for the homosexual subtext:

> I proposed the notion that the two had been adolescent lovers and now Messala has returned from Rome wanting to revive the love affair but Ben-Hur does not. He has read Leviticus and knows an abomination when he sees one. I told Wyler, "This is what's going on *underneath* the scene – they *seem* to be talking about politics, but Messala is really trying to rekindle a love affair," and Wyler was startled. We discussed the matter, and then he sighed, "Well. Anything is better than what we've got in the way of motivation, but don't tell Chuck [Charlton Heston]." I did tell Stephen Boyd, who was fascinated. He agreed to play the frustrated lover. Study his face in the reaction shots in that scene, and you will see that he plays it like a man starving.[106]

The scene to which Vidal refers depicts the first on-screen meeting between Judah and Messala, and begins with Messala entering a darkened room, lit only by rows of torches. Messala stands in the foreground of the frame with his back to the camera, which positions the audience as sharing his point of view. Messala spies Judah standing in the distance, perfectly framed by an illuminated doorway, which engenders the sense that, when seen through Messala's eyes, Judah is permanently surrounded by an incandescent glow. Judah and Messala approach one another and when they meet, they vigorously embrace and then stare into each other's eyes, while Miklós Rózsa's gloriously melodramatic score reaches its crescendo. The exchange of dialogue begins with the wide-eyed 'starving' Messala, voice quivering, telling Judah, 'I said I'd come back,' to which Judah, eyes welling up with tears, replies, 'I never thought you would.' The two proceed to physically embrace and exchange more highly suggestive dialogue ('Still close,' 'In every way'), before Messala asks rhetorically, 'Is there anything so sad as unrequited love?' and shows Judah to his private quarters. As John D'Emilio has detailed, the overwhelming emphasis on normalcy and conformity

Figure 1.9 The 'starving' Messala (Stephen Boyd) lovingly stares into the eyes of his boyhood friend.

that pervaded 1950s' America resulted in the common linkage of homosexuality and the menace of Communism.¹⁰⁷ Messala's overt attraction to Judah can thus be seen as positioning Messala as inherently antithetical to mainstream America, while at the same reaffirming the idealized hyper-masculinity of the strong and athletic Judah.

The presentation of Moses and Judah as paragons of hyper-masculinity is significant for it establishes both *The Ten Commandments* and *Ben-Hur* as key participants in the contemporaneous cultural campaign to privilege more traditional modes of masculinity. While the 1950s were a time in which normative sexuality and traditional conceptions of masculinity were intrinsically bound with idealized notions of Cold War Americanism, the hegemony of normative masculinity did not go completely unchallenged. This was a period in which alternative 'softer' modes of masculinity were beginning to take hold throughout America's cultural milieu. As Cohan argues in *Masked Men*, Hollywood cinema throughout the 1950s – a period that Cohan broadly defines as 'the span of time measured by the Truman and Eisenhower administrations,'¹⁰⁸ thus meaning 1945–61 – 'contributed to but also resisted and problematized the postwar articulation of masculinity as a universal condition.'¹⁰⁹ Among the prime cinematic signifiers of the burgeoning resistance to more traditional notions of the masculine ideal was the emergence of a new generation of performers whose look and acting style radically differed from that of the older, more established stars of the era. Young stars such as Marlon Brando, Montgomery Clift and James Dean, each of whom emerged from the Method school of acting out of New York, exhibited a neurotic sensitivity and subtle femininity that was diametrically opposed to the stoicism and rugged masculinity of older stars like John Wayne, Kirk Douglas, Burt Lancaster and Gary Cooper. It was a time in which, to quote Peter Biskind, Hollywood men 'were becoming more like women.'[110] This emergent, more feminized mode of masculinity was most notably conveyed in the wave of Method-inflected melodramas featuring the aforementioned new wave of male acting talent; see, for instance, *A Place in the Sun* (George Stevens, 1951) starring Clift, *A Streetcar Named Desire* (Elia Kazan, 1951) starring Brando, *From Here to Eternity* (George Stevens, 1953) starring Clift and *Rebel Without a Cause* (Nicholas Ray, 1955) and *East of Eden* (Elia Kazan, 1955) each of which starred Dean.

Cohan dedicates a chapter in *Masked Men* to the *The Ten Commandments* and its playing out of this clash of masculinities. However, he focuses primarily on how this conflict has the effect of positioning Brynner's Rameses as a repellent figure of racial Otherness within the historical setting of Cold War global politics.[111] Without contesting this claim, I would also argue that the affirmation of traditional masculinity in *The Ten Commandments* (and, indeed, *Ben-Hur*) could be seen as a response to the emergence of a more feminized mode of masculinity in the aforementioned melodramas.[112] Neither Brynner nor Boyd were ever readily associated with the new, 'soft' masculinity of Brando, Clift and Dean. However, as Cohan points out, 'As a consequence of the attention which his body – starting with his bald head – appeared to demand from female and male viewers alike, Brynner's star persona encouraged a visual treatment similar to that traditionally bestowed upon female stars.'[113] Moreover, in *The Ten Commandments* Rameses's character echoes those stars' vulnerability and weakness, while his androgynous appearance evokes their sexual ambiguity. Cohan positions the new wave of young male actors as having crossed 'the binarized axes of masculinity/femininity, straight/gay, authentic/theatrical, young/old that structured the virility of a traditional "he-man" movie star like John Wayne.'[114] Cohan adds, 'the new stars did not cross-dress literally, of course, but their association with melodrama gave their boyish personae an unmistakable "transvestite effect" nonetheless.'[115] However, as noted earlier, in *The Ten Commandments* Rameses essentially does cross-dress, and thus he crosses the binarized axis of masculinity/femininity identified by Cohan as presenting a challenge to the traditional conceptions of normalized fifties' masculinity. Similarly,

Boyd's Messala, who carries with him a love and desire for Judah, crosses the binarized axis of straight/gay. Meanwhile, standing in direct opposition to the androgyny-infused Otherness of Rameses and the sexual Otherness of Messala is the traditional masculinity of Heston. Whereas the new school of actors were wild ones and rebels without causes, irrepressibly resisting the fundamental tenets of mainstream American life, Heston proudly represented the quintessence of Cold War conservatism – straight, strong, pious and a crusher of deviant atheism. The celebration of Heston's 'hard' masculinity is significant for, as will be detailed throughout later chapters, Hollywood's subsequent imaginings of Israel would continue to deploy both the land of Israel, as well as Israel's conflict with the Arab world, as a means through which to unequivocally valorize traditional models of American hyper-masculinity.

Charlton Heston's star image

The construction of both Moses and Ben-Hur as symbols of traditional American masculinity is undoubtedly bolstered by the star image of Charlton Heston that emerged in the years following the release of *Ben-Hur* in 1959. As Richard Dyer asserts throughout his groundbreaking study *Stars* (1979), an actor's star image is central to a film's production of meaning.[116] Here it is crucial to understand that an actor's star image can inform the reception of films that were produced and released prior to the star image's formation through the phenomenon of what Patricia White terms 'retrospectatorship.'[117] White's formulation of retrospectatorship posits that the reception of films in the years after their production and exhibition has the potential to endow them with new meanings through their being 'experienced anew in a different filmgoing culture.'[118] Thus, just as an actor brings with them the accumulated history of past performances to each new role, their later films serve to re-inscribe past roles with ideological significance. Heston's biographer Emilie Raymond argues that, in the wake of Heston's performances as Moses and Judah Ben-Hur, a star image emerged 'that embodied responsibility, individualism, and conservative masculinity.'[119] This image remained with Heston throughout his career, as he continued to play larger-than-life characters whose actions carry with them a historical significance of often-Biblical proportions. In 1961, in what was only a slight deviation from his lead roles in *The Ten Commandments* and *Ben-Hur*, Heston played a legendary Spanish Christian warrior who leads the fight against Muslim invaders in *El Cid* (Anthony Mann); in 1965 he again ventured into Biblical territory as John the Baptist in *The Greatest Story Ever Told* (George Stevens); in 1966 he again faced off against fanatical anti-Western Muslims as the heralded English First World War general Charles Gordon in *Khartoum* (Basil Dearden); in 1968 he played the ill-fated American astronaut George Taylor in the science fiction classic *Planet of the Apes* (Franklin J. Schaffner). Here it is worth noting that Heston would reject scripts in which the characters did not represent the values with which he had become associated.[120] In building on his iconic roles of Moses and Judah Ben-Hur, the aforementioned films helped to consecrate Heston as, in the famous words of French film critic Michel Mourlet, 'an axiom' of the cinema who enables the mise-en-scene to 'confront the most intense of conflicts and settle them with the contempt of a god imprisoned, quivering with muted rage.'[121] Central to Mourlet's deification of Heston is the actor's physiognomy, described by Mourlet in the following terms: 'the sombre phosphorescence of his eyes, his eagle's profile, the imperious arch of his eyebrows, the hard, bitter curve of his lips, the stupendous strength of his torso – this is what he has been given, and what not even the worst of directors can debase.'[122] Here Mourlet effectively surmises what lies at the heart of Heston's fundamental appeal as an epic hero; the actor's unique physical presence and resonant delivery of dialogue conforms to traditional conceptions of the individualist hero that, dating back to the earliest stages of European settlement of the continent, has remained a central figure in the United States' national mythology. When projected via the widescreen format that prevailed throughout the 1950s and 1960s, and which profoundly heightens the effect of the cinematic image, Heston becomes less an actor and more a living paradigm of the inherent power and virtuosity of classical Hollywood cinema.

According to Dyer, 'A film star's image is not just his or her films, but the promotion of those films and of the star through pin-ups, public appearances, studio hand-outs and so on, as well as interviews, biographies and coverage in the press of the star's doings and "private" life.'[123] Consequently, audience reception of both *The Ten Commandments* and *Ben-Hur* continues to be informed by not only the iconic roles performed by Heston throughout the later stages of his career, but also by his corresponding emergence as one of Hollywood's most prominent conservatives. Once a highly visible civil rights activist who endorsed John F. Kennedy for president,[124] Heston had well and truly shifted to the right of the political spectrum by the early 1980s. Exemplifying Edgar Morin's assertion that 'The star is more than an actor incarnating characters, he incarnates *himself in them*, and they become incarnate in him,'[125] Heston the conservative, again quoting Raymond, 'publicly identified with the Cold War liberal values of anticommunism and personal freedom' so virulently espoused in the epic films in which he starred.[126] In addition to his anti-Communism Heston vociferously opposed abortion and progressive initiatives such as affirmative action, and later campaigned for Republican presidents Ronald Reagan, George Bush and George W. Bush, the latter of whom awarded him the Presidential Medal of Freedom in 2003. A staunch supporter of Second Amendment rights, Heston was also the president of the National Rifle Association (NRA) from 1998 to 2003, a role that ultimately came to define the final chapters of his life.

Dyer argues that: 'The star phenomenon consists of everything that is publicly available about stars.'[127] A star's image is thus at least partially predicated on 'what people say or write about him or her, as critics or commentators, the way the image is used in other contexts such as advertisements, novels, pop songs, and finally the way the star can become part of the coinage of every day speech.'[128] In the decade prior to his death in 2008, Heston's star image was largely predicated on the relationship that existed between his mutually determinative on-and-off-screen personas, and the ways in which these personas were mobilized across disparate texts. For instance, in two episodes of the absurdist Comedy Central sitcom *That's My Bush!* (2001) a mentally unhinged characterization of Heston appears in his capacity as NRA president, frequently spouting extreme right-wing rhetoric that is punctuated with famous lines of dialogue from his most memorable screen roles.[129] Heston's status as doyen and spiritual leader of American conservatism gained further currency as a result of Michael Moore's Academy Award-winning documentary *Bowling for Columbine* (2002), which explores the nature of gun violence in the United States. Heston appears throughout as the chiselled face of America's powerful pro-gun lobby, the ostensive 'villain' of the film. Reflecting the authority lent to Heston's political activism by the public image cultivated by his film roles, Moore conflates Heston the ideological icon with Heston the performer by intercutting footage of the real-world Heston with scenes from some of the more notable entries in the actor's filmography. Consequently, Heston the Hebrew deliverer also plays the role of saviour for the gun-toting, God-fearing American far Right. At one point in the film Heston is even deridingly referred to as 'Moses' by a gun control advocate who bemoans the toxic influence of the NRA over American public life. In the film's denouement Moore briefly interviews Heston – who appears seated in front of a poster of himself as Judah Ben-Hur – before Heston makes an abrupt exit after being challenged over what is presented as the NRA's insensitive response to a number of incidents involving the shooting deaths of children (but not before Heston suggests that a significant factor behind America's disproportionately high rate of gun violence is its 'mixed ethnicity'). The appearance of Heston, be it as caricature or political spokesman, in programmes such as *That's My Bush!* and *Bowling for Columbine*, effectively symbolizes the irrevocable conflation of Heston's past life as an actor who specialized in playing historical and mythical heroes and his contemporary status as an individualistic, hyper-masculine icon of the American far Right. This particular mode of representation crystallizes how the dialectic between Heston's on-and-off-screen personas over the decades since his iconic roles of Moses and Judah Ben-Hur continues to retrospectively feed into and embolden the Americanization of each character. It is also crucial to note that the conflation of Heston the actor with Heston the ideological icon has occurred in conjunction with the frequent airing of both *The Ten Commandments* and *Ben-Hur* on television throughout subsequent decades. As a result, the respective on-and-off-screen personas of Charlton Heston that have emerged throughout the last fifty years have continually intersected with his foundational roles of Moses and Judah, resulting in a perpetual re-informing of audience reception of both *The Ten Commandments* and *Ben-Hur* that ultimately serves to reaffirm their status as American Cold War parables.

The presentation of ancient Hebrews as stand-ins for Americans in *The Ten Commandments* and *Ben-Hur* for the purpose of articulating the notion of Americans as 'God's Chosen People' and America as the Promised Land would serve as the foundation for the alignment of Jewish-American identity that would pervade Hollywood's disparate representations of Israel throughout the following six decades. Furthermore, *The Ten Commandments* and *Ben-Hur* each establish Israel as a place that, while clearly evocative of modern-day America, nonetheless retains its own identity, thus rendering it an ideal site in which battles between competing masculinities can be effectively staged, and where a hardened masculinity that has been traditionally bound up with notions of American identity can be celebrated as being inherently superior without upsetting the fabric and values of contemporaneous American society. As will be discussed in detail throughout the following chapters, the privileging of the traditional hyper-masculine ideal would remain a central tenet throughout future invocations of Israel in Hollywood cinema. The historical and ideological significance of both *The Ten Commandments* and *Ben-Hur* will be further illuminated through the following chapter's examination of *Exodus*. Released just one year after *Ben-Hur*, *Exodus* builds on the motifs established by both *The Ten Commandments* and *Ben-Hur* in its presentation of modern-day Israelis as proto-Americans through the imagining of Israel as a 'New Frontier' akin to the Old West of American folklore, whereby the advancement of European civilization in the face of dark-skinned savagery can only be achieved through the will of intrepid, hyper-masculine heroism.

2

A new frontier: The birth of Israel as frontier myth in *Exodus* (1960)

The immense popularity of the historical epic with both studios and audiences throughout the 1950s was not merely attributable to the form's overt celebration of liberal democracy. Beginning in 1947, Hollywood entered a ten-year recession that saw movie attendance decline by 50 per cent.[1] In its attempts to regain this lost audience, Hollywood invested in the development of CinemaScope and other widescreen technologies that greatly enhanced the theatrical experience. The epic, with its grandiose narratives, gargantuan sets, gaudy accoutrements, casts of thousands and exorbitant production costs, was widely seen as the genre that could best demonstrate the magnificence of this new format. As Steven Cohan explains:

> The studios emphasized the increased size and scale of these films as a means of differentiating their product from competing leisure industries, not only television but also professional sports and amusement parks, legitimate theater and nightclubs, and the new developments in the recording industry, such as long-playing albums and high-fidelity equipment. To borrow a phrase of the State Department at that time, a biblical in widescreen, with its potential for impressing audiences with oversized spectacle, gave customers more bang for their buck.[2]

However, Hollywood's deployment of the widescreen format was not restricted to films that took the ancient world as their narrative setting. The era was also replete with big-budget, big-scale epics that narrativized more modern history, with notable examples including *Giant* (George Stevens, 1956), *The Alamo* (John Wayne, 1960), *The Longest Day* (Ken Annakin, Andrew Marton, and Bernhard Wicki, 1962) and *How the West Was Won* (John Ford, Henry Hathaway and George Marshall, 1963). The birth of the state of Israel also received the epic treatment in the form of *Exodus* (Otto Preminger, 1960), a lavish, 200 minute, widescreen extravaganza featuring an all-star cast including

Paul Newman, Eva Marie Saint, Sal Mineo, Lee J. Cobb, Peter Lawford, John Derek and Hugh Griffith.

Exodus was based on a novel of the same name written by American author Leon Uris, published in 1958. *Exodus* was a triumphant imagining of the birth of Israel, telling a story that, in the words of Matthew M. Silver, 'urged millions of readers to discard Holocaust-era images of Jews as defenceless, cowering victims and to see them instead as heroic masters of their own fate,'[3] in the process achieving outstanding commercial success, spending eighty weeks on the bestseller list and selling almost four million copies before the film's release.[4] MGM had originally commissioned Uris to write the book in 1956, with the intention of eventually adapting the novel into a film.[5] Uris's objectives in writing *Exodus* reveal themselves in a private letter he addressed to himself less than two months after MGM commissioned the project, in which he wrote:

> I am not writing this book for the Jews or the Zionists. I am writing this book for the American people in hopes I can present it in such a way that Israel gets what she needs badly – understanding. I am writing this book to bring a major film company into Israel which will produce a motion picture that will present this story to a billion people around the world on film.[6]

Uris achieved his goal of bringing Israel 'understanding' in the eyes of the American public. To quote David Ben-Gurion, Israel's first prime minister, 'As a literary work [*Exodus*] isn't much. But as a piece of propaganda, it's the greatest thing ever written about Israel.'[7]

Soon after the release of Uris's novel, Otto Preminger managed to persuade MGM to sell him the rights to the screen adaptation, telling them 'It is a great book, but if you make it the Arab countries will close all MGM theaters and ban all MGM films. You can't afford an Arab boycott, but I can. Since I am an independent producer, they can't hurt me too much.'[8] Preminger subsequently took the project to United Artists, who agreed to back the film with a sizable budget of $3.5 million.[9] After acquiring ownership of the property, Preminger discarded the screenplay written by Uris and brought in blacklisted screenwriter Dalton Trumbo to rewrite the script.[10] While Uris had been dismissed from the project, the success of his novel ensured that the film version constituted a major cultural event. Anticipation for the film was high, with advanced ticket sales setting a record of $1.6 million.[11] Released on 15 December 1960, *Exodus* claimed the number one spot at the box office during Christmas of that same year, and would go on to be one of the top five box office hits of 1961.[12]

To this day *Exodus* remains the most commercially successful and culturally significant cinematic rendering of the birth of the Jewish state produced within the Hollywood system. The profound impact of the book-and-film phenomenon is effectively summed up by Silver, who describes *Exodus* as 'a major event in the culture of Jewish revival after the Holocaust.'[13]

Preminger's *Exodus* mythologizes the ultimate victory of the Zionist movement on the grandest of scales. The film interweaves the story of the declaration of Israeli statehood with allusions to the history of European anti-Semitism and its catastrophic culmination in the Holocaust, the Zionist struggle against the British occupiers of Mandatory Palestine, and the outbreak of hostilities with the region's native Arab population. In its grandiosity, *Exodus* signals its affinity with the Biblical and historical epics that typified the era, while the film's tale of an oppressed people arduously striving for liberty was akin to that of both *The Ten Commandments* and *Ben-Hur*. Even the film's title, drawn from the name of a ship that successfully evacuated some 600 Holocaust survivors from Cyprus and relocated them to Palestine, explicitly recalls the narrative of *The Ten Commandments*. *Exodus* also echoes both *The Ten Commandments* and *Ben-Hur* by projecting an idealized conception of American identity through the narrativization of the Jewish struggle for national liberty.

The previous chapter argued that *The Ten Commandments* and *Ben-Hur* were only ostensibly about the ancient world, and that each film was, instead, primarily concerned with projecting an idealized notion of American identity in accordance with the rhetoric of the Cold War. In both *The Ten Commandments* and *Ben-Hur,* modern-day Americans are positioned as the spiritual descendants of the ancient Hebrews, thus advancing the notion that the citizens of the United States are 'God's Chosen People.' *Exodus* similarly conflates American and Jewish identity by explicitly encouraging its audience to envisage Israelis as proto-Americans, by presenting the birth of the Jewish state as a re-enactment of the expansion of the American frontier through the invocation of the language and form of the traditional Hollywood Western. It is important at this point to acknowledge that identifying *Exodus* as a pseudo-Western is not a particularly revelatory observation. Matthew M. Silver argues that 'the film's later phases, chronicling struggles at the time of the Jewish statehood declaration, play out as an Israeli cowboy replay of how the American West was won.'[14] Similarly, Lester D. Friedman describes the film as 'a Hollywood Western played out in the desert instead of on a prairie, a tale of brave men overcoming the dangers of a wild frontier to bring law, order, and civilization to a new land.'[15] Meanwhile, Omer

Bartov asserts that *Exodus* presents 'the idealized version of the heroic Jew, a combination of the white settler in the Wild West and the righteous victim of persecution seeking justice through war and peace.'[16]

While previous commentary has remarked on the film's superficial similarities to the Western genre, it has tended to focus on how such an approach contributes to a favourable imagining of both Jews and the state of Israel in the eyes of the film's American audience. For instance, Friedman positions *Exodus* as belonging to a wave of major Hollywood films produced during the mid-to-early 1960s, which also includes entries such as *Judgment at Nuremburg* (Stanley Kramer, 1961) and *The Pawnbroker* (Sidney Lumet, 1964), which 'reflect the feelings of acceptance and confidence prevalent among the majority of America's Jews during this period.'[17] Bartov claims that the film consciously renders for its American audience a 'new Jewish hero into a strangely familiar figure despite his involvement in a far-off and not entirely explicable conflict.'[18] Amy Kaplan argues that both the book and film versions of *Exodus*, by interweaving 'two apparently contradictory stories of a universal mission and a particular national triumph, the rebirth of humanity and regeneration through violence,' ultimately cast Israel 'as a mirror of American exceptionalism, as both unique and exemplary.'[19] What such commentary has generally overlooked is how the film's Americanization of Israel's birth serves to perpetuate and circulate a particular imagining of the United States. As we will see, *Exodus*'s appropriation of the language of the classic American Western serves to position the film as a vehicle for conveying a more traditional version of America's national mythology, and in so doing the film stands as a prime exemplar of Hollywood's tendency to mobilize the image of Israel for the purpose of articulating an idealized notion of American national identity.

Manifest destiny and the myth of the frontier

With the United States emerging as its region's pre-eminent power throughout the first half of the nineteenth century, the notion of American 'chosenness' would ultimately facilitate the emergence of the concept of 'Manifest Destiny.' In essence, Manifest Destiny asserted that the United States – or, more specifically, those of its citizens who were of European extraction – was 'chosen' by God to claim and conquer surrounding territory and to subsequently remake the world in accordance with American conceptions of liberty, democracy and civilization.

Journalist John O'Sullivan is credited with coining the term Manifest Destiny when, in 1845, on the verge of both the United States' acquisition of Oregon and also the Mexico-American War (the latter of which would ultimately result in the United States claiming more than half of Mexico's territory), he wrote that it was the United States' 'manifest destiny to overspread the continent allotted by Providence for the free development of our yearly multiplying millions.'[20] The term was soon adopted and debated by Americans of all political stripes, ultimately becoming, to quote historian Anders Stephanson, 'a staple of the political language of American history.'[21]

In addition to serving as a justification for the acquisition of Oregon and also much of Mexico, the notion of Manifest Destiny also served to validate westward migration and what would now be termed the 'ethnic cleansing' of the continent's indigenous population, who were generally considered to be a noxious obstacle to the inexorable progress of Euro-American civilization. Out of this westward migration emerged the so-called 'Frontier Myth,' which was most famously articulated by the historian Frederick Jackson Turner in his seminal paper 'The Significance of the Frontier in American History,' delivered to the American Historical Association at the Chicago World's Columbian Exposition in 1893.[22] Turner's thesis claimed that many aspects of the distinctively American national character – with its emphasis on self-reliance, individualism and democratic ideals – were born out of the collective experience tied to the expansion and eventual closure of the country's western frontier, which Turner labelled 'the first period of American history.'[23] For Turner, at the heart of this experience was the confrontation between advancing civilization and the untamed savagery of the wilderness. So widely accepted was Turner's thesis that it would ultimately come to serve as one of the central myths of the United States' national history. Indeed, it would contribute significant ideological capital to notions of Manifest Destiny and American exceptionalism, prompting historian Edward Countryman to describe it as 'the single most important piece of writing ever produced about the American past.'[24]

The Western genre of cinema, which is best understood as comprising films that take place within the symbolic landscape of the American West, roughly in the period between 1865 and 1890, with stories that centre on 'mining camps, the building of the railways, the Indian Wars, the cattle drives, the coming of the farmer,'[25] has doubtlessly served as the most widely consumed means through which both the notion of Manifest Destiny and the myth of the frontier have been dramatized within the American cultural sphere. In the words of film scholar Jim Kitses, 'the Western is American history.'[26] Through its perpetual retelling of stories that unfold during one of the defining periods of the United States' development into nationhood, the genre has played a central role in the construction and projection of the United States' national identity. A cursory look at some of the major thematic shifts within the genre up to and including the period surrounding the release of *Exodus* illuminates the ways in which the genre has functioned to affirm an idealized conception of Americanism in accordance with an ever-changing national cultural and political milieu.

The significance of the Western in early American film production is typified by the mythology that surrounds Edwin S. Porter's one-reel *The Great Train Robbery* (1903), which Richard Slotkin posits 'has long figured in the folklore of American mass culture as the progenitor of narrative cinema.'[27] In the decade following the release of *The Great Train Robbery*, the Western emerged as 'the first truly cinematic genre and the first distinctively American contribution to the new art form.'[28] From as early as 1910 through to the early 1930s, between a fifth and a quarter of all the films produced in the United States were Westerns.[29]

Production of Westerns declined in the early-to-mid 1930s amid changes to the industry initiated by the development of sound and the subsequent emergence of new film genres.[30] Scholars have also pointed to the social crises brought on by Great Depression as a factor in the Western's decline throughout the early years of the 1930s. According to Slotkin:

> The crises of the Depression undoubtedly had something to do with the genre's decline. The formulas of the silent Western (and especially of the epic) had developed during the boom time of the 1920s, and the historical or literary references of these films evoked a mythology ineluctably linked with the heroic age of American expansion and the dream of limitless growth. In 1932–35 it may have seemed that that vision of history was invalid, or no longer useful, that to speak to the needs of the moment projective fantasies had at least to entertain the possibility of historical catastrophe, the failure of the progressive dream that had been embodied in the Myth of the Frontier.[31]

However, the end of the decade ushered in a revival of the genre, with the major Hollywood studios more than doubling their production of 'A' Westerns.[32] Slotkin attributes the resurgence of the Western to the winding down of the Great Depression and the restoration of public faith in national institutions in the wake of Franklin Roosevelt's New Deal, which enabled American history to 'once again be read as a kind of "success story".'[33]

During the war years – and particularly between 1942 and 1945 (the years in which the United States was directly involved in the conflict) – production of Westerns significantly declined as Hollywood focused instead on reconstructing battles fought during the war rather than drawing on national mythology. However, as Slotkin has detailed, the Second World War combat films like *Bataan* (Tay Garnett, 1943) and *Operation, Burma!* (Raoul Walsh, 1945) essentially re-enacted the motifs of the classic Western, with the Japanese playing the role of the racially inferior dark-skinned antagonists.[34] These films serve to demonstrate one of the key arguments of Slotkin's *Gunfighter Nation: The Myth of the Frontier in Twentieth-Century America* (1992); namely, that the mythic language attached to American westward expansion has been consistently deployed as a tool to negotiate the disparate tensions that have pervaded American society throughout its historical development, and that Hollywood has often utilized this language in a wide range of settings and contexts that are exterior to the historical frontier. *Exodus* can be understood as performing a similar function as the aforementioned Second World War combat films, with Israel standing in for the United States' historical frontier, and the region's Arab population standing in for America's supposedly demonic indigenous population.

With the end of the Second World War and the subsequent ascension of the United States to a position of unrivalled global hegemony, the Western emerged as Hollywood's dominant mode of national mythmaking. Between the years 1947 and 1950 Westerns constituted roughly 30 per cent of Hollywood's total output.[35] Westerns produced during this period generally exalted the United States' mythical past while expressing optimism about its future. Notable examples of this type of Western include *My Darling Clementine* (John Ford, 1946), in which law and order is triumphantly installed in a hostile frontier town by Henry Fonda's Wyatt Earp, and *Red River* (Howard Hawks, 1948), which, through the conflict between a tyrannical cattle driver (John Wayne) and his adopted son (Montgomery Clift), metaphorizes the United States' progression from a land founded by rugged and ruthless individualists to one ostensibly defined by liberalism and democratic principals. Other examples of this celebratory cinema include John Ford's 'cavalry trilogy,' comprising *Fort Apache* (1948), *She Wore a Yellow Ribbon* (1949) and *Rio Grande* (1950), which overtly celebrated the United States' military tradition against the backdrop of the so-called 'Indian Wars.'

However, as the forties transitioned into the fifties, disparate social forces such as anxieties fuelled by the Cold War and also the burgeoning Civil Rights movement coalesced to present a formidable challenge to American self-assuredness and its self-appointed status as a global symbol of liberty, justice, and inherently benevolent power. This shift in the collective consciousness was reflected by a dramatic reinterpretation of the United States' national mythology. For instance, the early 1950s saw the emergence of a wave of so-called 'gunfighter' Westerns – best typified by such high-quality films such as *The Gunfighter* (Henry King, 1950), *High Noon* (Fred Zinnemann, 1952) and *Shane* (George Stevens, 1953) – in which a lone gunfighter faced off against seemingly insurmountable forces of evil. Slotkin argues that the typical protagonist of the gunfighter film served as the 'embodiment of the central paradox of America's self-image in an era of Cold War "subversion," and the thermonuclear balance of terror: our sense of being at once extremely powerful and utterly vulnerable, politically dominant and yet helpless to shape the course of crucial events.'[36]

In 1950 two revolutionary Westerns were released that depicted frontier conflict primarily from the Native Americans' perspective – *Broken Arrow* (Delmer Daves), starring the iconic Western hero James Stewart and Jeff Chandler as the legendary Chiricahua Apache warrior Cochise, and *Devil's Doorway* (Anthony Mann), featuring Robert Taylor as a heroic Native American who has valiantly fought for the Union in the Civil War. These films signalled the emergence of what Slotkin terms the 'cult of the Indian' subgenre,[37] and they were followed by a wave of Westerns that similarly adopted a relatively more positive view of Native Americans than had Westerns of previous decades; see, for example, *Sitting Bull* (Sidney Salkow, 1954), *Taza, Son of Cochise* (Douglas Sirk, 1954), *Apache* (Robert Aldrich, 1954) and *White Feather* (Robert D. Webb, 1955). According to Slotkin,[38] as well as scholars such as John H. Lenihan[39] and Thomas Cripps,[40] the cult of the Indian wave was motivated by the struggles over black civil rights in the late 1940s and early 1950s, with Native Americans serving as stand-ins for African Americans. Meanwhile, Edward Buscombe has argued that this wave of pro-Indian films constituted a concerted effort from Hollywood to redress the decades of racist depictions of Native Americans in the wake of a world war fought, at least in part, to combat institutionalized racism.[41]

Throughout the late 1950s and early 1960s John Ford directed a number of films such as *The Searchers* (1956), *The Man Who Shot Liberty Valance* (1962) and *Cheyenne Autumn* (1964) that, in stark contrast to his output in the years immediately following the end of the Second World War, candidly questioned the nation's traditional mythology and were marked by what John G. Cawelti calls 'melancholy about the passing of the Old West and ambiguity about the new society that replaced it.'[42] The decline in popularity of more traditional conceptions of America's frontier mythology at this time is also emblematized by the emergence of a series of Westerns set in the contemporary age such as *The Misfits* (John Huston, 1961), *Lonely Are the Brave* (David Miller, 1962) and *Hud* (Martin Ritt, 1963), each of which centred on the adversarial relationship between modernity and traditional American values and the inexorable death of the 'Old West.' It was in this context, in which Hollywood Westerns were beginning to trend away from traditional conceptions of the American historical narrative, that *Exodus* transposed the United States' traditional frontier mythology onto the birth of Israel.

Exodus as Western

According to Thomas Schatz, the setting of a genre film is not merely one of the ways a film can be identified as a genre film, but it is also a central component of the language deployed by a genre film to generate meaning. Because they exist 'within a familiar formula that addresses and reaffirms the audience's values and attitudes,' conventional narrative components such as setting 'assume a preordained thematic significance that is quite different from non-generic narratives.'[43] This is particularly true when speaking of the Western and its ritual reimagining of the frontier myth. As Schatz argues, the image of the land reified by the classic Western – so many of which were shot in Monument Valley in Arizona, a landscape famously typified by harsh sprawling terrain and a series of monolithic stone formations – is one that 'projects a formalized vision of the nation's infinite possibilities and limitless vistas, thus serving to "naturalize" the policies of westward expansion and Manifest Destiny.'[44] In their discussion of how the Hollywood Western naturalizes the notion of Manifest Destiny, Ella Shohat and Robert Stam remark upon how 'the land is presented as both empty and virgin, and at the same time superinscribed with Biblical symbolism – "Promised Land," "New Canaan," "God's Earth".'[45] The presentation of the land as both empty and virgin facilitates the Western's glossing over of the often violent appropriation of Native American territory by European settlers, while the superinscription of Biblical symbolism implies that the land was bestowed to those settlers by providence. As a result, the Western reinforces the notion of Americans as the modern-day 'God's Chosen

People,' in so doing signalling its kinship with Biblical and historical epics such as *The Ten Commandments* and *Ben-Hur*.

Throughout *Exodus* there is a similar sanctification of the land and the Jews' supposedly incontestable right to it, though with one subtle difference – in *Exodus*, which was shot in Israel, the land is literally Biblical rather than simply being inscribed with Biblical symbolism. The notion of Manifest Destiny that essentially underpins the entire genre of the Western thus carries with it an even greater ideological thrust. Indeed, Preminger has stated that he felt that the land of Israel was the real 'star' of the film, and upon laying eyes on the territory he reversed his original decision to film in black and white and instead decided to film in colour so as to better accentuate the aesthetic beauty of the landscape.[46] The scene in which the film's hero Ari Ben Canaan (Paul Newman) interrupts a journey to his parents' house to show his American girlfriend Kitty (Eva Marie Saint) a mountaintop view of the Jezreel Valley best typifies the film's sanctification of the land. A shot from Ari's perspective pans across a sprawling pastoral landscape redolent of the open frontier of the mythologized American West that presents Eretz Israel as a bucolic oasis of tranquillity; this distinctly echoes the traditional point-of-view conventions of the Western, which, as Shohat and Stam point out, 'consistently favor the Euro-American protagonists.'[47] In so doing, the shot can be read as projecting its own formalized vision of Israel's infinite possibilities as a newly (re)claimed Promised Land, just as similar shots serve an analogous ideological function in the traditional Hollywood Western. Accompanying this shot is Ari's narration of the history of the land, in which he identifies the ruins of Megiddo, pointing to 'the very same paving stones that Joshua walked on when he conquered it,' and then Mount Tabor, 'where Deborah gathered her armies ... and watched Barak march out to fight the Canaanites,' as told in the Book of Judges.[48] An increasingly ornery Ari regales Kitty with how 3200 years ago, upon Barak's defeat of the Canaanites, the Jews first came to the valley – that 'it wasn't just yesterday or the day before.' As in *The Man Who Shot Liberty Valance*, John Ford's classic meditation on the complex relationship between myth and history in America's old West, legend has become historical fact. This leads into a discussion regarding Ari's father and how after relocating from Russia to Palestine he took the name Barak Ben Canaan – meaning, 'Barak the Son of Canaan,' a title which is naturally passed down to Ari, who as a 'Sabra' (a Jew born in Mandatory Palestine or, after 1948, Israel) arguably possesses an even greater claim to the land than does his father. This presentation of Ari as a literal son of the land carries with it the inherent positioning of the region's Arab population as interlopers, a notion which is reinforced when Ari points out an Arab village in an aside before continuing on with his Judeo-centric history lesson (which conveniently neglects to identify the epoch in which Arabs began to call the region home). Here the film signals its fidelity with the classic Hollywood Western, which, to quote Shohat and Stam, 'turned history on its head by making Native Americans appear intruders on their own land.'[49] The scene ends with Ari defiantly declaring, 'I'm a Jew. This is my country.' As is the case in the classic Hollywood Western, the dark-skinned people may have lived on the land, but the white man is its rightful claimant. Americans are left to

Figure 2.1 Ari Ben Canaan (Paul Newman) and Kitty Fremont (Eva Marie Saint) look over the Promised Land of the Jezreel Valley in *Exodus*.

Figure 2.2 Julie Maragon (Jean Simmons) and James McKay (Gregory Peck) look over the Promised Land of the American West in *The Big Country* (William Wyler, 1958).

understand the birth of the Israeli nation as a re-enactment of their own, with the Promised Land of Zionist mythology mirroring the Promised Land of frontier mythology for another of 'God's Chosen People.'

A genre film is identified not solely by its physical setting, but also by the presence of a constellation of generic character types who help to define the narrative's community and animate the dramatic conflicts within.[50] According to Schatz, 'the generic character is psychologically static – he or she is the physical embodiment of an attitude, a style, a world view, of a predetermined and essentially unchanging cultural posture.'[51] The generic character type whose presence essentially defines a film as a Western is the cowboy hero, who Schatz identifies as 'an agent of civilization in the savage frontier,' representing 'both the social order and the threatening savagery that typify the Western milieu.'[52] Echoing Schatz, Douglas Pye describes the cowboy hero as 'a figure of confident identity and charismatic authority' who makes the land 'safe for White settlement.'[53] Here it is crucial to note that the ritualistic sanctification of the intrepid frontiersman in American culture predates the invention of cinema. As Slotkin details throughout *Regeneration Through Violence: The Mythology of the American Frontier* (1973), in which he examines the development of a uniquely American mythology during the first two and a half centuries of European settlement, the conflict between white settlers and the continent's native population and its subsequent mythologization through means such as the emerging medium of narrative literature firmly established the Indian-hunting frontiersman as the first prototypical American hero.[54] According to Slotkin, the figure of the frontiersman is so historically central to American conceptions of national identity that it is through the early mythologization of the legendary frontiersman Daniel Boone that 'we can trace the emergence of American national consciousness, the process of cultural differentiation that finally divided the Euro-Americans from the Europeans.'[55]

Paul Newman's Ari Ben Canaan clearly conforms to the conceptions of the cowboy hero put forward by Schatz and Pye. Ari is the charismatic and courageous leader of the Haganah (the pre-state Jewish defence organization in Palestine that eventually became the nucleus of the Israeli military, and which *Exodus* depicts as leading the fight for Israeli independence). However, it is not merely his charismatic persona coupled with his conquering of an untamed land and making it safe for Israeli settlement that positions Ari as an evocation of the traditional cowboy hero of American mythology. Peter Homans asserts that the cowboy hero, as a transcendent figure, 'rides into town from nowhere,' and is thus 'in some way dissociated from the people he must save.'[56] In *Exodus* Ari first appears, roughly fourteen minutes into the film, emerging shirtless from the Mediterranean Sea with the gleaming Star of David hanging from a chain that sits defiantly on his chiselled chest, after making a daring entrance into what was then Mandatory Palestine (in the process circumventing British attempts to restrict Jewish immigration). Throughout this sequence Ari is bathed in a bright light while all around him is darkness, engendering a halo effect that marks him as not merely an assertive, courageous hero, but as bordering on the divine in the tradition of the eponymous character in the self-consciously mythic classic Western *Shane*. Just as Shane's enigmatic arrival in the emergent frontier town distinguishes him as a hero in contrast to the defenceless small-town pioneers whose aid he comes to in their war against wealthy cattle barons, Ari's emergence out of the Mediterranean announces his status as a heroic Sabra. In this scene Ari resembles, in the words of Tony Shaw, 'a bronzed Adonis,' and is thus differentiated from the weak and vulnerable Jews of the Diaspora shown earlier in the film in the displaced persons camp in Cyprus, who after having miraculously survived the Holocaust are now fighting a seemingly losing battle for a nation of their own.[57]

Figure 2.3 Ari Ben Canaan makes his grand entrance out of the Mediterranean.

The estrangement of Ari from the Jewish victims of Nazi Germany is ideologically significant as it serves to divorce him from the so-called 'Ghetto mentality' long associated with the traditional ideal of the nebbish Jew of the Diaspora. This was a specific aim of Leon Uris who, in the words of the author's biographer, wanted to 'do no less than remake the image of the Jew in the post-Holocaust world' for the American audience his book was targeting.[58] Uris, who was a former US Marine, was repelled by the image of the 'soft' Jew and also publicly expressed a profound distaste for what he called 'introspective Jewish writing.'[59] According to Uris's declaration which preceded the book's title page, *Exodus* 'tells the story of the Jews coming back after centuries of abuse, indignities, torture and murder to carve an oasis in the sand with guts and blood,' and was 'about fighting people, people who do not apologize either for being born Jews or the right to live in human dignity.' Regarding his central protagonist and the character's prospective appeal to the book's target audience, Uris wrote in a correspondence with his father, 'I believe it will be like a breath of spring air for the American people to meet Mr. Avi [sic] Ben Canaan, the fighting Jew who won't take shit from nobody … who fears nobody. He will be a welcome departure from the Mailer … Morningstar apologetics.'[60] Indeed, Paul Breines characterizes the Ari of Uris's novel as 'the virtual prototype of the American image of the Israeli tough Jew,' and the literary version of *Exodus* as the foundational text in the primeval development of the Tough Jew archetype that would become fully formed in American culture in the wake of Israel's dramatic victory over its Arab neighbours in the 1967 War (also known as the 'Six Day War').[61] According to Breines, the figure of the Tough Jew played a central role in reshaping the image of the contemporary Jew in American society by presenting Jews as strong, rugged warriors, thus throwing off the age-old stereotype of the Jew as weak and nebbish and ultimately helping to turn the formerly alien Other into a familiar figure with whom American audiences could idealistically identify.

Ari Ben Canaan is also rendered more accessible to American audiences by virtue of a thorough de-ethnicization that echoes the respective constructions of the protagonists played by Charlton Heston in the Biblical epics discussed in the previous chapter. Ari is devoid of much that might be considered Jewish; he quotes the Bible but has no apparent religious feelings, and his participation in ceremonial traditions is limited to those that take place within his parents' home. Meanwhile, the casting of the handsome, fair-haired, blue-eyed Newman plays a key role in making the film's hero, in the words of Bartov, 'into a strangely familiar figure despite his involvement in a far-off and not entirely explicable conflict.'⁶² *Exodus*'s conscious de-ethnicization of its Israeli hero is reinforced by one of the film's more comical scenes. The anti-Semitic British Major Caldwell (Peter Lawford) unwittingly boasts to Ari that Jews 'look funny' and that he can 'spot one a mile away.' This prompts Ari to ask the officer to inspect his eye to see if there is something inside, to which the officer obliges, invariably finding nothing. Notably, this scene and its overt positioning of Ari as the physical clone of a handsome Anglo-Saxon is completely absent from Uris's novel; indeed, the book describes Ari as 'a strapping six-footer with black hair.'⁶³ The ideological significance of this sequence is stridently affirmed through its unfolding in the form of a close-up on the respective faces of Newman and Lawford. As Mary Ann Doane asserts, the close-up, as a result of its disavowal of off-screen space, exists as an autonomous image.⁶⁴ As such, it emerges as 'a sign, a text, a surface that demands to be read,' with the film star's face functioning as 'a privileged site of meaning,' and 'the intensification of a locus of signification.'⁶⁵ Through its focus on the aesthetically pleasing face of Paul Newman, whose 'classic looks' invoke, in the words of Yosefa Loshitzky, 'the beauty of an ancient Greek sculpture,' the aforementioned sequence unequivocally conveys to the film's American audience that the Israelis are, indeed, no different to themselves (or, perhaps more accurately, no different to how they wish to see themselves).⁶⁶ Furthermore, through the juxtaposition of Newman's attractive and apparently Anglo-American features with the bigotry espoused by Lawford's imperious British soldier, the sequence positions Israeli identity as emerging out of an opposition to British colonialism. Here it is pertinent to note that this binary is founded on a wholly ahistorical premise; as Adel Safty has extensively detailed, the Zionist movement succeeded in large part due to, rather than in spite of, the efforts of successive British governments.⁶⁷ In forging such an opposition, the film implicitly aligns Israeli settlers with the American revolutionaries of the late eighteenth century who successfully threw off the yolk of British colonial rule.⁶⁸ Moreover, *Exodus* positions Israeli toughness as being akin to the uniquely American conception of toughness. As Rupert Wilkinson argues, one of the primary factors underpinning the American concern with toughness – in addition, of course, to the experience of westward expansion – is the early American settlers' 'anticourtier tradition,' from which emerged the demand that 'the true American' be 'vigorous, manly, and direct, not effete and corrupt like the supposed Europeans.'⁶⁹ *Exodus*, by casting Paul Newman as its frontiersman hero – and by positioning him in

Figure 2.4 Major Caldwell (Peter Lawford) unwittingly looks into the eyes of a Jew.

direct opposition to detestable British overlords – presents the Israeli settler both as a carbon copy of the 'true American' and as a source of narcissistic identification for its American audience.

In constructing the Israeli hero in the image of the traditional American tough guy, *Exodus* echoes both *The Ten Commandments* and *Ben-Hur* in deploying the land of Israel as a stage upon which to celebrate a more traditional hardened mode of masculinity. *Exodus*'s aggrandizement of the hyper-masculine ideal is made even more conspicuous upon retrospectively examining the film in relation to the Newman screen image that emerged in the years following *Exodus*'s release. Unlike Charlton Heston, Newman was never the traditional he-man hero. Like Marlon Brando, James Dean and Montgomery Clift, Newman emerged in the early 1950s out of New York's Method school of acting, and ultimately came to serve as one of the prime signifiers of an emergent mode of Hollywood masculinity that was defined by introspection and sensitivity, which stood in stark contrast to the 'hard' masculinity of older stars such as John Wayne, Kirk Douglas and Gary Cooper. Through a string of roles including, most notably, an angst-ridden, method-inflected Billy the Kid in *The Left Handed Gun* (Arthur Penn, 1958), Eddie Felson in *The Hustler* (Robert Resson, 1961), Hud Bannon in *Hud*, Luke Jackson in *Cool Hand Luke* (Stuart Rosenberg, 1967) and Butch Cassidy in *Butch Cassidy and the Sundance Kid* (George Roy Hill, 1969), the Newman screen persona that ultimately emerged was one defined by, to quote one biographer, 'vulnerability, weakness, a hedonistic streak, and a full dose of antiauthoritarian cockiness and cynicism.'[70] However, the anti-heroism that underpinned the Newman persona is entirely absent from *Exodus*, with Newman instead playing the role of a stoic, laconic frontiersman so totally in line with a more traditional conception of American masculinity that Lester D. Friedman compares the character to those generally associated with none other than John Wayne.⁷¹ The incongruity between Ari Ben Canaan and what would emerge as the Newman persona affirms how *Exodus* can be understood as carrying on the Hollywood tradition established by the era's Biblical epics of deploying Israel as a stage upon which it can unabashedly celebrate generally outmoded models of 'hard' masculinity.

The film's positioning of Ari as a 'familiar figure' for American audiences is augmented by its construction of Ari's love interest, Kitty Fremont, an American nurse from Indiana.⁷² Throughout the course of the film Kitty undergoes an appreciable evolution – one that is in many ways reflective of shifting attitudes towards Jews within the United States. Initially, Kitty is the personification of the United States' once staunch isolationism. Her interest in the region is personal rather than ideological; her husband was recently killed while working in Palestine, and she subsequently suffered a miscarriage. Kitty is presented as a Midwesterner who has had little to no contact with American Jews, and thus to her the Israelis are an exotic and unusual people, leading her to remark early on in the film that she feels 'strange among them.' At this point in the film Kitty's feelings regarding Jews can be seen as representing the anti-Semitism that until the 1950s pervaded American social life. Throughout the film's first act Kitty prefers the company of the British officials in charge of administering the Cypriot refugee camp, in what is a reflection of both the United States' legacy of anti-Semitism as well as its pre-war identification with its ally from across the Atlantic that resoundingly trumped the cultural and political rapport it

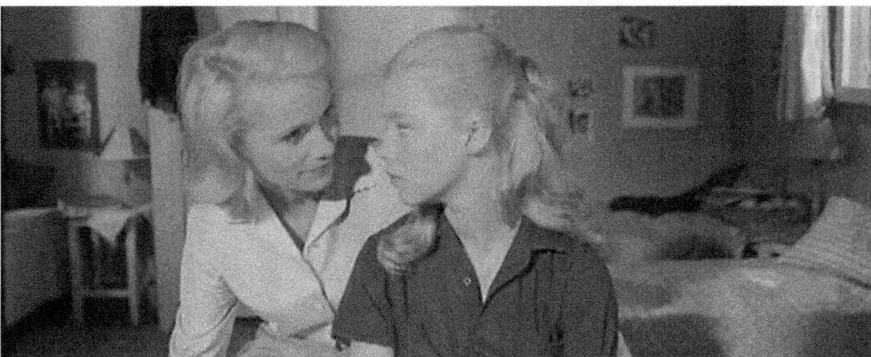

Figure 2.5 Kitty with Karen (Jill Haworth), her young Israeli clone.

enjoyed with any other nation.⁷³ However, in a development that can be seen as symbolizing the nation's increasing affinity for certain elements of Jewish history and tradition and the concomitant distaste for anti-Semitism in American postwar society that contributed to the emergence of the notion of the United States' so-called 'Judeo-Christian' heritage, Kitty comes to be repelled by the overt anti-Semitism of the British.⁷⁴ When the bigoted British Major Caldwell remarks to Kitty, 'I don't know how you can stand them,' Kitty responds by volunteering to deploy her skills as a nurse in a Jewish refugee camp. During her time at the camp, Kitty comes to appreciate that the differences between American Gentiles and the Jews who will go on to create the state of Israel are largely superficial. She even attempts to adopt a young Jewish girl named Karen (Jill Haworth) to whom she bears a striking resemblance, a narrative development that serves to reinforce the notion of Israel as an incipient facsimile of the United States.

The favourable characterization of Kitty following her turn away from the film's anti-Semitic British characters can be seen as reflection of the United States' concept of self in the post-war milieu. As discussed in the previous chapter, American policy makers in the post-war era sought to project the ideal of the United States' 'benevolent supremacy,' which positioned the United States as an altruistic force for good that sat astride the world like a colossus in a manner that starkly contrasted with the attitudes and behaviours of the pre-war colonial powers of Europe as well as the authoritarian Soviet Union.⁷⁵ This construction entailed the possession of an incomparably powerful military as well as an inherent sense of benevolence that ostensibly strived to help to secure liberty for all the nations of the world and spread democracy.⁷⁶ Kitty, as a nurse who selflessly volunteers to assist in a displaced person's camp, is the embodiment of this supposed altruistic benevolence. Her integral role in the success of the Zionist mission reflects the then popular conception of Israel as a newborn baby, which was delivered into the world with the assistance of the United States, who had played the role of midwife.⁷⁷

Ultimately Kitty swears to join Ari and his people in their struggle, in spite of his implorations that she go back to America as she's 'had her civil war.' This piece of dialogue not only reinforces the notion of Kitty as emblematic of the American nation, but it disingenuously implies that the Arab-Israeli conflict is a civil war akin to the American Civil War which gave birth to the modern American nation, and which has long been a central feature of many major Hollywood Westerns.⁷⁸ Kitty's consummating of her commitment to Ari (and, by implication, the state of Israel) also links *Exodus* to the traditional Western by mirroring the formation and implied integration into a community of a frontiersman and a civilized white woman that, according to Douglas Pye, is probably the most frequent ending in Western films.[79] Indeed, Kitty, who is urbane, espouses a Presbyterian faith and is frequently attired in white – and who is played by the snow-haired and angelically beautiful Eva Marie Saint, who was then best known for playing the innocent Catholic schoolgirl in *On the Waterfront* (Elia Kazan, 1954) – conforms to Robert Warshow's contention that women in Westerns represent 'refinement, virtue, civilization, [and] Christianity.'[80] In essence, Kitty is playing the role of what André Bazin termed 'the pure young woman,' recalling, for instance, the eponymous schoolteacher girlfriend (Cathy Downs) of Henry Fonda's Wyatt Earp in *My Darling Clementine*, and the Quaker wife Amy (Grace Kelly) of the hero Kane in *High Noon*.[81] In these films the pure young woman, as the personification of everything that is alien to the untamed frontier that is the classic Western's sphere of action, often comes from the East (Clementine is from Boston, while Amy is said to be from 'back east'), and it is her inevitable union with the cowboy hero that symbolizes not only the moral redemption of the protagonist, but also the emergence of the United States into a unified nationhood; it is a marriage of not only man and woman, but also of civilization and wilderness, of law and order, of East and West. *Exodus* transposes this same marriage onto the Israeli frontier; only the paradigm is inverted by presenting civilization as coming not from the East but from the American Midwest. Israeli nationhood, as it is constructed in *Exodus*, is born out of the coming together of the rugged Sabra frontiersman – who is himself modelled on the cowboy hero of America's Wild West – and twentieth-century American Presbyterian values, and is thus to be understood by American audiences as one that distinctly echoes the brand of American nationhood that has been engendered and projected throughout the annals of the Hollywood Western.

Arabs as Indians in *Exodus*

Another way in which *Exodus* explicitly recalls the Hollywood Western is through its presentation of the region's Arabs in a manner that mirrors the genre's traditional construction of Native Americans. Throughout the film's first two acts, in which the focus is primarily on the Zionists' struggle with the British overlords of Mandatory Palestine, the region is presented as being essentially devoid of a large Arab population; in reality, at the time of the United Nations' vote to partition Palestine there were roughly 650,000 Jews in Palestine, while there were some 1.3 million indigenous Palestinian Arabs.[82] The relative invisibility of the Arabs is important from an ideological standpoint for it facilitates a natural spectatorial identification with the film's white, Americanized Jewish protagonists. More significantly, this invisibility essentially promotes the notion of Israel as a 'virgin' land awaiting the arrival of Western civilization to help make it bloom – a notion that echoes the popular conception of the unsettled American frontier as an untilled 'garden.'[83] Subsequently, in the film's third act, the region's Arabs are explicitly demonized as, to quote Shohat and Stam from their examination of the representation of Native Americans in Hollywood Westerns, 'mean-spirited enemies of the moving train of progress.'[84]

Prior to discussing the ways in which *Exodus* presents the Arabs of the Mandatory Palestine as being akin to the Native Americans of traditional conceptions frontier mythology, it is first pertinent to touch on how the absence of Arabs throughout the film's first two acts is somewhat offset by the occasional appearance of Taha, a mukhtar (a head of a village or neighbourhood) played by John Derek, who is the film's only Arab character of any real significance. The fact that this character is played by a well-known Anglo-American actor recalls Hollywood's affinity for casting white men as Native Americans (a representational practice commonly known as 'redfacing').[85] Taha is introduced as a boyhood friend of Ari, and his father is said to have given the land of his village to the Jews so that they could build a village in which Jews and Arabs could happily live side by side. The obvious message, as Yosefa Loshitzky argues, 'is not that the Zionists took Arab lands but to the contrary: the Arabs (their brothers) gave them the land because they knew that the Jews would bring progress to the region.'[86] As embodied by Derek, who only four years earlier was the valiant Hebrew Joshua in *The Ten Commandments*, Taha is a classic example of the so-called 'noble savage' – a friendly 'good' Arab who embraces the inherently superior Westerner and the civilization he represents.[87] Taha can be seen as explicitly mirroring examples of altruistic dark-skinned characters from the annals of frontier mythology such as Blueback (Chief John Big Tree), the friendly, Christianized Native American who fights alongside the settlers against the coalition of Britons and Indians in *Drums Along the Mohawk* (John Ford, 1939); indeed, 'Taha' is not all that far removed from 'Taza,' the name of the friendly Indian played by Rock Hudson in *Taza, Son of Cochise* a mere six years prior to the release of *Exodus*. In a scene that simultaneously affirms the ties that bind Ari and Taha, the inherent nobility of Ari and his father, as well as the wickedness of the Arabs, Taha declares, 'When the Syrian Arabs murdered my father in his own mosque, Ari's father saved my life, and my heritage.' However, the relationship between Ari and Taha is irrevocably severed following the declaration of partition. While Ari insists that Jews and Arabs can live together in peace and harmony and that Jewish land will also be Arab land, a sober Taha replies that the two can no longer be friends, and that he 'cannot turn his back on his fellow Muslims.' When Taha next appears on-screen he is a corpse, hanging from a noose with the Star of David painted on his chest in blood after having been murdered by his own people for collaborating with a Jew. Crucially, this contrasts starkly with the novel, in which Taha dies in battle with the Zionists.[88] In the film's final scene Taha is buried alongside a fallen Jew, with Ari eulogizing Taha with the words, 'death should have come to him as an old friend offering the gift of sleep. It came instead as a maniac.' The film's lone Arab character of note is thus positioned as a martyr for the Zionist cause, existing purely to demonstrate the tolerance and humanity of Israelis against the inhumanity of Arabs, and to imply that, ultimately, there can be no hope for coexistence between the two peoples.

Aside from the character of Taha, Arabs only appear as a major presence in the film's final act when they launch an assault on Ari's peaceful ebullient kibbutz. The incursion immediately follows the declaration of partition by the United Nations, upon which Ari's father, Barak Ben Canaan (Lee J. Cobb), delivers an address where he states:

> To the Arab population of Jewish Palestine, we make the following appeal – the Grand Mufti has asked you either to annihilate the Jewish population, or to abandon your homes, and your lands, and to seek the weary path of exile. We implore you – remain in your homes and in your shops, and we shall work together as equals in the free state of Israel.

What follows is a variation of what Ella Shohat and Robert Stam identify as one of the most central topos of the Hollywood Western; the Indian raid on the fort.[89] The attack is imbued with an excessive wickedness by virtue of it taking place immediately after Jewish appeals for coexistence. During the assault a nameless, faceless Arab lunges from off-screen and snatches the angelic young Karen. With this sequence the film channels the classic Western by re-enacting what Slotkin calls 'the most sacred of the frontier myths, the tale of captivity and rescue,' in which an innocent white woman, who is emblematic of the virtuous and imperilled Puritan society, is taken captive by Native Americans.[90] According to the myth, the woman inevitably faces sexual contamination at the hands of the savage native, a figure that in early Puritan thought was often positioned 'as insatiably lustful, a being of overbearing sexual power,' before she is ultimately rescued by heroic white settlers.[91] The captivity narrative essentialized the disparate anxieties of the Puritan settlers that emerged out of their attempts to adjust to a strange and hostile environment, and would serve to define their attitudes towards the threatening aspects of the New World. As such, the tale of captivity and rescue manifested itself in various ways in early Puritan society, functioning as literary entertainment as well as material for sermons and political diatribes, dominating the publication of stories of the frontier between 1680 and 1716, and ultimately constituting 'the first coherent myth-literature developed in America for American audiences.'[92]

As the frontier continued to migrate further westward, the captivity narrative persisted as one of the core tropes of frontier mythology. For instance, the captivity narrative is a recurring development in James Fenimore Cooper's series of *Leatherstocking Tales* (published between 1823 and 1841), which Slotkin characterizes as 'the seminal fictions of American literary history.'[93] In the original dime novels authored by Ned Buntline which detailed the supposed exploits of Buffalo Bill, who Henry Nash Smith labels 'the most highly publicized figure in all the history of the Wild West,'[94] the action similarly consists of, in the words of Smith, 'a series of abductions of genteel females – principally Bill's twin sisters – and rescues according to the time-honored pattern.'[95] The ongoing centrality of the captivity narrative to frontier mythology can in turn be seen as contributing to the concomitant consecration of Manifest Destiny by helping to position the conflict between natives and settlers as a 'savage war' for civilization that is both noble and inevitable, and which can only end via the extermination of one side.[96]

The mythic resonance of the captivity narrative to notions of white American identity as constructed by Hollywood cinema is demonstrated through its centrality to D.W. Griffith's racist Civil War epic *The Birth of a Nation* (1915), a film that Miriam Hansen argues 'did lay unprecedented claim to the construction of American history,'[97] and which Michael Rogin describes as 'the movie that founded American mass culture.'[98] In *The Birth of a Nation*, Griffith co-opts the traditional captivity narrative and transposes it onto the postbellum South by having a lecherous freed slave (whom the intertitles describe as a 'renegade black buck') lust after a young white girl named Flora Cameron (Mae Marsh). Flora commits suicide rather than allowing herself to be defiled by the dark-skinned devil, before a valorized Ku Klux Klan rides to the rescue and exacts justice for what Griffith unambiguously positions as the divinely blessed white race. In reproducing a core tenet of frontier mythology *The Birth of a Nation* set the cinematic template for the Hollywood Western, which would similarly depict the birth of the American nation on the foundation of racial violence, while also, on occasion, utilizing the tale of captivity and rescue in its presentation of white civilization as being besieged by dark-skinned savagery.

As is the case with the genre itself, Westerns based on the tale of captivity and rescue evolved in line with the vicissitudes of the contemporaneous social and political climate. Earlier examples, such as *Northwest Passage* (King Vidor, 1940) and *Unconquered* (Cecil B. DeMille, 1947), deployed the captivity narrative in a traditional manner for the express purpose of projecting the image of Native Americans as lascivious savages capable of the worst kind of atrocity. However, by the mid-1950s, in correspondence with the emergence of the pro-Indian Western and a general contesting of frontier mythology, there emerged a number of films that featured tales of captivity and rescue that radically diverted from more traditional conceptions of the narrative. The most notable example of this is John Ford's *The Searchers*, which appeared just four years before the release of *Exodus*, and which has since emerged to be one of the most celebrated Westerns of the classical Hollywood period.

The captivity narrative in *The Searchers*

The narrativization of the captivity narrative in *The Searchers* differs profoundly from that of *Exodus*, and it is through a detailed examination of these differences that we see how the version of frontier mythology articulated throughout *Exodus* is one that is far more traditional than that generally being played out in contemporaneous Hollywood Westerns. *The Searchers* tells the story of an Indian-hating Civil War veteran named Ethan Edwards (John Wayne) and his mission to find his young niece Debbie Edwards (Natalie Wood) who has been kidnapped by Comanche Indians. Following her kidnapping, Debbie is subsequently raised as an Indian, and ultimately made the wife of the tribe's brutal chief Scar (Henry Brandon). In Ethan's mind Debbie has 'become

Indian' by virtue of her being sexually defiled by the Comanche chief. He is inspired to search for her with the intention of killing her, with the implication being that she is better off dead than to go on living, to quote the grotesquely racist parlance of Ethan, 'with a buck' (the same term derisively applied to the rapacious freed slave in *The Birth of a Nation*). After an arduous seven-year search Ethan finally finds Debbie alive, physically unharmed but ostensibly having turned 'savage.' Ultimately Ethan captures Debbie and abandons his plan to kill her, instead returning her safely to the community from which she was taken as a young girl.

The Searchers, perhaps more than any other 1950s Western, signifies the then increasingly problematic status of the United States' traditional frontier mythology. Prior to *The Searchers* the team of director John Ford and his frequent star John Wayne made their names in a series of highly popular Westerns that unequivocally celebrated America's supposedly glorious past, such as *Stagecoach* (1939), and the cavalry trilogy of *Fort Apache, She Wore a Yellow Ribbon* and *Rio Grande*. In each of these films – and, indeed, essentially every film that John Wayne ever appeared in – Wayne served as an unambiguous symbol of hyper-masculine heroism. However, the John Wayne character at the heart of *The Searchers* is one of Hollywood cinema's iconic anti-heroes. He is a mentally unhinged loner who frequently espouses racist epithets, mutilates the body of dead Comanche, shoots at buffalo for the sole purpose of eliminating the natives' primary food source, and who is, for much of the film, intent on murdering his innocent niece out of a virulent disgust at her having had sexual relations with an Indian. Moreover, as is commonly remarked upon by scholars, Ethan and Scar are repeatedly presented as mirror images of one another in what is an apparent suggestion by Ford that the historical construction of Native Americans as barbarous savages can be seen, at least in part, as the projection of white settler self-hatred onto the Indian Other.[99] In the words of Peter Lehman, the racism of Ethan is compounded by the fact that he is 'powerfully and charismatically played by John Wayne,' as this positions the character as a strong point of emotional identification for the audience by virtue of the actor's immense popularity and star image that was so readily associated with the conventional Western hero.[100] The result is a film that, to quote Pye, 'probably goes further than any other Western in dramatizing and implicating us in the neurosis of racism.'[101]

In addition to explicitly demonizing its racist protagonist, *The Searchers* proffers a relatively sympathetic depiction of Native Americans that is in stark contrast with the overwhelming majority of Hollywood Westerns produced before the 1950s. In *The Searchers* Native American raids on white settlers are not presented as senseless acts of barbarism, but instead as part of a cycle of strikes and counterstrikes launched by natives and whites alike. The audience is subjected to scenes that depict the aftermath of a massacre of a Native American village carried out by the US Cavalry that counts innocent women among its victims, signifying the broader institutionalization across American society of the racial hatred held by Ethan.[102] In addition, during the final confrontation between Ethan and Scar, Scar articulates to Ethan that he kidnaps white children to replace the children he has lost at the hands of the white man. Indeed, the mere fact that the film depicts Native Americans as members of a genuinely functioning community renders it an anomaly within the Western genre, for, as observed by Shohat and Stam, Westerns rarely show Native Americans 'as simply inhabiting the domestic space of their unthreatening daily lives.'[103]

In contrast to the nuanced interrogation of frontier mythology that is *The Searchers*, *Exodus* offers absolutely no suggestion that the snatching of Karen is in any way an act of retribution for Jewish transgressions against the native Arab population. Completely devoid of context, her kidnapping is instead presented as a reprehensible act of savagery – a point that is reaffirmed when she is soon found dead. Crucially, everything that happens to her between her kidnapping and the Israelis discovering her lifeless body occurs off-screen, thus inviting the audience to imagine the worst. To recall what Mikhail Bakhtin terms 'genre memory,' which posits that inherent within all genres is the memory of previous entries across that respective generic canon, this lacuna instils in an audience firmly grounded in Puritan mythology, as well as half a century of generically constructed anchored inferences regarding the rapacious lusting after white women by dark-skinned 'savages,' the implication that she has also been raped.[104] This of course further fuels the notion of the Arabs as barbarians while also positioning the frontier of the Holy Land as 'the meeting point between savagery and civilization,' as Frederick Jackson Turner described the American frontier.[105] As noted by Slotkin, the subject of the American captivity narrative 'symbolizes the values of Christianity and civilization that are imperilled in the wilderness war,'[106] and by virtue of killing (and by implication, raping) her Israeli equivalent and then tossing her lifeless body away, the Arabs of *Exodus* declare their complete and unequivocal incompatibility with the Israelis' civilizing mission. Rather than constituting an ill-fated rival civilization doomed to oblivion under the heel of the white man (as are the Comanche in *The Searchers*), the Arabs of *Exodus* are presented as an utterly irredeemable, licentious Other with whom the Israelis cannot live side by side in peace and harmony in their new Eden. It is an imagining that conforms to traditional formulations of the American myth of the 'savage war,' in which Native Americans are positioned as the instigators of a war of extermination.[107] As such, war with the Arabs is presented, from the Israeli perspective, as both noble and inevitable if civilization is to flourish.

To this day *Exodus* remains the most notable of Hollywood's adventures to have taken place in Israel. However, today its significance rests not so much in the commercial success that it achieved, but in its effective conflating of American and Israeli identity. Central to this conflation was the establishment of Israel as a 'New Frontier.' As a New Frontier, the setting of Israel enabled Hollywood to clearly express ideas that had long been central to traditional conceptions of American national mythology but which contemporaneous social conditions had dictated were no longer viable in narratives that unfolded within an obviously American context. Like Hollywood's cowboy heroes that came before him, the film's hero Ari Ben Canaan succeeds in 'winning a wilderness' against unforgiving conditions and its supposedly savage indigenous inhabitants. In so doing, he epitomizes a mode of hard heroic masculinity that American mythology identifies as being central to the taming of the frontier and the subsequent birth of the American nation, but which was becoming increasingly contested by the early 1960s. Meanwhile the film's overt demonization of the region's indigenous Arab population simultaneously recalls the Hollywood Western, while also distancing itself from the contemporaneous entries in the genre that were trending away from demonological depictions of Native Americans. As such, the film succeeds in proffering a virulent celebration of long outmoded conceptions of the mythology surrounding the United States' emergence into nationhood. The ultimate result of *Exodus*'s invocation of American frontier mythology in the narrativization of the birth of the Jewish state is the prejudicial framing of the Arab-Israeli conflict as one in which a demonic racial Other akin to the historical enemies of white American settlers strives to eliminate a people that are fundamentally 'like us' – a framing that would be further expanded upon in *Cast a Giant Shadow* (Melville Shavelson, 1966), the next major Hollywood production to centre on the birth of Israel.

3

The age of interventionism: American heroism in *Cast a Giant Shadow* (1966)

In *Gunfighter Nation: The Myth of the Frontier in Twentieth-Century America* (1992), cultural historian Richard Slotkin asserts that the United States' frontier mythology has engendered the notion that 'the conquest of the wilderness and the subjugation or displacement of the Native Americans who originally inhabited it' has been the single dominating factor in the United States' 'achievement of a national identity, a democratic polity, an ever-expanding economy, and a phenomenally dynamic and "progressive" civilization.'[1] Slotkin details how the mythic language that emerged out of the nation's westward expansion has been repeatedly deployed for the purpose of negotiating the disparate social and political struggles that have defined the American historical experience. Crucially, Slotkin argues that the Western is not the only film genre to articulate the myth of the frontier. Throughout *Gunfighter Nation* Slotkin elucidates how the mythic language of the frontier has been deployed by Hollywood across a myriad of temporal and geographical settings; for instance, as discussed in the previous chapter, Slotkin sees the combat films of the Second World War in which heroic American soldiers battle against villainous Japanese as a conscious re-enactment of the frontier conflict between settlers and Native Americans.[2] Through his discussion of the pervasiveness of the myth throughout American culture, Slotkin lucidly demonstrates how the myth of the frontier has wielded remarkable power 'in shaping the life, thought, and politics of the nation.'[3] Though it is afforded no critical attention in *Gunfighter Nation*, *Exodus* clearly attests to Slotkin's thesis through its deployment of the language and form of the traditional Hollywood Western in its narrativization of the birth of the Jewish state.

Six years after *Exodus* the durability and malleability of the mythic language of the frontier would again be on display with the release of *Cast a Giant Shadow* (Melville Shavelson, 1966), a film that would similarly mobilize the image of Israel as a New Frontier for the purpose of enunciating an idealized conception of the United States' national identity. *Cast a Giant Shadow* tells the purportedly true story of Mickey Marcus (Kirk Douglas), an American colonel from the Second World War who is recruited by the Haganah to aid them in their war against the Arabs following the partition of Palestine in 1948. Based on a bestselling biography of Marcus by Ted Berkman,[4] the film was produced by John Wayne's production company Batjac and featured an all-star cast including, in addition to Douglas, Frank Sinatra, Yul Brynner, Senta Berger and Angie Dickinson, with John Wayne also appearing in a minor role as an American general. Marcus, a lapsed Jew, initially refuses the Haganah's request but is ultimately unable to resist the lure of battle, at first assuming the role of a military advisor before eventually being appointed the first modern-day general of the Israeli military. After leading the Israelis to a glorious victory, Marcus is killed after being accidentally shot by a young Israeli soldier. This brief summary of the film's plot reveals the key difference between *Exodus* and *Cast a Giant Shadow*, while the former is best understood as a conscious attempt to frame the birth of the Jewish state as a re-enactment of the expansion of the American frontier, the latter is more explicitly concerned with valorizing American heroism. As this chapter will demonstrate, this valorization of American heroism in *Cast a Giant Shadow* is produced through the transposition of frontier mythology onto the birth of Israel, which serves to articulate a coded message of pro-interventionism that speaks directly to the United States' military presence in Vietnam, which had seen a dramatic escalation throughout the first half of the 1960s.

Cast a Giant Shadow was not a commercial success. Director Melville Shavelson lamented that the public agreed with more critical reviewers 'by staying away in droves.'[5] However, *Cast a Giant Shadow* constitutes an interesting case study due to the involvement of John Wayne in the film's production. By the time of the production of *Cast a Giant Shadow* Wayne had been a leading man in Hollywood for over twenty years, specializing in unadulterated paeans to the frontier myth and hyper-patriotic combat films which ultimately served to establish Wayne as, to quote Lawrence H. Suid, 'the model of the action hero for several generations of young males, representing the traditional American ideal of the anti-intellectual doer in contrast to the thinker.'[6] In an example of how a star's image emerges out of the relationship between barely distinguishable on-and-off-screen personae, Wayne's status as an archetypal American hero was further affirmed by his active engagement in the nation's politics. From the mid-1940s onwards Wayne served as one of Hollywood's most vocal and most visible

Republicans, frequently railing against Communists and liberals, publically endorsing conservative Republican presidential candidates Richard Nixon (in 1960, 1968 and 1972) and Barry Goldwater (in 1964), and offering frequent and unabashed support for the United States' military venture in Vietnam.[7] Wayne's political activism functioned in concert with his status as the traditional ideal of the anti-intellectual doer to engender the image of Wayne as a mythical figure of idealized masculinity, embodying traditional American values of toughness, militarism and rugged individualism. Consequently, at this point in his career Wayne functioned as, to quote Slotkin, 'a kind of folk hero, his name an idiomatic expression, a metaphoric formula or cliché that instantly invoked a well-recognized set of American heroic virtues – or, from a different perspective, inflated American pretensions.'[8] As evidence of Wayne's ideological resonance Slotkin points to the string of cameo appearances Wayne made throughout the sixties in films such as *The Longest Day* (Ken Annakin, Andrew Marton, and Bernhard Wicki, 1962), the epic Western *How the West Was Won* (John Ford, Henry Hathaway, and George Marshall, 1962) and the Biblical epic *The Greatest Story Ever Told* (George Stevens, 1965), each of which feature Wayne functioning in an almost purely iconic manner in order to 'invoke military and Western associations.'[9] *Cast a Giant Shadow* repeats this formula, with Wayne's screen image being deployed for the purpose of lending ideological clout to the unabashed championing of American interventionism in foreign conflicts.

Due to the fact that Wayne only appears on screen for a mere fifteen minutes, *Cast a Giant Shadow* has been generally overlooked in retrospective examinations of the legacy left by Wayne as both an actor and as an archconservative ideological icon. For instance, Emanuel Levy's *John Wayne: Prophet of an American Way of Life* (1988), which proclaims to be a comprehensive study of Wayne and 'his range of activities as an actor, star, folk hero, ideologue and political figure, and cultural icon,'[10] affords *Cast a Giant Shadow* a mere single mention, coming in a paragraph devoted to Wayne's cameo roles.[11] Gary Wills' biography entitled *John Wayne: The Politics of Celebrity* (1997), which similarly explores Wayne's impact on American political life, fails to mention *Cast a Giant Shadow* even once.[12] These and other analyses of Wayne overlook the fact that *Cast a Giant Shadow* is in many ways remarkably similar to two other Batjac productions, each of which starred and were directed by John Wayne: *The Alamo* (1960), the purported retelling of the Battle of the Alamo fought between Texian settlers and their supporters and Mexican troops under the command of the despotic general Santa Anna in 1836 during the Texas War of Independence,[13] as well as the notoriously jingoistic Vietnam War film *The Green Berets* (1968). This chapter establishes the kinship shared by these three films, thus demonstrating how *Cast a Giant Shadow* is best understood as the second instalment of an unofficial trilogy of increasingly propagandistic pro-interventionist cinema specifically designed to articulate John Wayne's archconservative conception of the United States' role in the Cold War world. Consequently, this chapter elaborates our understanding of the ways in which John Wayne, to paraphrase Eric Bentley, put his art at the service of his beliefs.[14] Furthermore, by positioning *Cast a Giant Shadow* as a vessel through which Wayne dramatized his political ideology, this chapter illuminates further how the state of Israel has been deployed by Hollywood as a means of articulating an idealized conception of the United States' political identity.

American interventionism in Vietnam

Film theorist Ismail Xavier posits that in consciously allegorical cinema, 'the narrative texture places the spectator in an analytical posture while he or she is facing a coded message that is referred to an "other scene" and not directly given on the diegetic level.'[15] In *Cast a Giant Shadow* the diegetic pertains to the outbreak of hostilities between Jews and Arabs following the declaration of Israeli statehood in 1948, and an American hero's intervention in the conflict on the side of the Israelis. Within the diegesis, there is no overt reference to the contemporaneous conflict in Vietnam. However, a cursory look at the political and cultural milieu in the years between the release of *Exodus* in 1960 and the release of *Cast a Giant Shadow* in 1966 reveals the difficulty in divorcing any cinematic treatment of American interventionism produced during this period from the increasingly escalating situation in Vietnam.

The election of John F. Kennedy as the thirty-fifth President of the United States of America in late 1960 effectively symbolized the collective mood of a nation that had by now enjoyed a full generation of unparalleled power and prestige. In June of 1960 Kennedy accepted the nomination of the Democratic Party with an address that invoked the rhetoric of America's frontier mythology. Kennedy declared that the United States stood on the precipice of a 'New Frontier.' Beyond this 'New Frontier' lay 'uncharted areas of science and space, unsolved problems of peace and war, unconquered problems of ignorance and prejudice, unanswered questions of poverty and surplus.'[16] With these words

Kennedy offered an explicit appeal to the idealized notions of courage and leadership that ostensibly defined the American people, foreshadowing what would be his administration's fundamental rejection of the conservatism of the Eisenhower presidency in the pursuit of an age of heretofore-unseen national greatness.[17] In his inauguration speech Kennedy made the ambitious pledge to 'pay any price, bear any burden, meet any hardship, support any friend, oppose any foe, in order to assure the survival and the success of liberty.' He called upon a 'new generation of Americans' to face up to its 'destiny,' to 'ask not what your country can do for you, but what you can do for your country,' and to commit its energies to the 'long twilight struggle' against 'the worldwide forces of oppression and poverty.' Kennedy would lead the charge in this long twilight struggle with a foreign policy in aid of the 'containment' of Communism that was significantly more aggressive than that of his predecessor. In accordance with the rhetoric of the New Frontier administration, the far corners of the Third World would fall under the sphere of influence of the once staunchly isolationist United States, who would now embrace the role of beneficent interventionist power. Furthermore, in his inauguration speech Kennedy declared:

> To those people in the huts and villages across the globe struggling to break the bonds of mass misery, we pledge our best efforts to help them help themselves, for whatever period is required – not because the Communists may be doing it, not because we seek their votes, but because it is right …

Crucially, Kennedy strove to portray this endeavour as one of altruistic 'nation building' rather than old fashioned imperialism, stating, 'To those new States whom we welcome to the ranks of the free, we pledge our word that one form of colonial control shall not have passed away merely to be replaced by a far more iron tyranny.'[18]

The Kennedy administration's execution of a more aggressive foreign policy in pursuit of the containment of Communism manifested itself most conspicuously in Vietnam. American involvement in Vietnam dated back to the late 1940s in the form of military aid provided to France, the original colonial masters of Indochina, who were engaged in an ongoing war with the North Vietnam-based Communist Viet Minh regime. In 1954 the French were expelled from Vietnam and American support transferred to the South Vietnam-based GVN (anti-Communist Government of Vietnam), who carried on the war against the Communists. The ascension of Kennedy signalled a dramatic increase in American presence in the region. For Kennedy Vietnam represented a microcosm of the broader global struggle between the forces of freedom and the so-called 'Communist conspiracy,' against which it was the United States' moral duty to lead the fight. Moreover, Vietnam constituted a crucible of American strength. As a senator, Kennedy described Vietnam as not only 'a proving ground for democracy in Asia,' but 'a test of American responsibility and determination'; years later, as President, Kennedy would confide to James Reston of the *New York Times*, 'we have a problem in making our power credible, and Vietnam is the place.'[19] Under Kennedy American troop presence in Vietnam escalated dramatically, with levels of 'military advisers' tripling in 1961 and again in 1962, and with said 'advisers' taking a far more active role in the execution of the counterinsurgency against the Communists.[20]

Following the assassination of Kennedy in November 1963 and Lyndon Johnson's subsequent assuming of the presidency, American involvement in Vietnam would continue to escalate. Following the so-called 'Gulf of Tonkin incident' in August 1964, in which the United States National Security Agency falsely claimed that an American ship had been the subject of an unprovoked attack by North Vietnamese Navy torpedo boats, Congress passed a resolution authorizing a massive bombing campaign of the North.[21] This was soon followed by the deployment of American ground troops in Vietnam, which signalled a complete takeover of the war effort against the Communists by the United States. Here it is crucial to note that polls taken in early 1965 indicated that the public overwhelmingly favoured Johnson's actions following the Gulf of Tonkin incident.[22]

As was the case under Kennedy, the Johnson administration saw Vietnam as a litmus test for American power. At the time of the American takeover of the war in 1964–5 the Johnson administration judged that the American stake in a victory in Vietnam was more than 70 per cent 'symbolic,' and that preserving American 'national honor as a guarantor' was far more important than helping the GVN to survive.[23] General Maxwell D. Taylor, American ambassador to South Vietnam from July 1964 to July 1965, effectively summed up this attitude by arguing shortly after the Gulf of Tonkin incident, 'if we leave Vietnam with our tail between our legs, the consequences of this defeat for the rest of Asia, Africa, and Latin America would be disastrous.'[24] Conversely, successful completion of the mission to eradicate the Communist element in Vietnam would validate the United States' self-appointed status as the benevolent protector of the world's downtrodden and oppressed.

Hollywood goes interventionist

Slotkin argues that one of the principal ways in which Hollywood circulated the popular imagining of the United States as a benevolent interventionist power was through the so-called 'Mexico Western,' which began to appear in the late 1940s and early 1950s. In these films 'a group of American gunfighters crosses the border into Mexico during the time of social disruption or revolutionary crisis to help the peasants defeat an oppressive ruler, warlord, or bandit.' Slotkin argues that this cycle of films reflexively mirrored the transformation of America's engagement with the Third World during the late-1950s and into the 1960s 'in response to the exigencies of Cold War power politics.'[25] A classic example of the Mexico Western is *The Magnificent Seven* (John Sturges, 1960), an American remake of the Japanese film *Seven Samurai* (Akira Kurosawa, 1954). Released in the spring of 1960, amid the election campaign that ultimately thrust Kennedy to power, *The Magnificent Seven* tells the story of a group of elite American mercenary gunfighters recruited by a poor Mexican farming community to aid them in their resistance against a cruel warlord. The film ends with a shootout that eliminates the warlord and his men, but which also claims the lives of four of the Seven, who in the film's denouement are buried alongside the fallen townsfolk. For Slotkin,[26] as well as scholars such as Michael Coyne[27] and Stanley Corkin,[28] *The Magnificent Seven* lucidly prefigures the United States' ideological commitment in Vietnam (albeit, with a profoundly more idealistic resolution). In addition to a narrative that fundamentally champions American interventionism in a Third World conflict, the film contains within it an assortment of tropes that soon after the film's release would come to be deployed in the rhetoric pertaining to the United States' presence in Vietnam. For example, the American protagonists, through both narrative convention and the heroic screen personae of many of the actors who play members of the Seven (including Steve McQueen, James Coburn and Charles Bronson), are positioned as inherently chivalrous and incapable of resisting the opportunity to right an injustice. As such, these characters anticipate the claim made by Kennedy in his inaugural address, less than three months after the release of *The Magnificent Seven*, that the United States would strive to assist 'those people in the huts and villages across the globe struggling to break the bonds of mass misery … not because the Communists may be doing it, not because we seek their votes, but because it is right.'[29] The gunfighters, who are presented as being experts in the violent arts, train the Mexicans in self-defence, with the Mexicans shown to be comically incompetent; at this point American involvement in Vietnam was ostensibly limited to the presence of 'advisers' who were helping to train an inherently weak and ineffectual South Vietnamese military. The protagonists behave in an unequivocally paternalistic fashion towards their beneficiaries, an attitude most strikingly typified by the character of Bernando O'Reilly (Bronson) who becomes a father figure to a group of Mexican children, in one scene even spanking them when they characterize their fathers as cowards; as Slotkin convincingly argues, an implicitly racialist paternalism underlined the ideological rationale of American engagement in Vietnam.[30] In contrast with the ennobling representation of the film's American interventionist heroes, the dark-skinned reprobates in *The Magnificent Seven* are brutal, uncivilized and show little regard for human life; throughout the war the Vietnamese would often be portrayed in a similar manner, as typified by General William Westmoreland, commander of US military operations between 1964 and 1968, who in the Academy Award-winning documentary film *Hearts and Minds* (Peter Davis, 1974) opined that 'The Oriental doesn't put the same high price on life as does a Westerner …. We value life and human dignity. They don't care about life and human dignity.' It is important to understand how *The Magnificent Seven*, as the definitive Mexico Western, allegorized a certain interpretation of the Vietnam War, as variations of each of these aforementioned tropes would appear six years later in *Cast a Giant Shadow* and its depiction of the Arab-Israeli conflict, at a time in which America's engagement in Vietnam cast a much greater pall over the national psyche.

According to Slotkin, the evolution of the Mexico Western 'proceeded in step with the development of American policy in the struggle for hearts and minds in the Third World.'[31] This cycle of films thus serves as a prime example of how during the era of Kennedy's ascension to power both Washington and certain dominant modes of Hollywood cinema were each animated by 'the same ideologically loaded images of heroism and savagery, the same narrow and essentially racist views of non-White peoples and cultures, the same hope that all problems can be solved by a burst of action and a spectacular display of massive yet miraculously selective firepower.'[32] However, the Mexico Western was not alone in articulating the interventionist spirit that pervaded the political and cultural milieu of the United States throughout the early to mid-1960s. The film version of *Cast a Giant Shadow* similarly mobilized ideological images of heroism and savagery, espoused narrow and essentially racist views of non-white peoples and cultures, and dealt with problems through the deployment of massive yet miraculously selective firepower, all while extolling the intervention of a white knight American hero in a foreign conflict. In so doing *Cast a Giant Shadow* distinguishes itself from the story of the birth of Israeli independence as told in *Exodus*, in which the heroes are undeniably Americanized, but are nonetheless presented as unequivocally Israeli. In *Cast a Giant Shadow* the hero, while Jewish, is never presented as anything less than a 'true' American.

The championing of American interventionism that lies at the heart of *Cast a Giant Shadow* is attested by the plethora of divergences the film makes from Ted Berkman's biography of Mickey Marcus. In Berkman's biography Marcus becomes involved in the Israeli fight for independence after a representative of the Israeli government employs Marcus, in his capacity as a lawyer, to find someone to advise and assist the Israeli military in their imminent war with the Arabs. After a fruitless search, Marcus assumes the role himself. At this point in the book much has already been made of Marcus's Judaism, with particular emphasis placed on the bullying he suffered as a Jewish youth growing up on the streets of New York.[33] The book also makes the point that Marcus's acceptance of the mission to help bring about a Jewish homeland is indelibly linked to his own very personal understanding of Jewish suffering; for instance, in his attempts to assuage his wife's disappointment at the revelation that he intends to go to Palestine, Marcus remarks that the death of Adolf Hitler merely left the job 'half-done.'[34]

Conversely, in the film, Marcus' Judaism, while never explicitly denied, is thoroughly downplayed as a motivating factor in his rush to assist the Israeli military. Instead Marcus, like the gunfighters of *The Magnificent Seven*, is at heart a protector and a liberator whose motivation is positioned as emanating from an insatiable desire to fight for the liberty of the world's downtrodden and oppressed. The film's marginalization of the protagonist's Judaism is established in the opening scene in which a Haganah agent (James Donald) approaches Marcus on the streets of New York. Whereas in Berkman's biography Marcus is asked to find someone to fill the role of advisor to the Israeli military, in the film the Haganah agent targets Marcus specifically. The agent introduces himself as a representative of 'the world's youngest, worst trained, least equipped and most outnumbered army.' He goes on to quote the extreme anti-Jewish rhetoric of Ibn Saud, the founder of the Kingdom of Saudi Arabia ('There are 50 million Arabs. What does it matter if we lose 10 million to kill all the Jews? The price is worth it.'), and Haj Amin al-Husseini, the Grand Mufti of Jerusalem ('I declare a holy war. Murder them. Murder them all.'), each of which firmly establishes Israel as a besieged nation fighting for its survival. The agent proceeds to solicit the help of Marcus by appealing to his Judaism, telling him that Israel is 'his country', only to have Marcus refute him with the words, 'I'm an American. Last time I was in Temple was when I was 13.' The Israeli then attempts to appeal to his Americanness, asking him, 'What is it you say in your schools? Liberty and justice for all – is it only for all of you?' It is the Haganah agent's invocation of the American Pledge of Allegiance that ultimately convinces Marcus of the sanctity of the mission, as demonstrated by the sequence's transition into a scene in which Marcus tells his wife (Angie Dickinson) that he is set to leave for Palestine to take up the role of 'military advisor' to the Jewish underground forces. Crucially, Marcus is here positioned as fulfilling an advisory role similar to that ostensibly played by the United States' military in Vietnam prior to the Gulf of Tonkin incident and the subsequent deployment of American ground troops. When his wife asks, 'Why there and why you?' Marcus refers not to his own Judaism, but to the fact that he knows 'a great deal about the business of killing and *they've* been killed by experts – someone has to help *them* fight back [emphasis added].' Marcus's acquiescence to the Israelis' request thus appears to emerge principally out of an innate sense of repulsion at the knowledge of injustice being perpetrated against a weak and vulnerable people. In essence, Douglas's Marcus, just like the cowboy heroes of *The Magnificent Seven*, personifies Kennedy's plea for the selfless New Frontiersman who 'pays any price, bears any burden, meets any hardship, supports any friend, opposes any foe, in order to assure the survival and success of liberty'.[35]

Upon his arrival in Palestine Marcus (operating under the nom de guerre Mickey Stone so as to not officially involve the United States military in the operation) is distinguished by not only his professionalism and strategic know-how, but by a confidence and fighting spirit that is unmatched by any of the Israelis under his command. The superiority of Marcus is frequently conveyed through the mise-en-scene that predominantly features the rugged, well-built Douglas standing up, often in the centre of the frame, while the comparatively frail Israelis – most of whom are played by actors that would be relatively unknown by the film's American audience – passively sit. This formal privileging of the American Marcus distinctly echoes the manner in which a clear superior/inferior relationship is constructed in *The Magnificent Seven*, whereby, in the words of Corkin, 'When the white men sit, the Mexicans sit lower. When the whites stand, the Mexicans squat'.[36]

While the Israeli leadership incessantly bemoan their inferior manpower and weaponry and speak of merely holding territory, Marcus implores them to always be on the attack, at one point telling them to 'stop thinking like losers,' commenting

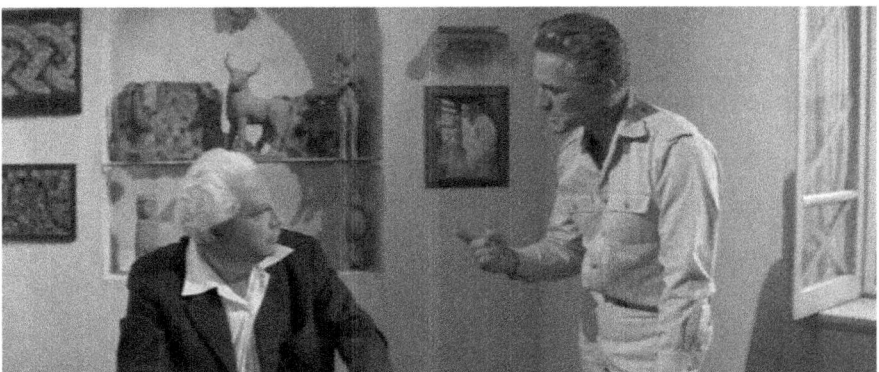

Figure 3.1 Mickey Marcus (Kirk Douglas) stands over the Israeli Prime Minister Jacob Zion (Luther Adler).

that there 'have been enough Masadas in this country' (a reference to the mass suicide of Jewish rebels in the Jewish fortress of Masada during the final stages of the Jewish revolt against Roman rule c. CE 73–4).[37] Here Marcus demonstrates all of the values that Rupert Wilkinson identifies as being central to American culture's definitions of toughness – namely, 'mastery, competence, informal assertiveness, and self-defense.'[38] Marcus is established as what Wilkinson terms 'the "can-do guy," the guy who delivers, who gets things done,' and who is 'not afraid to face down rivals and aggressors.'[39] During a raid on a British outpost, despite only serving as an 'advisor' and being told by the Israelis he is advising that the mission is too dangerous and that he should not participate, Marcus heroically charges into the battle, singlehandedly taking down an armed soldier and dragging a fallen comrade to safety while Israeli soldiers flee to safety. This scene exhibits Marcus's inimitable courage and tenacious fighting spirit, whilst simultaneously reflecting the contemporaneous reality in Vietnam whereby the Americans were officially operating in an advisory capacity, but were in actuality leading the anti-Communist forces. In another instance that reaffirms the superior courage and fighting spirit of Marcus, later in the film an Israeli unit retreats after sustaining only two casualties, outraging Marcus in the process. Although Shavelson would claim that the film 'counters the myth that Jews walked to the gas chambers because they didn't know how to fight,'[40] it instead presents the Israelis as a vulnerable people in desperate need of American assistance.

Marcus's superior qualities are eventually confirmed when the Israeli Defence Minister Jacob Zion (Luther Adler) – a character who bears an uncanny resemblance to David Ben-Gurion, the first prime minister of Israel – gives

Figure 3.2 Marcus plays the role of the heroic American 'advisor.'

him the title of 'Aluf,' which roughly translates to 'General.' Not long after being appointed 'the first general of the army of Israel in 2000 years,' Marcus finally refers to the Israeli army as 'us.' This comes after almost two hours of Marcus making clear distinctions between himself and the Israelis under his command. Patricia Erens argues that in this scene Marcus 'suddenly realizes where he belongs,' and that he at last 'understands the root of his compulsive need to move from war to war.'[41] However, not long after Marcus expresses his kinship with his Israeli comrades there is a scene that is entirely absent from Berkman's biography in which Marcus declares to his Israeli lover Magda Simon (Senta Berger) that he is returning to his wife in America. This scene undermines the character's earlier identification with the Jews of Israel and reiterates that Marcus is, above all else, an American soldier selflessly fighting for the liberty of a foreign nation. At the end of the scene Marcus is killed after being shot by an Israeli sentry who does not recognize him and calls out for Marcus to identify himself in Hebrew, a language Marcus does not speak. The film ends with Marcus dying a martyr for the Zionist cause in a fiery affirmation of his status as a patriotic American who is fundamentally a stranger in a strange land.

The manner in which *Cast a Giant Shadow* achieves narrative closure affirms the film's status as a pseudo-Western. Throughout the scene in which Marcus tells his Israeli lover that he is returning to America Marcus evokes the classic cowboy hero who, in the words of Peter Homans, invariably 'forfeits any opportunity to renounce his "beyond the town" origin and destiny.'[42] Furthermore, by ending with the martyrdom of Marcus, the film signals its kinship with not only the Mexico Western, but also the cycle of gunfighter Westerns that enjoyed a significant degree of popularity in the 1950s.[43] In these films a selfless, chivalrous gunfighter faced off against seemingly insurmountable forces of evil, usually to the defence of an inherently weak and vulnerable people (the previously discussed Mexico Western *The Magnificent Seven* can be seen as a second-wave variation of this cycle). According to Slotkin, the heroes of the gunfighter Western are defined by a 'professionalism in the arts of violence' and a fundamental 'characterological difference or alienation from their communities.'[44] The locus classicus of this cycle is undoubtedly *Shane* (George Stevens, 1953), in which a mysterious figure by the name of Shane (Alan Ladd) rides into a frontier community populated by honest, hardworking pioneer folk and single-handedly rescues them from a ruthlessly terroristic baron, before riding off into the sunset with what are presumed to be fatal wounds sustained in battle with the baron's henchman. As discussed in the previous chapter, *Exodus* echoes *Shane* through its construction of Ari Ben Canaan as a divine figure who brings salvation to the Israeli frontier, and in *Cast a Giant Shadow* there is a similar evocation of *Shane*. In *Shane* the eponymous gunfighter mysteriously emerges out of the wilderness as if sent by providence to protect the settlers of a land sanctified throughout the genre as a New Canaan for 'God's Chosen People.' In *Cast a Giant Shadow* Mickey Marcus, having been transported from the United States to an Israel that is populated by besieged settlers, similarly appears to the burgeoning community in which he enters as a mysterious stranger, well-schooled in the violent arts, having been sent to protect God's other 'Chosen People' in the literal Canaan. As noted by Slotkin, Shane's 'motives for helping the farmers are chivalric and romantic.'[45] Moreover, they are 'unique and arise from no visible history or social background, they appear to be expressions of his nature, signs of a nobility which is independent of history, like the attributes of a "higher race".'[46] In *Cast a Giant Shadow* Marcus is presented as a selfless American interventionist who, in coming to the aid of a besieged and vulnerable people ostensibly fighting for freedom and liberty, is also exhibiting the inherent nobility of a member of a 'higher race.' Finally, like Shane, Marcus sacrifices himself for a society to which he will never belong. As Slotkin says of Shane, Marcus 'is never part of the community, and his superior values are not seen as belonging to the community. He is an aristocrat of violence, an alien from a more glamorous world, who is better than those he helps and is finally not accountable to those for whom he sacrifices himself.'[47] Through its kinship with the gunfighter film, *Cast a Giant Shadow* reinforces how, as it is constructed by Hollywood, Israel is the quintessential New Frontier. As a result, the cinematic rendering of Israel enables not only the unadulterated celebration of frontier mythology, but also the valorization of traditional notions of hard masculinity and old-fashioned movie heroism.

Casting in *Cast a Giant Shadow*

The film's positioning of Marcus as a heroic, all-American force for freedom is reiterated through the casting of Kirk Douglas. Douglas is arguably best known for his many tough guy roles, with the most notable examples including a ruthlessly unscrupulous boxer in *Champion* (Mark Robson, 1949), an honourable French Colonel in *Paths of Glory* (Stanley Kubrick, 1957) and as the eponymous hero of *Spartacus* (Stanley Kubrick, 1960). In addition to the aforementioned films, Douglas appeared in a myriad of highly regarded Westerns throughout the 1950s and 1960s, including *Gunfight at the O.K. Corral* (John Sturges, 1956), *Last Train from Gun Hill* (John Sturges, 1959), *Lonely Are the Brave* (David Miller, 1962) and *The War Wagon* (Burt Kennedy, 1967), the latter of which was another Batjac production where he again appeared opposite John Wayne. These roles established Douglas as a paradigmatic figure of mid-century screen toughness who represented a quintessentially American ideal of hyper-masculinity. Crucially, the Douglas persona suffused this image with a resolute liberal pedigree, most famously epitomized by the central role he played in helping 'break the blacklist' by crediting the blacklisted writer Dalton Trumbo with the screenplay of *Spartacus* (of which Douglas was the executive producer).[48] As Leo Braudy explains, 'the continuity of an actor's image can supply complex filling for the gaps in his immediate characterization.'[49] The duality of the Douglas persona thus facilitates in *Cast a Giant Shadow* a valorization of both American intervention in foreign conflicts and the ideology of Zionism, in turn reaffirming the conflation of Cold War liberalism and Zionism first established by Hollywood in *The Ten Commandments* and

Figure 3.3 Kirk Douglas stands over Yul Brynner.

Ben-Hur. The casting of Douglas also demonstrates how the land of Israel functioned as a stage upon which Hollywood could overtly celebrate traditional conceptions of white American masculinity. Indeed, one of the Israelis whom Marcus frequently stands over is played by none other than Yul Brynner, who in *The Ten Commandments* played the emasculated Rameses opposite Charlton Heston's hyper-masculine Moses.

The film's championing of American interventionism also reveals itself through the invention of the character of Vince Talmadge, played by Frank Sinatra. An immensely popular singer, Academy Award winning actor (for his role in *From Here to Eternity* [Fred Zinnemann, 1953]), and the unofficial leader of the headline-grabbing 'Rat Pack,' Sinatra was an icon of American post-war popular culture. Although of Italian descent, Sinatra, to quote Leonard Mustazza, 'tapped into the psyche of a nation,' through work and behaviour that was 'uniquely American in style and outlook.'[50] Similarly, Rupert Wilkinson identifies Sinatra as a symbol of twentieth-century American toughness, arguing 'Sinatra and his "Rat Pack" took elements of underworld story, combined them with other subcultures, and forged them into a national stereotype of the tough and successful man.'[51] In the role of Talmadge, Sinatra plays a Texan aviator who arrives some seventy-eight minutes into the film as a volunteer fighter pilot for the fledgling Israeli army. Talmadge's most notable scene has him dropping seltzer bottles from his plane over Egyptian soldiers who flee in terror from what sounds like falling artillery. According to Shavelson's recounting of the film's production, this seemingly preposterous episode actually took place in the war that followed the declaration of Israeli independence due to the Israeli army's lack of bombs.[52] However, in what is a significant twist, Shavelson depicts the mission as being carried out not by an Israeli character, but by a Texan aviator played by an iconic American performer. Rather than a 'native' successfully defending his own territory, it is the white American hero who exhibits remarkable courage and ingenuity in the field of battle while selflessly intervening to defend the defenceless. The scene ends with Talmadge crashing his plane; as he is not seen again, the implication is that he has perished in the operation. Like Marcus, Talmadge dies a martyr who 'pays any price, bears any burden, meets any hardship, supports any friend, opposes any foe, in order to assure the survival and success of liberty.'[53]

The film's endorsement of American interventionism is also conveyed through the character of General Mike Randolph who, like Talmadge, is an invention of the film and is played by an American cultural icon (John Wayne). Randolph is introduced in a flashback as the leader of the squadron, of which Marcus is a member, which liberates the Dachau concentration camp at the end of the Second World War. This scene not only establishes the immensity of Jewish suffering that preceded the birth of Israel, but it affirms the image of the United States as a benevolent power by perpetuating the notion of Americans as the true vanquishers of Nazism. Later in the film, after Marcus has returned from his first excursion to Palestine, he and Randolph have an exchange in which Marcus pleads the Israeli case, claiming that they are helpless and 'surrounded by five Arab nations ready to shove them into the Mediterranean.' Randolph responds by derisively asking him, 'Then why did you come back?' before imploring him to 'stand up and be counted,' effectively encouraging Marcus to carry on his fight for Israeli independence. In a telling observation, *Time* magazine described Wayne's performance as 'an uncanny impersonation of President Johnson,' the man who, only two years prior, had dramatically escalated the United States' military involvement in Vietnam.[54]

It is entirely fitting that it is Wayne's character that explicitly articulates the sanctity of Marcus's mission. Although he only appears on screen for some fifteen minutes, it is Wayne who is most responsible for the film's ideology. In the ironically titled *How to Make a Jewish Movie* (1971), an amusing recounting of the film's production, director Melville Shavelson details how he was finding it impossible to secure funding for the project, with Hollywood producers frequently asking him, 'Who would want to see a picture about a Jewish general?'[55] Shavelson's response was to craft a treatment that told the story of 'a tough Jewish soldier who helped save the cradle of Judea by teaching a Jewish army how to fight a Jewish war that had nothing to do with Jews.'[56] Instead the focus would be on what Shavelson termed the protagonist's Kennedy-esque 'inbred American hatred for injustice,' and his willingness to 'fight for any underdog who came to him and asked.'[57] Shavelson took his treatment to Wayne, then the biggest star in Hollywood, whose commitment would guarantee the support of a major studio. Wayne's star image ostensibly exuded the 'inbred American hatred for injustice' more so than that of any other prominent Hollywood actor, and he responded to Shavelson's overtures by telling the director that the treatment for *Cast a Giant Shadow* was 'the most *American* story' that he had ever heard.[58] Wayne saw in Marcus's story a means through which to champion America's image as a beneficent interventionist power at a time when America's presence in Vietnam was becoming increasingly controversial. According to Shavelson, Wayne told him:

> Everybody's knockin' the United States today, claiming we're sendin' in troops all over the world to knock over some little country where we've got no right to be. They've forgotten who we are and what we've done. At a time like this, we *need* to remind them of how we helped the littlest country of all get its independence. How an American army officer gave his life to do it.[59]

Wayne agreed to produce the film under the auspices of Batjac, which helped to secure financial backing and distribution from United Artists. In addition, Wayne secured a co-producer role for his son Michael Wayne, and also recruited Kirk Douglas to play the role of Marcus.[60] Meanwhile, with Wayne now firmly in control of the picture the story proceeded to evolve from one of a Jewish-American soldier's fight for Israeli sovereignty to an unadulterated paean to American interventionism. Wayne is reported to have said to Mary St. John, his long-time private secretary, 'Shavelson is a nice fellow, but the film is a passion to him, a baby, a labor of love, a crusade. I'll be damned if I'm going to give free rein to a Jewish true believer making the movie of his lifetime with my money.'[61] The subsequent shift in tone was so profound that Shavelson later remarked, 'Duke [John Wayne] was so high on the Americanness of the picture that Kirk, who is of course a Jew, said to him, "Don't forget that Mickey Marcus was Jewish." And Duke said, "Jesus Christ was Jewish too, but he didn't go to West Point".'[62] In what is a further confirmation of the film's transformation once in the hands of Wayne, Shavelson claims that all of the marketing for the film 'eliminated all mention of the nation of Israel, the War of Liberation, the Jews, or Colonel Mickey Marcus.'[63]

The political cinema of John Wayne

Wayne's stated reasons for doing *Cast a Giant Shadow* mirror those that were behind Batjac's production of both *The Alamo* and *The Green Berets*. Through an examination of the similarities *Cast a Giant Shadow* shares with these productions, we can better understand the film as a conscious celebration of American interventionism. *The Alamo* is a variation on the Mexico Western that, like *The Magnificent Seven,* was released in 1960 in the midst of that year's presidential election. The film stars John Wayne as Davy Crockett in the familiar role of 'a kind of frontier everyman who disdains formal hierarchy but who is readily recognized as one of nature's noblemen.'[64] Crockett leads a small cadre of Tennesseans who have valiantly volunteered to aid the people of Texas in their fight for freedom. At the point in history in which the film is set, Texas was a part of Mexico rather than the United States of America, and thus the film centres on American heroes selflessly defending the liberty of people that belong to another nation, as in both *The Magnificent Seven* and *Cast a Giant Shadow*. *The Alamo* was a deeply personal project for Wayne, who was not only the film's star but also its director, while his son Michael was associate producer, fulfilling a role similar to the one that he would later play in the production of *Cast a Giant Shadow*. In promoting the film Wayne declared that he was aiming it at 'all who have an interest in a thing called freedom,' because 'I think we've all been going soft, taking freedom for granted.' He viewed Texas's struggle for independence not only as 'one of the most heroic moments in American history,' but also as a 'metaphor of America.'[65] Such ideals reveal themselves in the film's often-preachy dialogue, such as when Wayne, as Crockett, pontificates about the sanctity of republicanism with the following eulogy:

> Republic. I like the sound of the word. It means people can live free, talk free, go or come, buy or sell, be drunk or sober, however they choose. Some words give you a feeling. Republic is one of those words that makes me tight in the throat – the same tightness a man gets when his baby takes his first step or his first baby shaves and makes his first sound as a man. Some words can give you a feeling that makes your heart warm. Republic is one of those words.

Wayne frequently aligned the narrative of the film to the rhetoric of the Cold War and the supposed necessity for American leadership in the fight against Communist aggression; 'These are "perilous times," he felt, "when the eyes of the world are on us," and "we must sell America to countries threatened with Communist domination".'[66] Here Wayne is explicitly appealing to the same ideal of American exceptionalism as would Kennedy in his inauguration speech just three months after the release of *The Alamo*. Wayne also claimed to hope that 'something more than profits will result from *The Alamo*,' and that 'the battle fought there will remind people today that the price of liberty and freedom is not cheap.'[67] Again, the film explicitly articulates these ideals through its dialogue. For instance, when one of Crockett's men expresses a desire to return home based on the fact that 'It ain't our oxen being gored,' Crockett convinces him to stay on and fight with the words, 'Figure this. A fellow gets in the habit of gorin' oxes, it whets his appetite. He may come up north and gore yours.' Crockett's retort is not merely a clear imploration of the supposed necessity to meet aggression with force, but it serves as a crude colloquial summation of the so-called 'domino theory,' which speculated that once one state in a particular region came under the influence of Communism then the surrounding countries would naturally follow, and which would serve to justify American intervention across the world throughout the Cold War era.[68]

Five years after the release of *The Alamo*, and only one year before the release of *Cast a Giant Shadow*, Wayne purchased the film rights to Robin Moore's bestselling Vietnam War novel *The Green Berets* (1965). Released in 1967, *The Green Berets* not only featured Wayne as its star but it would be the only project besides *The Alamo* for which Wayne would receive a directorial credit. Like both *The Alamo* and *Cast a Giant Shadow*, *The Green Berets* was produced under the auspices of Batjac and featured his son, Michael, as a producer. Also, *The Green Berets* would explicitly mythologize the United States as a chivalrously interventionist redeemer nation. However, unlike *The Alamo* and *Cast a Giant Shadow*, *The Green Berets* is entirely devoid of allegorical pretensions. Instead, it constitutes Hollywood's only attempt to directly address America's involvement in Vietnam during the period in which the war was being fought. Whereas Wayne had previously deployed both the legend of the Alamo and the outbreak of Arab-Israeli hostilities to allegorically champion his own right-wing interpretation of America's role in the Cold War world, *The Green Berets* served as a means through which Wayne unobtrusively articulated his archconservative views regarding the United States' presence in Vietnam, which he equated to America's opposition to Nazism in the Second World War.[69] Wayne's fiercely pro-interventionist ethos and propagandistic intentions are made unequivocally clear in a letter he wrote to President Johnson in which he appealed for the Defense Department's cooperation in the making of the film. He explained that the aim of the film was to 'inspire a patriotic attitude on the part of fellow Americans.'[70] In regards to Vietnam Wayne said it was 'extremely important that not only the people of the United States but those all over the world should know why it is necessary for us to be there …. The most effective way to accomplish this is through the motion picture medium.'[71] Wayne insisted that he could make the 'kind of picture that will help our cause throughout the world.'[72] Jack Valenti, then Special Assistant to President Johnson (and soon-to-be President of the Motion Picture Association of America), reportedly told Johnson, 'Wayne's politics [are] wrong, but in so far as Vietnam is concerned, his views are right. If he made the picture he would be saying the things we want said.'[73] Consequently, Wayne received the governmental assistance he coveted.

In line with Wayne's simplistic view of the world – replying to a question about his personal politics Wayne once famously declared, 'They tell me everything isn't black and white. Well, I say, why the hell not?'[74] – *The Green Berets* presents what was a profoundly complex conflict in terms that are both Manichaean and contemptible, producing an 'us and them' tale in which the Americans are courageous good guys who defend helpless Vietnamese women and children from the barbarous Viet Cong in one scene, and then bring the ebulliently grateful villagers toys and medicine in the next. As in *The Alamo* and *Cast a Giant Shadow*, characters frequently pontificate about the righteousness of America's role in the war; indeed, the film begins with a scene in which a soldier responds to a journalist's question regarding the Vietnamese desire for American assistance by saying, 'They need us … and they want us.' Wayne even challenges the growing opposition to the war in America through the character of a dovish American journalist who Wayne openly mocks, and who later converts to the cause after having been exposed to the savagery of the Viet Cong. Crucially, *The Green Berets* presents the conflict as little more than a re-enactment of the racial warfare that typified the expansion of the American frontier. The film's depiction of the Viet Cong clearly draws on traditional Hollywood representations of Native Americans; for instance, the Viet Cong are shown attacking Americans with crossbows, and when they take the American base they wail like screen Indians. Producer Michael Wayne summed up the film's debt to the Western in the following terms, 'We're not making a political picture; we're making a picture about a bunch of right guys … Cowboys and Indians … The Americans are the good guys and the Viet Cong are the bad guys … Maybe we shouldn't have destroyed all those Indians, but when you are making a picture, the Indians are the bad guys.'[75] Furthermore, as noted by John Belton, the climactic scene of the film recreates the climax of *The Alamo*, in which the camp is surrounded and besieged by the enemy; the only difference is that, on this occasion, the Americans win the battle, thus 'providing an ideologically correct, upbeat ending to a downbeat Western myth.'[76] In what is an effective encapsulation of Wayne's conception of Vietnam as a New Frontier that needs to be tamed by the white man and made safe for Western civilization, the camp that houses the American Special Forces unit is identified as 'Dodge City,' evoking the famous frontier town that was once home to the legendary American lawman Wyatt Earp.

Reviewers savaged *The Green Berets*, with its simplistic conception of the Vietnam conflict being a primary source of critical animus. Renata Adler in the *New York Times* described the film as:

So unspeakable, so stupid, so rotten and false in every detail that it passes through being fun, through being funny, through being camp, through everything and becomes an invitation to grieve, not for our soldiers or for Vietnam (the film could not be more false or do a greater disservice to either of them) but for what has happened to the fantasy-making apparatus in this country. Simplicities of the right, simplicities of the left, but this one is beyond the possible. It is vile and insane. On top of that, it is dull.[77]

In a similar vein, *The Hollywood Reporter* dubbed the film, 'a cliché-ridden throwback to the battlefield potboilers of the Second World War, its artifice readily exposed by the nightly actuality of TV news coverage, its facile simplification unlikely to attract the potentially large and youthful audience whose concern and sophistication cannot be satisfied by the insertion of a few snatches of polemic.'[78] However, in spite of the overwhelmingly caustic critical reception the film elicited, *The Green Berets* was a major commercial success, earning a domestic box office of over $20 million, which was more than double its production costs.[79] While this speaks to the incredible popularity of John Wayne, it also suggests that in mid-1968, a period still more than a year prior to the revelations of the My Lai massacre as well as the killing of anti-war protestors at Kent State University by members of the Ohio National Guard, the ideal of American interventionism still held great appeal to a significant proportion of the American public.

Both *The Alamo* and *The Green Berets*, in their unabashed valorization of American interventionism, lucidly illustrate Eric Bentley's claim that John Wayne put his art at the service of his beliefs.[80] Similarly, *Cast a Giant Shadow* transforms the story of Mickey Marcus and his role in the birth of the state of Israel so as to align it with Wayne's personal ideals. However, it is not merely the marginalization of Marcus's Judaism and the invention of the jingoistic characters played by Sinatra and Wayne that signify this transformation. The film contains a number of other major divergences from Berkman's biography of Marcus that evoke both *The Alamo* and *The Green Berets*, and in so doing serve to position the film as an explicit celebration of American interventionism. For instance, the film's construction of the Arabs of Palestine is distinctly reminiscent of traditional screen representations of Native Americans, directly mirroring the ways in which *The Green Berets* represents the North Vietnamese. This manner of representation is established in the first scene following Marcus's arrival in Palestine in which Marcus gets on a bus that includes amongst its passengers a cross-section of (Jewish) Israeli society – a business man, an elderly woman, children and male and female soldiers. Eventually the bus reaches part of the city that is teeming with armed Arabs who bombard it with rifle fire, wounding a young woman in the process. This sequence recalls a scene in the classic Western *Stagecoach* (John Ford, 1939) (perhaps not coincidentally, starring John Wayne in one of his earliest major roles) in which a cross-section of nineteenth-century (white) American society travels through hostile Indian country and is eventually raided by Apaches. As was the case in *Exodus*, *Cast a Giant Shadow* establishes the Arab-Israeli conflict as one, to quote the words of historian Rashid Khalidi, 'between near equals and where, if either party is a victim, it is the Israelis.'[81] Moreover, *Cast a Giant Shadow* echoes the more traditional formulations of American frontier mythology, in which, as Slotkin notes, 'the myth of "savage war" blames Native Americans as instigators of a war of extermination.'[82] This scene sets the tone for all future confrontations between the Israelis, who are distinctly personalized and through whom the audience witnesses all of the events contained within the narrative, and the Arabs, who are nameless, faceless villains with essentially no sense of individuality, akin to the Native American savages of the classic Western (and, also, the Arabs of *Exodus*).

The film also includes a sequence that is absent from Berkman's biography of Marcus which is a variation of the rape/rescue trope that is so central to countless captivity narratives set on the American frontier (and which also appears in *Exodus*). This sequence begins with the Israelis transporting a convoy through hostile Arab territory. Magda, Marcus's Israeli lover, volunteers to drive one of the vehicles. During the operation her truck breaks down, and upon realizing that she is alone amongst a sea of Arabs Marcus shouts, 'Come on, Magda!' Suddenly, what seems like hundreds of Arabs are cackling and tormenting her by screaming, 'Come on, Magda!' Meanwhile, the audience is subjected to a succession of tight close-ups on a procession of salivating rapacious Arabs in a scene that exemplifies Edward Said's claim that Hollywood has traditionally depicted the Arab as being 'an oversexed degenerate, capable, it is true, of cleverly devious intrigues, but essentially sadistic, treacherous, low.'[83] To again recall what Mikhail Bakhtin conceptualized as 'genre memory,' for an audience raised on Puritanical frontier mythology the implication is obvious; Magda is to be subjected to what *The Birth of a Nation* (D.W. Griffith, 1915) frames as a 'fate worse than death' – a sexual assault at the hands of dark-skinned savages – as was Karen in *Exodus*, and as were countless white victims of Indian barbarism throughout a half century of Hollywood Westerns.[84] Magda is as discernibly aware of this inevitability as any member of the audience, and subsequently goes into shock. Meanwhile, the Yul Brynner character with whom Marcus is riding tells him that the situation is far too dangerous for them to stop. Brynner, who projected the soft, weakened masculinity in *The Ten Commandments*, lacks the requisite gallantry a rescue attempt would require. Marcus, the classic American 'can-do guy' who gets things done and who is unafraid to face down rivals and aggressors, courageously extricates himself from the vehicle and single-handedly goes off to save Magda. In a line of dialogue that effectively encapsulates the film's construction of America as a benevolent interventionist power rescuing the downtrodden of the world from their barbarous oppressors, Magda pleads, 'Help me, Mickey! Help me!' The scene then fades out and Marcus is next seen escorting a catatonic Magda to a doctor, signifying the success of his rescue mission. With Magda's safety secured, Kirk Douglas's Marcus emerges as a modern-day successor to the self-willed Indian-fighter legend made famous by the likes of Daniel Boone, Davy Crockett, William 'Buffalo Bill' Cody, and, it must be said, the film's producer, John Wayne.

On the surface this sequence may appear to be a mere correlative of the captivity narrative that is played out in *Exodus*. However, as detailed in the previous chapter, in *Exodus* the captivity narrative primarily functions to vilify the Arabs as inhumane savages with whom the Israelis cannot live side by side in peace and harmony. Conversely, in *Cast a Giant Shadow*, while the scene undoubtedly demonizes the Arabs as lecherous barbarians, its primary function is to valorize the white American as a saviour. It is a more traditional imagining of the captivity narrative that affirms Slotkin's claim that the purpose of the myth is to enact 'the triumph of civilization over savagery' through 'the hunter/warrior's rescue of the White woman held captive by savages.'[85] For this reason in *Cast a Giant Shadow* the woman is rescued before any physical harm can come to her, whereas in *Exodus* the victim is found dead. This clear distinction in the way each film plays out the captivity narrative is reflective of the divergent ideologies that underpin each production.

Here it is instructive to note that similarly vulnerable female characters appear throughout the Wayne oeuvre. For instance, one of the subplots of *The Alamo* centres on a relationship between Davy Crockett and a young Mexican woman (Linda Cristal) whom Crockett rescues from a forced marriage. Two variations of this character also appear in *The Green Berets*; one is a beautiful Vietnamese woman who is employed by the Americans as a honey-trap to ensnare a lascivious Viet Cong general; the other is a young Vietnamese girl who is found dead after being gang-raped by Viet Cong soldiers.[86] Crucially, neither *The Alamo* nor *The*

Green Berets features a strong, native-born male character opposite the strong, decisive American characters played by Wayne and Douglas, respectively. As a result, the weak, vulnerable women who are in desperate need of rescue by the hyper-masculine Americans serve as the principal representative of their respective nation. This dynamic can be understood as a subtle variation on what Ella Shohat terms 'gendered metaphors' of national identity. According to Shohat gendered metaphors interweave colonial and patriarchal discourses for the purpose of legitimating European dominion of the Third World.[87] As Shohat argues, from its earliest days of film production Hollywood has deployed gendered metaphors in its representations of the Third World; notable examples cited by Shohat include *Intolerance* (D.W. Griffith, 1916) and *Cleopatra* (Cecil B. DeMille, 1934), both produced during the age of empire building, and both of which present the Orient as a feminized 'scene of carnal delights' awaiting European/American penetration.[88] In the case of *The Alamo*, *The Green Berets*, and *Cast a Giant Shadow*, each of which was produced and exhibited against the backdrop of increasing American presence in Vietnam, female characters are employed as gendered metaphors to instead position the Third World as a proverbial damsel in distress for the purpose of legitimating the United States' self-appointed status as the world's defender of freedom and liberty.

Like *Exodus*, *Cast a Giant Shadow* deploys the establishment of the modern state of Israel for the purpose of projecting an idealized notion of the United States' political identity. However, whereas *Exodus* depicted the birth of Israel as a re-enactment of the expansion of the American frontier, *Cast a Giant Shadow* presents Israelis as a besieged, freedom-loving people crying out for valiant Americans to help them build a nation of their own in a manner that distinctly echoes John Wayne's construction of the Texians in *The Alamo* and also the South Vietnamese in *The Green Berets*. In so doing *Cast a Giant Shadow* articulates the ideology of the New Frontier by reimagining its hero as a Special Forces type figure who embodies the United States' supposed eagerness to come to the rescue of the world's downtrodden and oppressed. Apart from the film's functioning as an overt expression of Wayne's political ideology, what makes *Cast a Giant Shadow* particularly interesting in regards to the evolution of Hollywood's representation of Israel is the time of its production and exhibition. The half-decade that followed the release of *Cast a Giant Shadow* was a period of tremendous tumult in the United States typified by increasing opposition to the war in Vietnam, race riots, campus demonstrations, political assassinations and the emergence of second-wave feminism. Hollywood responded by attempting to tap into this climate of dissent and disillusionment through the production of films marked by overt anti-authoritarianism, with notable examples including *The Graduate* (Mike Nichols, 1967), *Bonnie and Clyde* (Arthur Penn, 1967), *Easy Rider* (Dennis Hopper, 1969) and *Midnight Cowboy* (John Schlesinger, 1969). Against the backdrop of crumbling social edifices the Production Code met its belated demise, allowing for more frank depictions of sex and violence and a general challenging of the traditional social order. Chauvinistic celebrations of American interventionism such as *Cast a Giant Shadow* would largely disappear from view, not to be seen again until the era of Ronald Reagan and John Rambo. Concomitant to this profound shift in the social and political life of the United States was a radical altering of both the geopolitical landscape of the Middle East and Israel's image in the United States as a result of the Jewish state winning an emphatic victory in the Six Day War of 1967 against a coalition of Arab nations. By virtue of this constellation of developments, *Cast a Giant Shadow* constitutes not only one of the last films produced by Hollywood during this era to unequivocally valorize American military interventionism, but the last time that Hollywood would depict Israel as a damsel in distress nation requiring the assistance of the United States.

4

Rise and fall: Israel and America in counterterrorist cinema, 1977–86

The countercultural zeitgeist of late-1960s America was reflected by profound changes in the tastes of the movie-going public. Audiences turned away from traditionally bankable genres like the escapist musical, the historical epic, and the classical Western, and turned towards the films of the so-called 'New Hollywood' movement initiated by an emergent generation of acting and filmmaking talent whose arrival is widely understood to have initiated a 'renaissance' period of American cinema.[1] One of the principal ways in which old Hollywood attempted to push back against the incursions of New Hollywood was through the production of big-budget, special effects-driven disaster films whereby, 'a manmade systems failure or a force of nature, often monstrously perverted, threatens to destroy a group of characters brought together more or less by chance ... and while many of them die, a few prevail through their courage and resourcefulness.'[2] The cycle is generally thought of as beginning with *Airport* (George Seaton, 1970), a star-studded thriller about an endangered 707 airliner that grossed over $100 million in the United States alone.[3] The disaster film proceeded to become one of the predominant subgenres of the 1970s, with the enormous success of *Airport* matched by similarly iconic titles such as *The Poseidon Adventure* (Ronald Neame, 1972), *Earthquake* (Mark Robson, 1974) and *The Towering Inferno* (John Guillermin, 1974). In so doing, the cycle provided a platform for the still active remnants of old Hollywood (*Airport*, for instance, featured stars of Hollywood's golden age such as Burt Lancaster, Dean Martin and Van Heflin, while the hero of *Earthquake* – as well as forgettable facsimiles such as *Skyjacked* [John Guillermin, 1972] and *Two-Minute Warning* [Larry Peerce, 1976] – was none other than that archetypal exemplar of traditional masculinity, Charlton Heston), as well as the explicit celebration of old-fashioned movie heroism.

Among the myriad of disaster films to emerge during this period was *Black Sunday* (John Frankenheimer, 1977), produced by Paramount. *Black Sunday* constitutes something of an anomalous entry in the disaster film canon, for the inciting incident is no manmade systems failure or a force of nature. Instead, the narrative speaks to contemporaneous anxieties regarding the proliferation of international terrorist incidents throughout the 1970s.[4] The film tells the story of a deranged Vietnam veteran named Michael Lander (Bruce Dern) who colludes with members of the Palestinian terror group Black September to detonate a Goodyear blimp filled with 200,000 steel darts over the Super Bowl, with the intention of killing 80,000 spectators (including the President of the United States). A heroic Israeli intelligence agent named David Kabakov (Robert Shaw) saves the day by uncovering the plot in the nick of time, killing the terrorists and towing the blimp out to sea where it harmlessly explodes.

Building on the commentary on the film proffered by Melani McAlister in her book *Epic Encounters: Culture, Media, and U.S. Interests in the Middle East, 1945–2000* (2005),[5] this chapter argues that the politics of *Black Sunday* are principally informed by America's defeat in Vietnam, with the Arab-Israeli conflict functioning as a prism through which the film valorizes hardened Israeli heroism against American weakness. As will be demonstrated, the film performs this juxtaposition as a means of negotiating the United States' own anxieties in response to the purported 'softening' of the United States in the wake of its retreat from Vietnam, as well as the social destabilization produced by a constellation of social forces, particularly the emergence of second-wave feminism. Opposition to the latter of these developments manifests itself in *Black Sunday* through the film's demonization of its principal female character, the analysis of which is supported by a detailed comparison with Frankenheimer's earlier film *The Manchurian Candidate* (1962), which similarly critiqued American supposed decline through the representation of a manipulative, maniacal woman.

The second half of the chapter will examine the action film *The Delta Force* (Menahem Golan, 1986), which inverts *Black Sunday* by depicting American Special Forces as the saviours of Jews (both American and Israeli) held hostage by Lebanese terrorists. A production of Cannon, who was then the world's pre-eminent purveyor of B-grade schlock cinema, *The Delta Force* depicts Arab terrorists hijacking a plane predominantly filled with American passengers, and the plane's subsequent liberation by an American Special Forces unit (the Delta Force) led by Major Scott McCoy (Chuck Norris) and Colonel Nick Alexander (Lee Marvin). Again building on the scholarship of McAlister and also Tony

Shaw, the latter of whom claims that the film 'underscores Israel's influence on the representation of terrorism on the big screen' and 'in many ways marks the apogee of cinema's hawkish reaction to the threat posed by "international terrorism" during the 1970s and 1980s,'[6] I argue that the *The Delta Force* overtly draws on the real-life counterterrorism operations of the state of Israel, while at the same time serving as a highly politicized imitation of the iconic post-Vietnam action film *Rambo: First Blood Part II* (George P. Cosmatos, 1985). Through the positioning of *The Delta Force* as an ersatz *Rambo*, it will be asserted that the film is a classic example of Reagan-era triumphalism that shamelessly expropriates a key chapter in Israeli history as a means of redeeming the United States' military failures both in Vietnam and during the Iran hostage crisis in 1980. Through my analysis of *Black Sunday* and *The Delta Force* this chapter elucidates the precise manner in which, throughout the two decades that followed the release of *Cast a Giant Shadow* (1966), Israel evolved from a helpless damsel in distress in need of American assistance into a highly proficient warrior state, ultimately assuming the mantle of a heroic model of action for a United States that was routinely seeing challenges to the previously irrefutable notion of American exceptionalism.

Based on a bestselling novel of the same name by Thomas Harris, *Black Sunday* was expected to be one of the biggest films of 1977. Preview screenings were so well received that Charles Bluhdorn, head of Gulf and Western Industries (which controlled Paramount Pictures), supposedly kissed the film's producer Robert Evans, telling him, 'In the eleven years I've owned Paramount, this is the most exciting moment I've ever had.'[7] Paramount executives were so impressed that Frankenheimer was awarded an exclusive five-year deal with the studio, while a number of pieces were published in various journals, magazines and newspapers that proclaimed the inevitable revival of the director's moribund career.[8] The hype surrounding the film's release was so overwhelming that a number of articles from the time suggested that it would go on to replicate the record-breaking success of *Jaws* (Steven Spielberg, 1975).[9] However, *Black Sunday* would fail to meet such lofty expectations, ultimately earning around $15 million at the box office (against a budget of $7.8 million), in the process failing to achieve the iconic status that many contemporary commentators anticipated.[10] Nonetheless, the film remains one of the most significant mobilizations of Israel in the history of Hollywood, constituting a prime exemplar of Hollywood's tendency to deploy images of Israel for the purpose of articulating American national identity.

In the wake of the events of 11 September 2001 and the United States' subsequent launching of the 'Global War on Terrorism,' there has been increased scholarly interest in the history of cinematic depictions of terrorism,[11] as well as the manner in which Arabs have been represented by Hollywood cinema.[12] *Black Sunday*, as the first major Hollywood film to depict Arabs launching a terrorist attack within the United States, has not surprisingly been the subject of renewed attention.[13] To quote Corey K. Creekmur, the events of 9/11 rendered *Black Sunday* 'disturbingly prophetic, instantly rescuing the film from two decades of easy dismissal as ludicrous.'[14] Creekmur goes on to position *Black Sunday* as a retrospectively significant cultural event, by virtue of it being 'one of the first films to acknowledge terrorist acts as spectacles carefully staged for the greatest possible mass media exposure.'[15] Another scholar who has recently proffered a retrospective analysis of the film is Stephen Prince in his book *Firestorm: American Film in the Age of Terrorism* (2009). Prince positions Black September as the masterminds of the attack on the Super Bowl while essentially dismissing the central role that is played by Dern's deranged American veteran, and in so doing exemplifies the recent tendency to see the film through the lens of 9/11.[16] Tim Jon Semmerling has provided perhaps the most notable recent examination of *Black Sunday*. Semmerling devotes to the film an entire chapter in his book *'Evil' Arabs in American Popular Film: Orientalist Fear* (2006), in which he argues that cinematic representations of Arabs throughout the history of Hollywood have generally conformed to egregious Orientalist stereotypes.[17] According to Semmerling, while *Black Sunday* overtly speaks to the anxieties of a United States that was still reeling from its defeat in Vietnam, the film's primary aim is to engender 'Orientalist fear by showing the savagery of Palestinian Arabs infiltrating a weakened and feminized America.'[18]

Semmerling is of course correct in his assertion that the film presents its Arab characters in a wholly unfavourable light. However, *Black Sunday* contains elements that problematize a reading of the film as a traditionally Orientalist text. Take for instance the film's fundamental downplaying of the ethnicity of its principal Arab villain, Dahlia Iyad, who is played by Swiss actress Marthe Keller. Dahlia is a far cry from the veiled, passive mute that has for so long been central to mediated representations of Arab women within the American cultural sphere. Instead, Dahlia looks, to quote the review of the film by critic Vincent Canby of the *New York Times*, 'as beautiful and healthy and uncomplicated as a California surfer.'[19] Keller's character not only appears to be of European descent, but she also speaks with a thick German accent. Also, the actress was at this

Figure 4.1 The distinctly non-Arab Dahlia Iyad (Marthe Keller).

point known in the United States almost exclusively for her performance in *Marathon Man* (John Schlesinger, 1976), where she played a Germanic Mata Hari who helps lead the title character (Dustin Hoffman) into the clutches of a sadistic Nazi War criminal, memorably played by Laurence Olivier. This particular construction of the character of Dahlia constitutes a significant departure from Harris's novel, which is completely devoid of any suggestion that Dahlia is of European extraction. As a consequence, the character can be seen as functioning less as a symbol of Arab extremism and more as a general stand-in for any number of revolutionary groups that came to prominence in the 1970s; indeed, the character's apparently Teutonic background evokes the image of West Germany's Red Army Faction (RAF; also known as the Baader-Meinhof Group), a leftist organization comprised both men and women that, while often expressing solidarity with the Palestinian cause, was principally known for a series of highly publicized terrorist attacks on Germany's civil society throughout the latter half of the 1970s.[20]

While promoting the film both Frankenheimer and Evans frequently asserted its apolitical nature. An article published in the *New York Times* at the time of the film's release quotes Frankenheimer as saying, 'If I wanted to make a film about the Mideast crisis I wouldn't make this movie. It's no more a film about the Mideast crisis than it is about football …. This isn't a political movie.'[21] An interview published in *Film Criticism* had Frankenheimer pushing a similar line, as he proclaimed that he was not a supporter of either the Israelis or the Palestinians, and that he 'didn't want to make a propaganda film for the Israelis,' citing as evidence of his impartiality the film's invention of an Egyptian character who articulates for the audience the lifetime of suffering endured by the

Palestinian antagonist.[22] Evans echoed such sentiments, declaring, 'I just want to make pictures that are captivating to an audience. I have no message,' and that he and Frankenheimer were making *Black Sunday* 'as apolitical as possible.'[23] Evans also made the truly astounding claim that none other than Henry Kissinger provided 'the key on how to make the picture' by telling him, 'You can't make it a political picture. You can't take sides. You can't make it anti or pro anyone.'[24] However, in spite of the protestations of Frankenheimer and Evans, *Black Sunday* is indeed a political film that functions as a clear response to the sociopolitical context surrounding its production and exhibition. To clearly illuminate this point we must first go back one decade to the milieu that saw the release of the unabashedly pro-interventionist *Cast a Giant Shadow*.

Vietnam and American decline

As was detailed in the previous chapter, throughout 1966 – the year in which the allegorical celebration of American interventionism that was *Cast a Giant Shadow* was released – opinion polls consistently revealed widespread support among the American public for the war in Vietnam.[25] However, amid a substantial increase in both American troop numbers and military operations in Vietnam, this support gradually dissipated. According to Stanley Karnow, by late 1967 'a plurality of Americans had concluded that the United States had "made a mistake" in committing combat troops to Vietnam.'[26] Crucially, Karnow notes that dissatisfaction with the war stemmed not only from peace advocates, but also from a significant number of Americans who felt that President Lyndon Johnson 'was not prosecuting the war dynamically enough.'[27]

In January of 1968 the Viet Cong launched simultaneous attacks on more than 100 cities and towns across South Vietnam, taking American forces almost completely by surprise. The Tet Offensive, as the campaign would come to be known, represented a major turning point in the war; while it ultimately resulted in a military defeat for the Communists, it had a devastating effect on the morale of Americans who watched the events unfold on television.[28] After Tet the American news media became particularly critical of the war,[29] while it also marked the point that public opinion genuinely turned against American involvement in Vietnam.[30] So widespread was the general sense of dissatisfaction among the American populous that Lyndon Johnson announced that he would not seek a second full term as president.[31]

Throughout the administration of Johnson's successor, Richard Nixon, the war would remain an unmitigated disaster punctuated by events that inflicted tremendous trauma upon the collective consciousness of the nation. In late 1969 the atrocities committed by American soldiers in the village of My Lai in March of 1968 were revealed to the world. In what became known as the My Lai massacre, American soldiers murdered somewhere between 450 and 500 innocent villagers. A significant proportion of the victims were women, children and the elderly.[32] The *Philadelphia Inquirer* described the massacre as 'the kind of atrocity generally associated with the worst days of Hitler and Stalin and other cruel despotisms.'[33] *Time* magazine proclaimed that the crisis of American confidence as a result of the My Lai revelations 'is a graver phenomenon than the horror following the assassination of President Kennedy. Historically it is far more crucial.'[34] In sum, the affair shattered the conception of the United States as a benevolent power intent on making the world safe for democracy, as promoted in films such as *The Green Berets* and, indeed, *Cast a Giant Shadow*.

Anti-war sentiment was further bolstered when on 4 May 1970, six months after the revelations of the massacre at My Lai, the Ohio National Guard opened fire on anti-war protestors at Kent State University, killing four students and wounding nine others. Eleven days later police in Jackson, Mississippi, shot and killed two students and wounded twelve others during an anti-war protest at Jackson State College. The slayings incited a nationwide student strike and a 100,000-person demonstration in Washington against the war. Throughout 1970 polling consistently found that a significant majority of Americans believed that the United States should withdraw all troops from Vietnam by the end of the following year.[35] Just over two years later, in January of 1973, Nixon signed the Paris Peace Accords, which officially ended the United States' military operations in Vietnam.

As discussed in the previous chapter, the administrations of both Kennedy and Johnson saw Vietnam primarily as a litmus test of American power. This attitude was similarly held by Nixon, who in 1970 declared in an address to the nation, 'If, when the chips are down, the world's most powerful nation, the United States of America, acts like a pitiful, helpless giant, the forces of totalitarianism and anarchy will threaten free nations and free institutions throughout the world.'[36] Furthermore, Nixon argued, defeat in Vietnam would reduce the United States to, in the eyes of the rest of the world, a 'second-rate power.'[37] The United States' withdrawal from Vietnam and the eventual fall of Saigon to Communist forces in April of 1975 could thus only be seen as bringing to a close one of the most shameful chapters in the annals of the nation's history, to the point where, in the American lexicon, 'Vietnam' no longer signifies a foreign nation, but is instead a metaphor for American humiliation, and a symbol of its decline as a moral and military force in the world. Indeed, the supposed reluctance of successive American governments to impose its will militarily in the developing world following the fall of Saigon was widely seen as a manifestation of a so-called 'Vietnam syndrome.'[38] In the words of sociologist Daniel Bell, 'The American Century foundered on the shoals of Vietnam.'[39]

In addition to shattering the long-standing myth of American exceptionalism, defeat in Vietnam constituted a profound challenge to the collective consciousness of the American public by initiating what the poet Robert Bly termed an 'erosion of male confidence.'[40] According to Bly, this erosion was a consequence of both the United States' humiliating retreat, and the dishonourable manner in which the war was executed. Meanwhile, a constellation of domestic-based forces coalesced with the stigma of Vietnam to engender a so-called 'crisis of masculinity,' the most significant of which was the dynamic revival of the age-old struggle for gender equality into a broad social movement that would eventually come to be known as second-wave feminism. Bly argues that, owing to the emergence of second-wave feminism, 'women came out of the Sixties and Seventies with considerable confidence in their values,' whereas 'men lack this clarity and belief.'[41] Echoing the sentiments of Bly, Michael Kimmel writes in *Manhood in America: A Cultural History* (1996):

> The erosion of confidence in a masculinity based on martial values that attended our involvement in Vietnam was only part of the problem for American men in the 1960s and 1970s. Men were besieged at home; the social movements of those two decades – the women's movement, the civil rights movement, and the gay liberation movement – all offered scathing critiques of traditional masculinity and demanded inclusion and equality in the public arena. No longer could the marketplace and the political arena be the preserve of heterosexual white men. The very groups who had been so long excluded from American life were making their own claims for identity.[42]

As Kimmel goes on to claim, 'Feminism posed perhaps the greatest challenge to a masculinity based on exclusion and affected men both personally and politically.'[43] The supposed crisis of masculinity that emerged out of the trauma of Vietnam and the rise of second-wave feminism was symptomatic of the apprehensions and self-doubt that plagued the nation's collective consciousness throughout the late 1970s. This resulted in the launching of a 'war against women' which raged across a broad spectrum of American cultural output throughout the 1980s, and that sought to, in the words of Keith Beattie, 'renovate structures of masculinity and patriarchy perceived to have been damaged during the war years by the putative threat posed by women.'[44] Released in 1977, *Black Sunday* constitutes an early attempt to renovate the structures of American white masculinity and patriarchy. Moreover, the film constitutes a particularly unique attempt to renovate these structures, by virtue of its overt invocation of a militarized Israel.

Israel's emergence as a military power

In stark contrast to the supposed 'softening' of the United States in the decade between 1966 and 1976, throughout this same period the image of Israel underwent a profound masculinization by virtue of the Jewish state's emergence as a widely respected military power. It was a time in which, according to Ruth R. Wisse, 'the cliché of the bronzed warrior emerged ready to replace the older cliché of a wizened rabbi,' which ultimately gave rise to the ideal of 'new Jew.'[45] The key event in this transformation was what is generally known in Israel (and much of the Western world) as the Six Day War, and what the Arab world refers to as an-Naksah (The Setback). The two decades that followed the declaration of Israeli statehood were punctuated by the seemingly ceaseless exchange of hostilities between Israel and its Arab neighbours. The mid-1960s also saw the establishment of el-Fatah and the Palestinian Liberation Organization (PLO), two entities that were each committed to bringing about Palestinian statehood and who would soon be frequently launching guerrilla attacks against Israeli targets. The tension between Israel and the region's Arabs spectacularly came to a head in 1967 in the form of a conflagration between Israel and a coalition of Arab states led by Egypt, Syria, Jordan and Iraq.[46] However, in a mere six days the war was over with Israel having achieved an emphatic victory. In the process Israel claimed the Syrian territory of the Golan Heights, while also gaining control of East Jerusalem, the West Bank and Gaza, giving Israel control of the entire former British mandate of Palestine. Historian Michael B. Oren describes the war as 'the greatest military triumph in the Middle East since the British defeat of the Germans at El Alamein twenty-five years earlier.'[47] The war's impact on the Arab-Israeli conflict was effectively summed up by Yitzhak Rabin, Chief of Staff of the Israeli Defense Forces in 1967 and future two-time Prime Minister of Israel, who concluded that the war changed the context of the Arab-Israeli conflict, 'not by making Israel any less repugnant to the Arabs, but by convincing them that it could never be eliminated by force of arms.'[48]

Coverage of the war in the United States was overwhelmingly one-sided. A report conducted by the American Institute for Political Communication found that of eighteen syndicated columnists with Washington outlets, nine viewed the crisis 'chiefly or primarily from the perspective of American foreign policy,' six columnists 'took a strong, persistent pro-Israeli position,' and only one writer authored a column which 'set out the difficulties, problems and needs of the Arabs.'[49] Janice Monti-Belkaoui, who examined the representation of Arabs and Israelis between the years 1966 and 1974 in two newspapers – the *New York Times* and the *New York Daily News* – as well as three magazines – *Newsweek*, *Time* and *U.S. News & World Report* – similarly found that in 1967 Israeli leaders were cast as 'heroes,' 'winners,' and 'splendid performers,' while Israel's military was 'powerful, efficient, skillful and proud.' Conversely, Egyptian president Abdel Nasser was presented as a 'typical villain.'[50] The American media's effusive praise of Israel's performance was, at least in part, undoubtedly a consequence of what Eytan Gilboa termed 'the concomitant American failures in Vietnam and the psychological need for Americans to identify with a winning cause.'[51] Gilboa's assertion is supported by the words of Harry McPherson, special counsel to President Johnson, who visited Israel soon after the outbreak of war and reported back to his president, 'After the doubts, confusions, and ambiguities of Vietnam, it was deeply moving to see people whose commitment is total and unquestioning.'[52] An unnamed United States military official quoted in *U.S. News & World Report* echoed the sentiments of McPherson, stating, in what was an obvious allusion to America's failure to defeat the Viet Cong, 'The Israeli performance was proof of the only sound military strategy: When a country decides to go into a war, it goes in "wham" – to win.'[53] McAlister effectively sums up the American response to Israel's military success in the following terms; 'As questions raged both about the morality of the US war in Vietnam and about the role of the US military more generally, Israel came to provide a political model for thinking about military power and a practical example of effectiveness in the use of that power.'[54] The United States' new found admiration for Israel's military prowess had a dramatic effect on American-Israeli relations. American policymakers who had long been preconditioned to view world affairs through the lens of the Cold War were now persuaded to regard Israel as, to quote Oren, 'a small but muscular cohort' that could serve as a bulwark against the twin assaults of Arab nationalism and Soviet penetration of the oil-rich Middle East.[55] The Six Day War and its aftermath constitute the period in which the special relationship between the United States and Israel truly began to blossom. Meanwhile, the American government's regard for the region's Arabs sunk to a new low, with the CIA citing their defeat as proof that they 'simply weren't up to the demands of modern warfare and that they lacked understanding, motivation, and probably in some cases courage as well.'[56]

The image of Israel as a highly proficient military power was further bolstered in July 1976 following an impeccably executed hostage rescue mission carried out by Israeli commandos at Entebbe Airport in Uganda. Codenamed Operation Thunderbolt, the mission resulted in the liberation of 102 hostages held by members of the Popular Front for the Liberation of Palestine, who one week earlier had hijacked an Air France plane, redirected it towards Uganda and held all of its Israeli passengers as hostages. Each of the four hijackers died in the counterstrike, along with three hostages and one Israeli commando (Lt. Col. Yonatan Netanyahu, the unit's commander).[57] As was the case with the Six Day War in 1967, Israel's success at Entebbe was widely lauded in the United States. President Gerald Ford sent a telegram to Israeli leader Yitzhak Rabin expressing 'great satisfaction' that the hijackers had been thwarted.[58] William Scranton, the United States' chief delegate to the United Nations, expressed his admiration before the UN Security Council, declaring 'the government of Israel invoked [sic] one of the most remarkable rescue missions in history, a combination of guts and brains that has seldom been surpassed. It electrified millions everywhere, and I confess I was one of them.'[59] The United States' national media proffered similar encomiums. The *New York Times* declared, 'The civilized world owes the Government and armed forces of Israel a permanent debt of gratitude for the courageously conceived and brilliantly executed rescue of more than 100 hostages from pro-Palestinian terrorists at Entebbe airport,' and that the operation would 'serve as an inspiration to other countries.'[60] The *Chicago Tribune* reported, 'Plucky little Israel once again had performed a military miracle, and this one saved American lives that only the Israeli government could save.'[61] Such was the excitement that the operation generated in the United States that two made-for-television movies based on the incident were immediately put into production. *Victory at Entebbe*, directed by Marvin J. Chomsky and featuring a star-studded cast including, among many others, Anthony Hopkins, Burt Lancaster, Kirk Douglas, Elizabeth Taylor and Richard Dreyfuss, aired on ABC in December of 1976. Soon after, in January of 1977, *Raid on Entebbe*, directed by Irvin Kershner and featuring a cast including Peter Finch, Charles Bronson, Martin Balsam, Jack Warden and Silvia Sidney, aired on 20th Century Fox. The swift development and production of these films confirms Paul Breines's claim that 'The successful and much-publicized Israeli rescue mission did more than any other single event to generate in America a full-blown myth of the Jews as nearly superhuman in their bravery, physical strength, and military skill.'[62]

American admiration for Israel's actions at Entebbe was indelibly linked to the United States' own failures in Vietnam. *National Review* commented, 'Once again, and most strikingly, the Entebbe operation showed that in political and military matters, *will* is the decisive factor'; meanwhile, the article referred to the post-Vietnam American government as being 'flabby-willed.'[63] Similarly, *U.S. News & World Report* ran a laudatory piece on Israel's success at Entebbe alongside a story titled 'When U.S. Rescue Mission Fizzled,' which recounted the failure of an American effort to rescue fifty-five prisoners of war from the Son Tay Prison near Hanoi in 1970.[64] Israel had demonstrated to a superpower that had just suffered a humiliating defeat at the hands of a third-world guerilla army and whose collective consciousness was consequently plagued by pangs of self-doubt how to effectively resolve a situation through the decisive application of force. For the many Americans who subscribed to the notion that the United States was now suffering from the so-called Vietnam Syndrome, Israel constituted a militaristic model of action worthy of reverence and emulation.[65]

Hollywood's response to Vietnam

In *The Remasculinization of America: Gender and the Vietnam War* (1989) Susan Jeffords contends that American cultural representations of the war in Vietnam are 'more than a comment on a particular war,' and that, instead, they are 'an emblem for the presentation of dominant cultural ideology in contemporary American society.'[66] Jeffords's assertion is particularly applicable to many of the representations of the Vietnam War that appeared in American popular cinema throughout the second half of the 1970s. As a consequence of the ever-increasing domestic opposition to the United States' presence in Vietnam, Hollywood had largely avoided overt depictions of the war throughout the decade following the release of *The Green Berets*. When Hollywood finally did begin to directly touch on the subject of Vietnam in the mid-to-late 1970s, it tended to produce films that were only superficially concerned with the actual waging of the war, and which were instead focused on veterans who were often depicted as psychologically traumatized, physically weakened victims of the conflict. Notable examples of this cycle include *Taxi Driver* (Martin Scorsese, 1976), a brooding character study of a disaffected veteran who embarks on a murderous mission to rescue a teenage prostitute from her junkie pimp and his gangster associates; *Rolling Thunder* (John Flynn, 1977), about a similarly disturbed ex-POW who hunts down the murderers of his wife and son; *The Deer Hunter* (Michael Cimino, 1978), an examination of the impact of the war on a small town from which a trio of friends volunteer to enlist and who each come to suffer various physical and psychological traumas; and *Coming Home* (Hal Ashby, 1978), in which a physically wounded and psychologically scarred veteran (Bruce Dern, in his first role after *Black Sunday*) has his return to American life juxtaposed with that of a paralysed veteran with whom the wife of Dern's character has become romantically involved. The veteran protagonists of each of these films are best understood as metaphorizing the ideal of a 'wounded' United States whose once supposedly self-evident status as a paragon of military supremacy and moral superiority has been irrevocably lost in the jungles and hamlets of Southeast Asia.[67] In emphasizing the traumatic effects of the war on American serviceman while at the same time essentially ignoring the pain and suffering inflicted on the Vietnamese people, this first wave of 'returning veteran' films go beyond the risibly absurd notion propagated by then president Jimmy Carter that the destruction wrought by the war 'was mutual,' and instead assert that it was the United States, rather than Vietnam, who was the war's true victim.[68]

As in the aforementioned 'returning veteran' films, *Black Sunday* lucidly articulates the notion of American post-Vietnam victimhood. The film's central American character is Michael Lander, a blimp pilot and Vietnam veteran who has gone psychotic after spending six months in a North Vietnamese prison as a prisoner of war, before being court-martialled by the US Military. However, unlike *Taxi Driver*'s Travis Bickle (Robert De Niro) and *Rolling Thunder*'s Major Charles Rane (William Devane) – who each direct their psychotic rage towards society's lowlifes – Lander's insanity drives him to plot to kill innocent Americans. For Lander the attack is motivated purely by a desire to exact revenge for the pain and suffering he experienced in Vietnam. Indeed, Dahlia Iyad, who is both Lander's lover and his accomplice, at one point accuses him of being completely devoid of any convictions or political beliefs, reinforcing the idea that Lander is deeply disturbed and that the attack is nothing more than a misguided attempt to avenge the horrible wrongs that have been committed against him.

Lander is introduced in the film's opening scene as a frail prisoner of war, appearing in a Viet Cong propaganda film that is being screened by members of Black September.⁶⁹ The apparently cheaply made, black and white film within a film evokes the iconic black and white television images of the murder of Israeli athletes at the Munich Olympics by members of Black September only five years prior to the film's release. Such a device situates *Black Sunday*'s characters and the dramatic attack on the Super Bowl within the same world that the audience resides. Lander trudges towards a microphone that is placed before the camera, bows to his captors, then, squinting as a bright light is shone in his face, proceeds to admit to committing war crimes. He apologizes for his deeds and for the fact that his country has killed Vietnamese children, and calls on the American people to stop the war; while it is not explicitly stated, it is assumed that this 'confession' is the catalyst for his court-martial. Arousing feelings of pity and contempt, Lander serves as the personification of the United States' status as what Nixon termed 'a pitiful, helpless giant'.⁷⁰ Semmerling writes that in this scene Lander 'shows himself to be repentant about his destructive actions, which sought to eliminate his enemies, and about the suffering he has caused'.⁷¹ However, Lander clearly appears to be under extreme distress, and he is surrounded throughout the scene by other prisoners of war who are also palpably suffering. The confession thus has the appearance of having been coerced, possibly by way of torture. Indeed, the characterization of the Vietnamese as cruel and heartless torturers was at the time widely held in the wake of the broadly perpetuated myth that the Vietnamese were still imprisoning thousands of American POWs (scenes of Americans being tortured by sadistic Vietnamese would appear in the soon-to-be released films *Rolling Thunder* and *The Deer Hunter*).⁷² This implicit

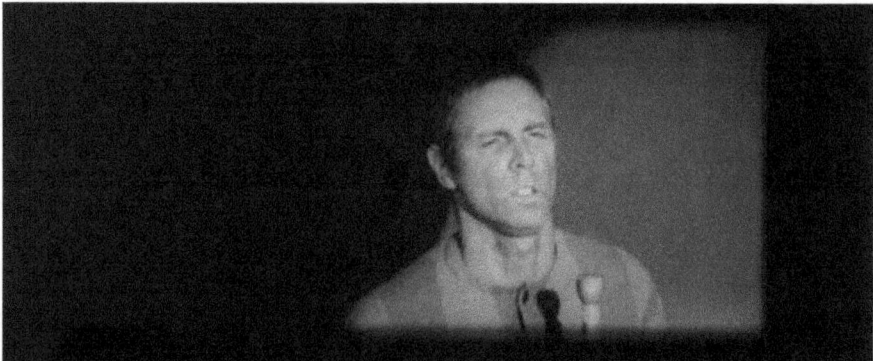

Figure 4.2 A tortured Lander confesses to his (and America's) crimes.

positioning of Lander as having been tortured by his captives undermines the notion that he is sincerely atoning for what he considers to be sins, and instead pitches him as a victim of the innately inhumane Vietnamese enemy.

Crucially, the film positions Lander as not only being wounded by the Vietnamese, but as being victimized by certain elements within his own country. This is felt most notably in an early scene in which Lander visits the Veterans Affairs office. Lander is met with callous disrespect from the office receptionist, and despite having an appointment he is told to take a number and wait until he is called. He takes the number fifty-two and sits down in the waiting room that is crowded with fellow veterans, after which the receptionist calls 'number 23', signalling that he has an extended wait ahead of him. A montage of shots follows in which a noticeably agitated Lander is shown sitting, waiting and anxiously shaking his legs (an image that is juxtaposed by the receptionist casually filing her nails), until finally his number is called. Lander enters the caseworker's office and is asked how his wife and children are faring. Lander responds by revealing that he is estranged from his family, sardonically remarking that his children 'don't know much about my rights'. The caseworker apologizes for unnecessarily bringing up painful memories before attributing responsibility for the gaffe to his predecessor whom he accuses of failing to update Lander's file in what is a clear indictment of American bureaucracy. Lander then expresses suspicion that a military official told his wife of the high rate of homosexuality and impotence among POWs, before then sleeping with her. Through the contrasting of the heroic, effective soldier (it is remarked upon in this scene that Lander earned four decorations) with the cold and ineffectual bureaucracy, as well as the subsequent suggestion that Lander was cuckolded by a higher ranking official, this scene speaks to the then burgeoning notion of the American soldier being 'stabbed-in-the-back'.[73] Meanwhile, the suggestion of Lander's impotence exemplifies how the film metaphorizes the notion of America having 'gone soft' following both the nation's traumatic defeat in Vietnam and the subsequent development of a supposed crisis of masculinity in the wake of the emergence of second-wave feminism.[74]

Frankenheimer's femme fatales

In stark contrast to the impotence of Lander, Dahlia is strong-willed, assertive, independent and possesses a palpable sexual potency. Dahlia's character is established in the film's opening sequence, which tracks her journey from

Beirut airport to Black September's headquarters. Dahlia stands out in the austere landscape overwhelmingly populated with Arabic men (and the occasional veiled Arab woman) as she traverses the bustling streets without male accompaniment and dressed in what appears to be a high-priced designer outfit, demonstrating a degree of mobility rarely seen in Western representations of Middle Eastern women. On her journey, which is conveyed through a series of extended handheld tracking shots, as if she is being followed and surreptitiously filmed, Dahlia passes by a funeral procession and a phalanx of armed soldiers, all of which signals an overwhelming sense of danger. Nevertheless, Dahlia strides confidently through the city before reaching her destination where she joins the various members of Black September in watching the film of Lander's 'confession.' Doubts are expressed over Lander's capacity to carry out the attack on the Super Bowl, to which Dahlia responds by confidently assuring the group that he is under her total control. As previously noted, Lander is devoid of political convictions, and thus Dahlia's claim of total control over him can be seen as reflecting a confidence that his submission to her derives almost entirely from the power she wields over him sexually. At the denouement of this scene Dahlia goes to bed with a high-ranking member of Black September where, as noted by Semmerling, she 'bites at him like a lioness biting at her mate during copulation.'[75] This sequence can be seen as laying the foundation for the rest of the film by positioning aggressive female sexuality as a source of fear and extreme danger.

Following this sequence Israeli commandos raid the Black September compound and proceed to summarily execute every member of the terrorist group that they encounter. The character we eventually come to know as David Kabakov, the film's protagonist, finds Dahlia in the shower, naked and cowering in fear. Through a series of shot/countershots the audience is led to infer that the vulnerable and beautiful woman captivates Kabakov, who, after having apparently determining that she poses no threat, lets her live. Here Dahlia's status as an aesthetically pleasing young woman helps to keep her alive, enabling her to carry out horrific attacks on innocent Americans. Later in the film there appears another instance in which Dahlia's sexuality enables her to commit deeds with potentially catastrophic results for society at large. On the eve of the Super Bowl an increasingly unstable Lander is replaced as the blimp pilot for the big game. Dahlia poses as an employee of the hotel in which the new pilot is staying. While delivering room service, Dahlia manages to gain access to the replacement's room after he attempts to seduce her. Having gained entry, Dahlia shoots the new pilot dead with a pistol that has been mounted with a silencer that functions as a phallic symbol of her potent sexuality, thus enabling Lander to reassume his role as blimp pilot for the big game. This sequence, which is notably absent from Harris's novel, compounds the opening sequence's affirmation of unbridled female sexuality as a force of uncontrollable evil.

The sexual potency and distinct non-Arabness of Dahlia signifies the film's relative lack of concern with the realities of the Arab-Israeli conflict, as well as its appeal to the crisis of American masculinity that emerged out of the coalescence of the loss in Vietnam and the rise of second-wave feminism. As I have detailed, the film presents its principal American character as a former serviceman who has been rendered a physical and psychological cripple as a result of his experience in Vietnam. This emasculated representative of American manhood attempts to unleash Armageddon on his countrymen by attacking the Super Bowl – that most hyper-masculine of American rituals – but only after falling under the spell of a vicious seductress who exudes an unbridled sexuality. In essence, Dahlia is a descendent of the classic film noir femme fatale who routinely led forlorn men to their doom in the urban crime dramas of the 1940s and early 1950s. However, unlike, for instance, Barbara Stanwyck in *Double Indemnity* (Billy Wilder, 1944), or Lana Turner in *The Postman Always Rings Twice* (Fritz Lang, 1946), Dahlia signals catastrophe for an entire country rather than one cursed individual, and the subject of her malevolent manipulation has been rendered defenceless to her wiles out of not blind love, but out of humiliation and hatred. She is a femme fatale that is a direct product of the peculiar circumstances that came to define post-Vietnam America.

Black Sunday's mobilization of the image of the castrating female in its construction of American nationhood has its antecedent in Frankenheimer's most well-known film, *The Manchurian Candidate*. The protagonist Raymond Shaw (Laurence Harvey) and his mother Eleanor Shaw Iselin (Angela Lansbury) have a relationship that is highly evocative of that of Lander and Dahlia; however, this is but only one of a number of similarities shared by the two films. Whereas *Black Sunday* is set in the immediate aftermath of the Vietnam War, *The Manchurian Candidate* largely takes place in the wake of the conflagration on the Korean Peninsula that lasted from June 1950 to July 1953. Unlike the war in Vietnam, the Korean War did not end in American defeat. Nevertheless, the film presents the conflict as having a traumatic effect on a number of American combatants in a manner that anticipates *Black Sunday* and its depiction of Lander. At the beginning of *The Manchurian Candidate*, a platoon of American soldiers have been captured by the enemy. Through a series of dream sequences, the audience comes to learn that while in captivity the soldiers have all been brainwashed by the Communist enemy. The film focuses on two of the soldiers; one is Captain Bennett Marco (Frank Sinatra), who works for Army Intelligence and is plagued by nightmares that recall the brainwashing, which he devotes his energies to investigating; the other is Shaw, who is the film's equivalent of Lander in that he is cold, anti-social, quite obviously mentally disturbed and a victim of both the Communists of Southeast Asia as well as elements within his own country. Eventually the audience discovers that Shaw has been programmed to assassinate a presidential nominee as part of an elaborate scheme to help propel to the White House the vice-presidential candidate – a buffoonish right-wing demagogue clearly based on Joe McCarthy, who also happens to be Raymond's stepfather – upon which he will govern as a puppet of Raymond's mother, who is in fact a Communist agent. The film ends with an apparently deprogrammed Shaw shooting not the presidential nominee but his mother and stepfather before also shooting himself, in the process preventing the Communist takeover of the US government.

In both *Black Sunday* and *The Manchurian Candidate* it is a demonic woman who manipulates a psychologically crippled veteran to launch a violent attack that threatens the very viability of the American way of life, and each film lucidly articulates the anxieties plaguing the collective consciousness of the respective Americas in which they were produced and exhibited. As we have seen, *Black Sunday* deploys the figure of the fiendish female Arab terrorist as a symbol for the prospective dangers facing an America whose status as an invincible superpower had disintegrated and in which the traditional domestic social order had been resolutely challenged. In *The Manchurian Candidate* the diabolical woman is a highly manipulative, sociopathic mother and Communist agent who has been read by scholars such as Michael Rogin and Rebecca Bell-Metereau as an overt caution against what Philip Wylie famously termed 'momism'.[76] Wylie introduced the concept into the popular lexicon in 1942 with his bestselling book *Generation of Vipers*, in which he delivered an invective-laden diatribe that attributed a diverse array of evils besieging American society to the supposedly rapacious and repressive nature of American matriarchy and its raising of a generation of lethargic eunuchs.[77] As detailed by Michael Kimmel, Wylie's thesis retained significant cultural capital well into the 1970s.[78] Bell-Metereau argues that for *The Manchurian Candidate*, 'Hatred of the feminine resides at the emotional core of the film, and at a more profound level rests fear and hatred of the feminized male.'[79] Bell-Metereau specifically points to momism and the anxieties it elicited in contemporary America as the cultural force to which the film's ideology is appealing.[80] Similarly, Rogin positions the film and its pairing of anti-Communist rhetoric with a familial constellation of 'an intrusive, sexually unsatisfied mother, a weak father, and a cold, isolated son', as an explicit articulation of the supposed relationship between Communist subversion and 'the entrapping, repressed, oedipal love that Wylie made the source of momism.'[81] *The Manchurian Candidate* and its personification of an existential threat in the form of an evil, domineering female can thus be read as an appeal to the peculiar set of anxieties plaguing post-war American society.[82] With *Black Sunday* Frankenheimer repeats the formula, only in this instance the film serves as an incipient exemplar of the cinematic war against women that functioned as a 'Backlash' against the feminist advances of the previous decade, and the supposed crisis of masculinity to which they contributed.[83]

Israel to the rescue

The most notable difference between *The Manchurian Candidate* and *Black Sunday* can be seen in their respective representations of the hero. Through an analysis of these divergent representations, we can better understand how *Black Sunday* mobilizes the notion of a militarized Israel as a model of action for post-Vietnam America. The hero of *The Manchurian Candidate* is Marco who, as noted earlier, is played by the iconic Frank Sinatra. As discussed in the previous chapter, Sinatra was a paragon of twentieth century American toughness, representing, in the words of Rupert Wilkinson, 'a national stereotype of the tough and successful man.'[84] Throughout *The Manchurian Candidate* Sinatra's Marco is diligent, intelligent, sexually attractive (a character played by Janet Leigh breaks off her engagement with her unseen fiancé and enters into a relationship with Marco literally one day after meeting him), and is highly effective at his job. While it is Raymond who foils the Communist plot to take over the government, it is implied that Raymond's actions in the film's penultimate scene are the result of him being successfully deprogrammed by Marco. Just prior to Raymond receiving the order from his mother to assassinate his stepfather's running mate, Marco hypnotizes Raymond and drills into him that he is no longer under Communist control, telling him 'the wires have been pulled.' There is nothing to immediately indicate that the deprogramming is successful, and thus Raymond's killing of his mother and stepfather comes as a surprise to both the audience and to Marco. However, given the manner in which the denouement unfolds, it is natural to assume that Marco was successful in deprogramming Raymond, who proceeded to feign submission to his mother while internally plotting to kill her (in the Richard Condon novel upon which the film is based it is made clear that Marco successfully hypnotizes Shaw and reprograms him to kill his mother and stepfather). The ambiguity in the film version is a direct consequence of the Production Code. John Frankenheimer is on record as stating that during that period one couldn't make a film in which its hero 'advocates killing people,' and thus Shaw's actions had to appear to be guided by his own free will.[85] Nevertheless, it is Sinatra's Marco who must be understood as being responsible for saving the day – just as he would help to do four years later in *Cast a Giant Shadow* as an American pilot aiding the Israelis in their war against the Arabs.

In *Black Sunday* it is a strong-willed Israeli hero named David Kabakov, played by the English actor Robert Shaw, who saves the day. This element distinguishes the film not only from *The Manchurian Candidate*, but also from the majority of the similarly constructed films of the contemporaneous disaster cycle in which the valorized models of action were usually played by iconic symbols of American masculinity. Shaw's British heritage marks him as an outsider in American film culture, while also facilitating a clear ethnic delineation between the Israeli Kabakov and Lander, played by the American Dern. Moreover, Shaw was best known for playing tough guy characters such as the vicious crime boss Doyle Lonnegan in *The Sting* (George Roy Hill, 1973), and the fearless shark hunter Quint in *Jaws*. Conversely, Dern was, at that point, most widely known as a supporting actor with a penchant for memorable turns of unscrupulous villainy; in *Hang 'Em High* (Ted Post, 1968) he attempted to hang Clint Eastwood, and in *The Cowboys* (Mark Rydell, 1972) he memorably killed John Wayne after shooting him in the back. Meanwhile Fritz Weaver, who plays the ineffectual FBI agent Sam Corley whom I will discuss later in more detail, was at the time best known as a TV actor; his lone notable appearance in a major Hollywood film came in *Fail-Safe* (Sidney Lumet, 1964), where he played a mentally unbalanced colonel whose actions help to bring about a nuclear apocalypse. Among the three major male performers there exists a clear hierarchy in terms of masculinity and star power that unequivocally privileges the Israeli character as a hero.

From the moment of Kabakov's first appearance on-screen, the film builds on the image of Israel as a highly proficient military power. Whereas Lander is introduced as a pathetic victim who is aligned with diabolical terrorists, Kabakov is introduced as the ruthless leader of a counterterrorist unit executing a highly successful, efficient raid on Black September's Lebanese compound, thus exemplifying the film's juxtaposition of the weakened American and the admirable Israeli. Immediately following a scene in which Dahlia and the rest of Black September detail the plan to attack the United States, we see Kabakov emerging from the inflatable rafts he and his team have used to access the compound (an entrance that bears more than a passing resemblance to that of Paul Newman's Ari Ben Canaan in *Exodus*). As the raid takes place at night the scene is cloaked in darkness, all except for Kabakov's face which is illuminated by the modicum of available light and shown in an extended close-up. Through the juxtaposition of Black September declaring their plans to attack the United States and Kabakov's emergence out of the water, the film asserts the Israeli's status as the saviour of helpless Americans. The camera proceeds to frequently assume Kabakov's point of view as he confidently navigates the terrorists' headquarters, prompting the audience to identify with the Israeli hero as his unit systematically executes every person they encounter. As previously discussed, Kabakov arrives upon a bathing Dahlia and, according to Frankenheimer, the character ultimately concludes that 'She's probably just a tramp and why one more killing?'[86] Kabakov's reluctance to execute Dahlia is significant not only because it enables her to proceed with the plot to attack the Super Bowl, but because it demonstrates Kabakov's own capacity for human weakness.

Figure 4.3 Kabakov (Robert Shaw) encounters the bathing Dahlia.

However, whereas the United States struggled to overcome its psychological trauma in the wake of Vietnam, Kabakov appears to be immediately aware of his mistake, and the remainder of the film depicts a relentless striving for personal redemption. In the following scene Kabakov and a trio of US government officials listen to a recording that was retrieved during the raid in which Dahlia speaks of an imminent terrorist attack to take place on American soil. Kabakov correctly infers that the recording does not constitute a threat but is instead to be used after the attack has occurred. He proceeds to warn his skeptical American counterparts of the seriousness of the threat posed by Black September, before articulating his own personal disappointment in allowing Dahlia to live.

As detailed throughout previous chapters, the language deployed by the earliest examples of Hollywood cinema's representations of the Arab-Israeli conflict perpetuated an image of Arabs that explicitly recalled the traditional cinematic construction of Native Americans. In expressing his superior knowledge of Black September's objectives and capacity for catastrophic violence, Kabakov can be understood as a variation of what Richard Slotkin has termed 'the man who knows Indians'.[87] Slotkin defines this character as a frontiersman who:

> Stands between the opposed worlds of savagery and civilization, acting sometimes as mediator or interpreter between races and cultures but more often as civilization's most effective instrument against savagery – a man who knows how to think and fight like an Indian, to turn their own methods against them. In its most extreme development, the frontier hero takes the form of the "Indian-hater," whose suffering at savage hands has made him correspondingly savage, an avenger determined at all costs to "exterminate the brutes."[88]

Throughout *Gunfighter Nation: The Myth of the Frontier in Twentieth-Century America* (1992), Slotkin details how 'the man who knows Indians' has been a central figure throughout the evolutionary development of America's frontier mythology, having been embodied by such luminous cultural icons as Daniel Boone, Davy Crockett, William 'Buffalo Bill' Cody and John Wayne. However, by the 1970s, this character had essentially gone the way of the Indian, with the production of Westerns by Hollywood all but coming to a complete halt (with the odd exception coming in the form of 'revisionist' Westerns such as *Little Big Man* [Arthur Penn, 1970] and *The Outlaw Josey Wales* [Clint Eastwood, 1976], in which the Indian is representative of a superior nobility). Where *Exodus* utilized the establishment of Israeli statehood as a means of articulating a more classical version of the frontier myth at a time when the Western was heading in new directions, *Black Sunday* mobilizes the contours of the Arab-Israeli conflict to celebrate the ruthless frontiersman who conquers dark-skinned savagery and delivers salvation to American civilization at a time in which the cinematic frontier was essentially closed.

The American officials' failure to appreciate of the seriousness of the recording sets the tone for the rest of the film in which there exists a clear delineation between the prescience and proficiency of Kabakov, and the ignorance and incompetence of his American counterparts. This distinction is most notably characterized by the ongoing juxtaposition between Kabakov and the FBI agent Sam Corley. In stark contrast to the perceptiveness of Kabakov, Corley is weak-minded and myopic, as exemplified by the sequence in which he is shown obliviously walking past Dahlia only minutes before she murders Kabakov's partner. Corley, who insists that he and his men 'follow the rule of law', also lacks the cold-blooded ruthlessness possessed by Kabakov that enables the latter to effectively perform his duty. In a telling sequence, American agents under the command of Corley botch an operation to capture Mohammed Fasil (Bekim Fehmiu), one of the leaders of Black September and the figure said to have masterminded the real-world massacre of Israeli athletes at the 1972 Munich Olympics. As soon as the plan is put into motion Fasil becomes aware that he is being watched, and he attempts to escape after taking a young woman hostage and holding a gun to her head. In this sequence, which was invented for the film, *Black Sunday* recalls both *Exodus* and *Cast a Giant Shadow* by enacting a variation of the captivity narrative, in which the white woman taken captive by dark-skinned savages symbolizes the values of civilization 'that are imperilled in the wilderness war'.[89] Using the young woman as a shield, Fasil manages to shoot down a number of American agents, and after abandoning the hostage he attempts to blend in to a crowd that is gathered at the shore of Miami Beach. Kabakov manages to catch up with him and shoots the terrorist dead just as Fasil takes aim at Corley, who is unarmed, affirming Kabakov's status as a 'hero-as-Indian-fighter'. The sequence ends with a visibly disgusted Kabakov remarking to the pathetically anaemic Corley, 'I should have let him shoot you.' The ruthlessness of Kabakov is similarly glorified in a scene – which, again, is not to be found in Harris's novel – in which he sticks a gun in the mouth of a citizen named Muzi (Michael V. Gazzo) whom he is interrogating. The camera alternates between a low-angle over the shoulder shot taken from Muzi's perspective that exaggerates the size and authority of Kabakov, and tight close-ups of Muzi as he blubbers his way through Kabakov's questioning while sucking on the Israeli hard man's revolver. This contrasting of power and terrified submission serves to encourage the

Figure 4.4 Muzi (Michael V. Gazzo) sucks on Kabakov's revolver.

audiences' awe and admiration for the film's unscrupulously brutal protagonist, who here echoes the practices of the wildly popular vigilante hero Inspector Harry Callahan (Clint Eastwood) of the contemporaneous 'Dirty Harry' series, while the phallic imagery employed throughout functions as a microcosm of the film's constant juxtaposition of the weakened, feminized Americans and the hyper-masculine power of the Israeli Kabakov.[90]

The dichotomy engendered by the lionization of Kabakov and the excoriation of the feeble Corley is maintained throughout the film's climactic sequence in which the two agents attempt to foil what they know to be a pending terrorist attack on the Super Bowl. During the singing of the American national anthem, Corley is shown with his hand on his heart and his eyes fixed on the singer whereas Kabakov is alert and anxiously scanning the crowd. Throughout the game Kabakov stands out as the only person on the side line not totally immersed in the action on the field, signifying both his professionalism and his status as a non-American. Once the precise details of the plot have been discovered Kabakov and Corley pursue the blimp in a helicopter, with Kabakov eventually shooting and killing Dahlia while Corley is taking cover. Kabakov proceeds to courageously abseil from the helicopter down to the blimp and miraculously manages to attach the blimp to the helicopter. The helicopter drags the blimp out to sea where it harmlessly discharges its payload of projectiles. The film's final shot depicts Kabakov swinging from a cable that hangs from the helicopter in what is an unadulterated celebration of the character's infallible heroism. Here the ending unfolds in a manner different to that of the novel, in which Kabakov, upon learning that the attack is going to be launched from a flying machine, brings into the operation an American helicopter pilot whose job it is to pay close attention to an Arab pilot whom Kabakov suspects will be the responsible for the attack, and who subsequently enables Kabakov to foil the plot by skilfully flying his helicopter to the blimp just before the plot is executed. Crucially, this character also served in Vietnam; his excision from the film thus leaves the traumatized and impotent Lander as the sole representative of the American serviceman. The film version instead positions the Israeli hero Kabakov as the figure who is solely responsible for thwarting the attack, while it simultaneously affirms the ineffectuality of American counterterrorist officials.[91]

In a society experiencing a supposed crisis of masculinity in the wake of Vietnam and the social upheaval of the 1970s, where unconventional, soft-bodied leading men such as Al Pacino and Dustin Hoffman came to the fore, Shaw's Kabakov represents a throwback to the era of John Wayne, Charlton Heston, Kirk Douglas and Alan Ladd. Like Douglas's Mickey Marcus in *Cast a Giant Shadow*, and Ladd's archetypal Shane from the film of the same name, Kabakov is a frontiersman who is both 'an aristocrat of violence' and 'an alien from a more glamorous world' whose heroism preserves a community to which he will never belong.[92] However, unlike the aforementioned interventionist films, in *Black Sunday* it is the United States that is the besieged, and its salvation comes in the form of a ruthlessly proficient Israeli hard man. *Black Sunday* can thus be seen as continuing the Hollywood tradition of deploying images of Israel as a means through which to articulate a more traditional model of hyper-masculinity. What makes *Black Sunday* unique amongst the group of films that mobilize Israel in this manner is that, whereas earlier films presented Israel as standing in for the United States, the hyper-masculinity of *Black Sunday*'s protagonist is affirmed by his *opposition* to the United States.

The Delta Force (1986)

In retrospect, *Black Sunday*'s underwhelming box office performance should not have come as a great surprise. The film mobilizes the image of a militaristic Israel for the purpose of presenting Americans in the post-Vietnam milieu as feminized, vulnerable and in desperate need of the intervention of a heroic Israeli; in sum, the United States is characterized in a manner that is wholly antithetical to the United States' long-standing perception of itself as a fundamentally exceptional nation, as well as the post–Second World War ideal of the United States as the world's foremost defender of liberty and freedom. Conversely, in, for example, *Jaws* – the blockbuster whose tremendous success *Black Sunday* was widely expected to replicate – a small beachside community is rescued from a demonic shark by an all-American everyman played by Roy Scheider with whom millions of American filmgoers could easily identify. Meanwhile, the watershed release of 1977, George Lucas's *Star Wars: Episode IV – A New Hope* (then known simply as *Star Wars*), was a simplistic space opera depicting a Manichaean clash between good and evil seen through the eyes of a boyish blonde-haired, blue-eyed protagonist. Clearly, American audiences in the mid-to-late 1970s were more interested in old-fashioned American heroism and fantastical escapism than in revisiting the traumas of the nation's recent past.

Nearly a full decade after the release of *Black Sunday* another film – Menahem Golan's 1986 film *The Delta Force* – would explicitly draw on the image of a ruthless and courageous Israel, only on this occasion that image would be projected onto the United States itself. Though not a huge critical success, *The Delta Force* found an audience in a United States that is perpetually hungry for depictions of American heroism, eventually earning over $17 million at the box office (against a budget of $9 million).[93] The events depicted in the film are based on the real-life hijacking of TWA Flight 847 on 15 June 1985, by members of Islamic Jihad and Hezbollah (in the film, the airline is subtly rebranded *ATW*). In the case of TWA Flight 847 the freedom of the hostages was secured after a number of the hijackers' demands were met – which included Israel releasing over 700 Shi'a Muslims it was holding prisoner – and largely as a result of the intervention of the Syrian government, while promises of US military retaliation made by President Reagan were never realized.[94] However, in the fantasy world of *The Delta Force* the Americans save the hostages essentially single-handedly, overpowering the dastardly Arabs with a combination of courage, ingenuity and overwhelming firepower, while receiving only minor assistance (in the form of intelligence) from the Mossad – their protectors in *Black Sunday*.

Another difference from the real-life hijacking of Flight 847 is that in *The Delta Force* the terrorists make no specific demands, and are not members of Hezbollah or Islamic Jihad. They are instead members of the wholly invented New World Revolution, and they have 'declared war against the American imperialists, Zionist terrorists, and all other anti-Socialist atrocities.' In this film Islamic terrorism and leftist extremism are subsumed into a singular nefarious entity that is fundamentally antithetical to the liberal democracy of the United States. As such, the terrorists' plot should not be seen as one specifically designed to elicit a certain response from Israel, but instead as one that is principally motivated by intense anti-Americanism, and ultimately as part of the broader Cold War struggle. Here it is pertinent to acknowledge that the passengers are mostly anonymous with the notable exception of an American priest played by George Kennedy, and two elderly couples comprising characters played by well-known American entertainers with whom American audiences would both sympathize and identify (Martin Balsam and Shelley Winters, and Joey Bishop and Lainie Kazan). As highlighted by Tony Shaw, the casting of Kennedy (the only actor to appear in all four entries in the *Airport* series) and Winters (star of *The Poseidon Adventure*) serves to link the film 'explicitly with the disaster genre from the 1970s.'[95] In addition to positioning the United States as the primary target of the hijacking, the film's casting also serves to unambiguously frame Americans as heroes; whereas in *Black Sunday* America was personified by a combination of the unbalanced and (literally) impotent Bruce Dern and the relatively unknown and (metaphorically) impotent Fritz Weaver, in *The Delta Force* America is represented by the celebrated tough guys Chuck Norris and Lee Marvin. Norris was at this point at the peak of his popularity, having starred in a string of highly profitable, overtly right-wing action films such as *Missing in Action* (Joseph Zito, 1984), *Missing In Action 2: The Beginning* (Lance Hool, 1985), *Code of Silence* (Andrew Davis, 1985) and *Invasion U.S.A.* (Joseph Zito, 1985). There was very little that distinguished one Norris vehicle from another, and on the back of these films Norris's screen image emerged as one defined by super-patriotism and taciturn heroism that frequently saw contemporaneous commentators compare Norris to tough guy icons like John Wayne, Clint Eastwood and Charles Bronson.[96] Meanwhile, Marvin, for whom *The Delta Force* was his last film, was at the end of a 35-year career abound with memorable turns as cops, cowboys, hoodlums and soldiers, wherein hardboiled toughness reigned as the defining feature.[97] Through the casting of Norris and Marvin as the squadron's heroic leaders, *The Delta Force* succeeds in gendering the United States as a hyper-masculine male endowed with a palpable potency.

The Delta Force as Reaganite entertainment

To understand *The Delta Force* as an exercise in projecting an idealized conception of American national identity, it is important to recognize the film as part of a contemporaneous cycle of populist action-based big-budget

Hollywood cinema that Yvonne Tasker appropriately terms 'muscular cinema.' This cycle centred on expertly violent, hyper-masculine protagonists frequently played by figures such as Sylvester Stallone, Arnold Schwarzenegger, and the aforementioned Norris, and triumphantly asserted more traditional ideas of white male power through the fetishization of the actors' powerful physiques, the systematic marginalization of women and the privileging of violent spectacle over dialogue and narrative complexity.[98] As such, muscular cinema can be seen as existing under the umbrella of 'Reaganite entertainment.'[99] Film critic Andrew Britton applied the term Reaganite entertainment in 1986 in a notable essay that critiqued the 'general movement of reaction and conservative reassurance in the contemporary cinema.'[100] Speaking to a broad and diverse array of films – from the blockbuster *Raiders of the Lost Ark* (Steven Spielberg, 1981) to the independently produced slasher film *Hell Night* (Tom DeSimone, 1981) – Britton claimed that throughout much of the cinema of the late 1970s and early 1980s there prevailed an overwhelming propensity towards the promotion of the virtues of the traditional American family, the affirmation of paternal structures and lucid conceptions of good and evil utterly devoid of nuance and complexity. Robert Kolker similarly invokes the image of Reagan while arguing that American popular cinema of the 1980s had 'an affinity for contemporary conservative discourse.'[101] Kolker claims that the then president and former Hollywood actor '(re)entered cinema as the guiding patriarch offering maternal care,'[102] and 'was not so much an individual as an ideological representation of the tough movie hero.'[103]

The frequent invocation of Reagan in discourse pertaining to the ideological underpinnings of popular cinema in the 1980s stems not only from the fact that he was president for eight of the decade's ten years and was thus one of the truly defining personalities of the era, but also because the inherent conservatism of much of Hollywood's output during this period was a clear manifestation of Reagan's political identity. Reagan was elected president in 1980 in the wake of not only the retreat from Vietnam, but also the 'failed' one-term presidency of Jimmy Carter, a widely maligned figure who 'did not appear as a strong or aggressive president,' and who was widely perceived as 'incompetent, inept, and unable to deal with the problems confronting America.'[104] Such was the perceived weakness of the Carter persona that in a 1984 article in the *Wall Street Journal* John Mihalic, a speechwriter for former president Gerald Ford, described Carter as America's first 'woman' president, and this alleged inability of the presidential office to exude strength was widely seen to exacerbate the degenerative effects on the body politic that resulted from the failure of Vietnam and a subsequent crisis of masculinity.[105] In stark contrast to his predecessor, Reagan was 'the quintessential macho president.'[106] Building on his former life as a star of B-westerns such as *The Bad Man* (Richard Thorpe, 1941), *The Last Outpost* (Lewis R. Foster, 1951) and *Law and Order* (Nathan Juran, 1953), Reagan was frequently marketed to the public as a modern-day cowboy in an attempt to project the image of old-fashioned all-American heroism.[107] Reagan's macho image also aligned with his affinity for offering simple solutions to complex problems. In his inaugural address he declared that 'In this present crisis, government is not the solution to our problem; government is the problem,' signalling the onset of what would become an eight-year assault on regulation and bureaucracy.[108] Two years later, speaking before the National Association of Evangelicals, Reagan delivered his famous 'Evil Empire' speech in which he articulated his reductively Manichaean conception of the world, framing the arms race with the Soviet Union as 'the struggle between right and wrong and good and evil.'[109] In so doing Reagan presented the ostensive justification for increased military spending and what was a far more aggressive foreign policy than that of Carter, who had repudiated the so-called 'imperial presidency' most readily associated with Richard Nixon, while at the same time minimizing American military involvement in foreign conflicts. Furthermore, where Carter had dared to suggest that Vietnam was a mistake,[110] Reagan, as both a presidential nominee and president, wholly reimagined the memory of Vietnam by insisting that the war was a 'noble cause,' and that if the army lost the war it was only because the government was 'afraid to let them win,' in turn reviving and indeed legitimating the stabbed-in-the-back myth alluded to in *Black Sunday*.[111] Here Reagan not only exemplified his commitment to the restoration of American honour and pre-eminence in the wake of a decade-long decline, but he again demonstrated his remarkable capacity to position himself as both a populist anti-bureaucrat who existed outside of 'the system,' and an authoritative patriarch leading the nation towards and beyond a cathartic regeneration – a duality that would persist throughout the tenure of his two-term presidency. As Kolker asserts, 'With the actor's talent for assuming a persona requisite to the situation at hand and a national audience ready to become subject to a discourse of security, power, and self-righteousness, he was able to focus various ideological elements. More, he became an ideology.'[112]

What makes Reaganite entertainment such an appropriate term to describe this wave of films is not merely the fact that they lucidly promote the fundamental aspects of the Reagan ideology, but that Reagan himself actively participated in fostering an alignment between his own political identity and contemporaneous popular cinema. Michael Rogin notes that while promising to veto a proposed tax increase, Reagan told Congress to 'Go ahead. Make My Day,' quoting a line spoken by Clint Eastwood's vigilante hero 'Dirty Harry' Callahan to a hoodlum who has threatened to kill a woman he has taken hostage in the film *Sudden Impact* (Clint Eastwood, 1983).[113] Also, Tasker points to the existence around this time of a widely reproduced poster of a character dubbed 'Ronbo' who sported the head of Reagan and the muscular torso of John Rambo (Sylvester Stallone), the protagonist of the hyper-violent action blockbuster *Rambo: First Blood Part II* (from hereon is referred to as *Rambo*).[114] *Rambo*, which told the story of a lone American ex-soldier who goes back to Vietnam to reclaim abandoned POWs and who, in the process, defeats not only brutal Russian Communists and their sadistic Vietnamese acolytes but also a black-hearted American bureaucrat, stands as perhaps the definitive exemplar of Reaganite entertainment. In another widely cited example of Reagan fusing his own identity with that of the heroes of eighties action cinema, Reagan again invoked *Rambo* in the wake of the hijacking of Flight 847, telling a reporter, 'I saw *Rambo* last night. Now I know what to do the next time this happens.'[115]

In *The Delta Force* it is not Reagan but Norris and Marvin who follow Rambo's example in dealing with the Arab hijackers, and the film itself is little more than a Middle East-based *Rambo* clone. *Rambo*, through its staging of the American soldier's triumphant return to Vietnam and his subsequent destruction of both the North Vietnamese and their Soviet overlords, serves, to quote Tasker, 'to cinematically correct the national humiliation of a defeat in Vietnam.'[116] Similarly, Jeffords identifies *Rambo* as a prime example of Vietnam representation in the Reagan-era functioning as an emblem for the 'remasculinization' of American culture.[117] Kolker refers to the film as 'the full fantasy of winning the war – "this time".'[118] Kolker here is referring to what is arguably the film's most famous line of dialogue in which Rambo, after having accepted the mission to rescue the long-lost POWs, solemnly asks Colonel Trautman (Richard Crenna), his former commanding officer, 'Do we get to win this time?' Trautman replies, 'This time, it's up to you.' The scene functions as a Reaganite articulation that defeat in Vietnam was a consequence of the soldiers being stabbed in the back, and is an affirmation of the film's righting of ignominious wrongs for a United States unaccustomed to defeat in the field of battle.

Like *Rambo*, *The Delta Force* is a right-wing revisionist fantasy that, while generally framed by American humiliation in Vietnam, draws more specifically on the indignities suffered by the United States in the Middle East throughout the late 1970s and early 1980s. These indignities include the Reagan administration's aforementioned inability to secure the freedom of the Americans taken hostage by the Flight 847 hijackers; the holding of fifty-two American citizens for 444 days in Iran after that country's US Embassy was taken over by Iranian student revolutionaries in November of 1979; and also the retreat of the American military from Lebanon after its barracks in Beirut were bombed by Islamic militants in October of 1983 in an attack which resulted in the deaths of 241 Americans. The film's status as an exercise in catharsis for the nation's real-life military and diplomatic humiliations is established in its opening sequence. The film opens with a shot of a military helicopter, and the accompanying chyron text identifies the scene as taking place in the Iranian desert, 200 miles southeast of Tehran, on 25 April 1980. Seconds later the helicopter explodes, and it is quickly revealed that many of the other surrounding helicopters are also in flames. What seems like hundreds of American soldiers, many of them injured, flee the scene in a mad panic. As the overwhelming majority of the film's audience at the time of its release would have understood, this sequence is a recreation of Operation Eagle Claw, the infamous failed attempt by the American Special Forces to rescue the American hostages held captive in Iran. In reality, Operation Eagle Claw was aborted after a series of unforeseen events left the unit without enough helicopters to carry out the mission effectively; in the course of leaving the base of the mission in the Iranian desert one of the remaining helicopters crashed into another vehicle, resulting in an explosion that killed eight American servicemen.[119] For a United States still reeling from the shock of defeat in Vietnam the episode was yet another shameful symbol of American weakness and decline, with the spectacular failure of the rescue serving to reinforce the widely held perception that Carter was an inept and ineffectual leader, and thus helping to ensure that he would be nothing more than a one-term president.[120] In a development that effectively symbolized the succession from a 'weak' president to a quintessential 'macho' president, the hostages were finally released on 20 January 1981, the day of Reagan's inauguration.

Like John Rambo before them, the heroes of *The Delta Force* align themselves with the political identity of Reagan by attributing the failures of the American military to the incompetence of bureaucrats and government officials. This populist anti-bureaucrat ethos is evidenced by the following exchange of dialogue between McCoy and Anderson as they are evacuating the scene:

McCoy: Why wouldn't they listen, Nick? We told 'em it's too dangerous to launch this operation at night.
Alexander: They thought their plan was better.
McCoy: I spent five years in Vietnam watching them do the planning, and us the dying. Well, I'm resigning when I get back.

McCoy does indeed resign and adopts the life of a civilian. However, as soon as word of the hijacking gets out he rushes to rejoin his squad where he is met by Anderson, who tells him that had he not come back voluntarily he was to have been issued a presidential decree ordering him to return to duty. Here we see the very conscious positioning of Reagan as being aligned with the soldiers and against the bureaucracy. This point is reinforced by film's depiction of the military brass stating that they don't even know who McCoy is at the same time that he is being fawned over by the men of Delta Force. *Rambo* similarly begins with its protagonist not as a serving member of the military, but as a prisoner doing penance after rampaging through a small town populated by sadistic rednecks in *First Blood* (Ted Kotcheff, 1982), the first entry in the *Rambo* series. Despite being incarcerated Rambo is recruited by Trautman to locate the missing POWs, and like McCoy he is unable to resist the lure of combat. In each instance the heroic soldier who was 'stabbed-in-the-back' comes out of retirement to intervene where the bureaucrats have failed. When the Delta Force are reunited following the hijacking of the plane they resolve to 'Let's not screw this one up'; like Rambo, who resolves to 'win, this time,' they know that the success of their mission will not only secure the freedom of those being held by America's enemies, but it will also regenerate the image of strength and prestige for an America plagued by a series of humiliations suffered in Southeast Asia and in the Middle East.

The mirroring of the relationship between Trautman and Rambo with that between Anderson and McCoy demonstrates how each film reflects the Reaganite ideology. Kolker argues that Reagan was 'more than an external guiding force' for 1980s' popular cinema, and instead became 'a disguised narrative figure … taking the form of an older man who teaches and legitimizes the hero and, perhaps even more importantly, protects the audience.'[121] For Kolker Trautman is the classic example of the Reagan surrogate, guiding, directing and controlling Rambo as he fulfils his society's desire for revenge.[122] In *The Delta Force*, Anderson is the Trautman to McCoy's Rambo.[123] Anderson guides, directs and controls McCoy, enabling the film to celebrate patriarchal authority while supplying 'the ideological demand for family without the need to bring forth the insoluble problems regarding the family's viability' that Kolker identifies as a tenet of Reaganite entertainment.[124]

In both *Rambo* and *The Delta Force*, the overt celebration of patriarchy is further enabled by the elimination of the feminine. In *Rambo* the only woman of note is the Vietnamese girl Co Bao (Julia Nickson), the daughter of a South Vietnamese intelligence officer who was killed during the war. Co aids Rambo in his battle with the Communists, at one point rescuing him from his Russian torturers (deploying, it must be noted, not strength but sexuality by posing as a prostitute), before a Vietnamese soldier kills her roughly one hour into the film. For Jeffords, this forceful elimination of Co from the traditionally male realm of the battlefield is essential to the film's regeneration of American masculinity, for it enables Rambo to single-handedly rescue the abandoned POWs and thus project the essentialness of the hyper-masculine male.[125] Women are similarly eliminated from the narrative of *The Delta Force* when midway through the film all of the women and children taken hostage by the terrorists are released, only to be seen again at the end of the film when the male hostages rescued by the Delta Force touch down in Israel. As in *Rambo*, narrative closure is achieved when strong American men rescue vulnerable American men, while masculinity and national supremacy is conveyed through the domination and defeat of fanatical but inherently weak dark-skinned men. Each film functions as a pushback against the supposed crisis of masculinity that emerged out of Vietnam, Iran, and the rise of second-wave feminism, and which was so pitifully embodied by Lander and Corley in *Black Sunday*.

Both *Rambo* and *The Delta Force* also conform to the Reaganite logic that imagines America's enemies as agents of evil that are both loosely aligned and vaguely defined, and which unequivocally privileges military prowess as the appropriate means of eliminating said evil. *Rambo* sees a subtle conflation of dishonourable American bureaucrats with the Russians and the Vietnamese (who, as pointed out by Kolker, are represented in a manner that evokes the way the Nazis and the Japanese were represented in the Second World War films), while in *The Delta Force* the terrorists are anti-American/anti-Zionist socialists with no clear political platform.[126] In each instance the super-villain is no match for the superior fighting skills of the American hero. Rambo, after single-handedly rescuing the POWs and killing seemingly every Communist left in Vietnam, triumphantly blows the Russian torturer extraordinaire into smithereens with a rocket launcher. Meanwhile, McCoy, in a classic example of what Britton termed Reaganite entertainment's 'ecstatic celebration of technology,'[127] despatches the leader of the New World Revolution with a projectile that he despatches from his custom-built motorcycle. Both films constitute the enactment of what Kolker calls 'the ideology's great fantasy of wish fulfillment: destruction of the other, ending opposition by annihilating it.'[128] The agents of the 'Evil Empire' have been thoroughly destroyed, along with the ghosts of the great American nation's past failures.

Israel as America's muse in *The Delta Force*

While there is an abundance of similarities shared by *Rambo* and *The Delta Force* that signify the status of each film as overtly ideological paragons of muscular cinema and Reaganite entertainment, what differentiates *The Delta Force* from *Rambo* and *Rambo*'s many imitators is that it evokes the real-world exploits of the Israeli military, and also the Israeli hero of *Black Sunday*. In *Black Sunday* the Israeli Kabakov is defined by an acute loathing of American bureaucracy and a ruthless efficiency that ultimately saves the lives of American civilians. This paradigm is inverted in *The Delta Force* with Americans traveling to the Middle East to save Americans while exuding the same loathing of bureaucracy and the same ruthless efficiency; there is even a scene in which an American soldier sticks his gun in the mouth of an Arab in order to get information in what is a direct mirroring of Kabakov's tactics in *Black Sunday*. Furthermore, while Israel's willingness to release some 700 Shi'a Muslims it was holding prisoner was central to securing the release of the Flight 847 hostages, in *The Delta Force* the only assistance offered by Israel comes in the form of intelligence. In accordance with the rules of Reaganite entertainment, in this restaging it is the Americans alone who must save the day. The Israelis express a desire to join in the 'fun,' to which Marvin's character responds, 'You boys have done it before, now it's our turn.'

While Israel doesn't 'join in the fun' – which the audience can only interpret as being a euphemism for slaughtering nefarious Arabs – it nevertheless remains ever-present throughout the raid, playing the role of the Americans' muse. The mission that erases the pain and humiliation of the failure to rescue Americans held hostage in Iran is clearly based on the raid on Entebbe, a subject explored by Golan nearly a decade earlier in his 1977 Israeli film *Mivtsa Yonatan* (a.k.a. *Operation Thunderbolt*).[129] The storming of the compound that houses the hostages by the Delta Force is almost a carbon copy of the raid on Entebbe airport by the Israel Defense Force depicted in *Mivtsa Yonatan*, relying on precise planning, the element of surprise and overwhelming firepower. In each instance the commandos effortlessly eliminate untold numbers of inept terrorists while only suffering one casualty; the only difference is that in *The*

Delta Force the soldier who loses his life is an anonymous character played by an unknown character actor (William Wallace), whereas at Entebbe the fallen soldier was the squadron's commander Yonatan Netanyahu (the older brother of future Prime Minister of Israel Benjamin Netanyahu). In *The Delta Force* the recognizable American heroes embodied by Norris and Marvin save the day and live to fight another battle, thus affording the American revenge fantasy an appropriately happy ending. It is also worth acknowledging that the final scenes of *Mivtsa Yonatan* and *The Delta Force* are practically identical. Both films depict the liberated hostages and their saviours landing in Israel and being met by a rapturous crowd, and in each instance the ebullience of the liberated hostages is juxtaposed with the solemnity of the soldiers who silently mourn the death of their fallen comrade. In *Mivtsa Yonatan* the liberated and their families joyously sing the ancient Jewish folk song *David Melech Yisrael* (*David Is the King of Israel*). In *The Delta Force* the liberated hostages sing *America the Beautiful*. The exuberance with which it is sung by the characters of *The Delta Force* lies in stark contrast with the melancholic manner in which the same song is delivered in the famous final scene of *The Deer Hunter*, in which that film's characters mourn the loss of both a close friend and their country's innocence, each of which was lost in Vietnam. In its unrelenting affirmation of American valour and supremacy Reaganite entertainment triumphantly restages the Vietnam War, and in this particular instance, it also restages one of the most famous scenes from the first wave of Vietnam War cinema. American greatness has been restored and it can be declared without any hint of irony or ambiguity, and it is Israel that has served as the inspiration.

The written histories of Hollywood will devote few, if any, pages to either *Black Sunday* or *The Delta Force*. However, both films constitute reasonably significant cultural artefacts by virtue of each being accurate encapsulations of the political and social zeitgeist of the time of their production. In drawing explicitly on the burgeoning threat of international terrorism, as well as the so-called 'crisis of masculinity' that emerged out of the confluence of the trauma of Vietnam and the rise of second-wave feminism, *Black Sunday* serves as a cinematic manifestation of the constellation of collective anxieties that defined late-1970s' America. Moreover, through its valorization of a ruthless, rule-breaking, hyper-masculine crime fighter, *Black Sunday* can be seen as a harbinger of the conservative, reactionary cinema that largely defined popular America cinema of the 1980s. Indeed, the precursory nature of *Black Sunday* is affirmed by the production of *The Delta Force*, a classic example of Reaganite entertainment that cinematically 'corrects' the myriad of military failures that had stained America's recent past by similarly drawing on the Arab-Israeli conflict and unabashedly glorifying ruthless hyper-masculinity. The significance of both *Black Sunday* and *The Delta Force* is also augmented by the fact that in each instance it is a militaristic Israel that brings salvation to America – either through the direct intervention of an Israeli warrior, as in *Black Sunday*, or by serving as the model of action for American warriors, as in *The Delta Force*. Together, the two films signify how throughout the annals of Hollywood cinema the image of Israel has continually evolved in line with the vicissitudes of the contemporaneous social and political climate, for the purpose of constructing and circulating American political identity – a phenomenon that would continue beyond the turn of the millennia and the subsequent launching of the 'War on Terror' with Steven Spielberg's *Munich* (2005).

5

The 'War on Terror' in *Munich* (2005)

A mere three years after the release of *The Delta Force* in 1986, the Berlin Wall came crashing down and with it the Cold War essentially drew to a close. Not surprisingly, this development would have significant implications for Hollywood, for, in the words of Robert Kolker, 'With the end of the Cold War, all the representations of anticommunist rage and victory collapsed along with the regime the dominant capitalist ideology so hated, so perversely loved, and so needed.'[1] The necessity of the Communist regime that ruled the Soviet Union throughout much of the twentieth century derived from what Michael Rogin terms the 'countersubversive tradition at the center of American politics.'[2] For Rogin, the creation of monsters has long been a central tenet of the 'historical construction of an American political identity.'[3] Crucially, Rogin points to Hollywood cinema as a primary mobilizer of this demonological impulse, arguing 'Movies make political demonology visible in widely popular and influential forms ... they speak to the fundamental countersubversive impulse to ingest historical, physical, and personal reality.'[4]

Following the collapse of the traditional Cold War paradigm, Hollywood was impelled to conceive of a new enemy against which idealized conceptions of Americanism could be constructed and celebrated. Perhaps not surprisingly, Middle Easterners came to fill the demonological void, their succession easily facilitated by centuries of European Orientalism as well as ever-increasing tensions between the West and the Arab and Islamic worlds throughout the second half of the twentieth century (and, it must be said, films such as *Exodus*, *Cast a Giant Shadow*, *Black Sunday* and *The Delta Force*). Throughout the 1990s there emerged a number of big-budget Hollywood films in which Arabs and Muslims were cast as ideologically driven demonic figures intent on carrying out attacks on Americans, in the process filling the roles that had previously been played by Russians or by third world Communists intrinsically associated with the Soviet Union. In the action blockbuster *True Lies* (James Cameron, 1994), a Palestinian terror organization attempts to detonate a nuclear bomb in the Florida Keys and is only prevented from doing so by the superhuman heroism of an American special agent played by Arnold Schwarzenegger. In *Executive Decision* (Stuart Baird, 1996) an Arab terrorist group hijacks a plane with the intention of detonating a bomb that is onboard over United States' airspace, only to be thwarted by an American special operations counterterrorism team that manages to board the plane mid-flight. In *The Siege* (Edward Zwick, 1998) Arab terrorists carry out a series of attacks across New York City until a heroic FBI agent (Denzel Washington) puts an end to their dastardly campaign. Each of these films mobilized a demonological image of the Arab in order to construct an idealized conception of American heroism in a manner that echoed the moral polarization of Cold War cinema, and in so doing signalled the ascendance of Middle Easterners to the status of 'Public Enemy #1' in the United States' post-Cold War cultural imaginary. The attacks on the United States by Arab terrorists on 11 September 2001 only served to reinforce this notion. In what was an all too predictable replaying of Hollywood's former positioning of Communists as the epitome of evil, in the years following the 9/11 attacks and the subsequent launching of the 'Global War on Terror' centred in Afghanistan and Iraq a great number of films and also television programmes were produced in which Arabs and Muslims were cast as diabolical villains opposite American heroes.[5]

As a result of the figure of the diabolical Arab Other now serving as the principal existential threat to the American homeland, representations of Israel were largely absent from Hollywood productions throughout the 1990s and early 2000s. If Arabs were to effectively play the role of Public Enemy #1, there was little to be gained in muddying their malevolence by telling stories that took place within the context of a highly contentious and controversial conflict. It would not be until the release of Steven Spielberg's *Munich* in 2005 that Israel would again be the subject of a major Hollywood film. *Munich* was based on George Jonas's book *Vengeance* (1984), which told the purportedly true story of the Israeli government's covert campaign of targeted assassinations – codenamed Operation Wrath of God – of Palestinian militants whom they linked to the massacre of Israeli athletes at the 1972 Munich Olympics.[6] In spite of what would prove to be highly controversial subject matter the film was a significant commercial and critical success, taking in over $130 million at the box office and being nominated for five Academy Awards, including Best Picture.[7]

Following in the footsteps of *Schindler's List* (1993), *Amistad* (1997) and *Saving Private Ryan* (1998), *Munich* appeared to be another example of Spielberg's proclivity for self-consciously significant dramatizations of major historical events. Due to the immense success of these aforementioned films, as well as their realistic mode of narration, they not only constituted a divergent mode of cinema for a filmmaker traditionally associated with fantastical escapism, but they also elevated Spielberg to the status of a public historian whose fictionalized narratives came to define within the public imaginary the actual historical events they were depicting.[8] No doubt as a result of the implicit authenticity of Spielberg's history-based narratives, *Munich*'s depiction of Israel's vengeful operation was the source of much controversy and debate, and the film was particularly excoriated by conservative commentators in the United States and also in Israel. However, this chapter argues that *Munich* is only ostensibly concerned with proffering an authentic history of the Mossad's execution of Operation Wrath of God, and is instead best understood as a meditation on the United States' own response to terrorism in the wake of the September 11 attacks by Islamic militants. The analysis of *Munich* proffered by this chapter is underpinned by a three-pronged approach. Firstly, the film is examined in relation to the hostility it elicited from sections of the mainstream media in the United States and Israel as a consequence of its supposedly critical depiction of the Israeli response to the Munich massacre. As a result, it will be established that the film is not, in fact, anti-Israel, and that it instead presents its Israeli characters as virtuous victim-heroes specifically designed to elicit the sympathy and admiration of its audience. In addition, this approach illuminates the contentious political climate in which the film was circulated and subsequently received by audiences, thus elucidating how the film's allegorical status was effectively suppressed. Also, as in the case of previous chapters, the film is read against events detailed in its source material. Examples of dissimilarity, excision and narrative invention are identified in aid of getting to the heart of the film's ideology. Finally, the manner in which the film makes a myriad of overt allusions to the United States and its launching of its own War on Terror are examined in detail. Ultimately this chapter will demonstrate how the film is largely unconcerned with historical verisimilitude regarding Israel's response to the Munich massacre, and is instead appropriating this period of Israeli history for the express purpose of articulating American anxieties in the wake of 9/11. Furthermore, it is argued that the film is a typically Spielbergian reflection on the post-9/11 United States. By this I mean that *Munich* attempts to satisfy mass desires by, on the one hand, championing an aggressive response to terrorism, while simultaneously placing the United States in the position of victim for having been the target of terrorists, and for having to forego its moral superiority by being essentially forced to launch retaliatory attacks. Consequently, this chapter positions *Munich* as a clear manifestation of what Linda Williams has described as American post-9/11 culture's 'ongoing effort to construct itself ... as the special locus of wronged innocence and virtue.'[9] In so doing, this chapter enables an understanding of *Munich* as yet another example of the long-standing Hollywood tradition of deploying Israel for the purpose of articulating the United States' own national identity.

7 September 1972

Munich opens with members of Black September infiltrating the Olympic Village in Munich and taking the Israeli athletes hostage. The film then proceeds to intercut scenes that represent the event itself with scenes depicting people watching the event unfold on television in the form of actual news reports from the time featuring well-known journalists such as Peter Jennings, Jim McKay and Howard Cosell. In the film's re-enactment of these events, a Black September member, whose face is covered by a stocking, looks down from the balcony attached to the Israelis' room in the Olympic village, while at the same time a television is shown broadcasting the same development in the form that would ultimately constitute the most iconic image of the tragic event. The sequence ends with German police making what was ultimately a botched rescue attempt, which is followed by a montage of palpably distressed television news reporters announcing the deaths of each of the hostages. This fusing of re-enactment with the actual mediated coverage of the massacre in the form of television news stories reinforces for the audience that the horrors they have just witnessed are not the stuff of Hollywood fantasy, but an event that actually occurred. Through such a subsumption of iconic historical images into the diegesis, *Munich* presents the illusion that the film that follows is a wholly authentic and objective historical document.

This opening sequence functions as a sort of prologue that sets the stage for the narrative that follows, in which the focus is on the manner of the Israeli government's response to the massacre, and the effects of the response on the respective psyches of those assigned to carry out the task. Immediately following the massacre, the audience is made a witness to a crisis meeting helmed by the

Figure 5.1 A Black September member looks down from the balcony attached to the Israelis' room in the Olympic village.

highest levels of the Israeli government. Prime Minister Golda Meir (Lynn Cohen) states that the situation is 'just like Eichmann' – a reference to the notorious Nazi functionary who managed the logistics of the deportation of millions of Jews from German-conquered territories to the ghettos and death camps that gave rise to the Holocaust, and who in 1960 was captured by the Mossad in Argentina and brought to trial in Israel where he was eventually executed for crimes against humanity. She continues, 'You say to these butchers, "You don't want to share this world with us, then we don't have to share this world with you". While there is no record of the real Meir ever speaking these words, they do bear a striking resemblance to words written by Hannah Arendt in the epilogue to her famous study *Eichmann in Jerusalem: A Report on the Banality of Evil* (1963) where, in passing judgment on Eichmann, she wrote:

> And just as you supported and carried out a policy of not wanting to share the earth with the Jewish people ... we find that no one, that is, no member of the human race, can be expected to want to share the earth with you. This is the reason, and the only reason, you must hang.[10]

In the pursuit of *Munich*'s ideological ethos, this passage stands as being particularly revelatory; in taking the language famously used by Arendt to condemn Eichmann and deploying it to refer to the perpetrators of the Munich massacre, the film is indirectly positioning anti-Israeli terrorism as an extension of the Holocaust. Where the Eichmann narrative differs from that of *Munich*, however, is whereas Eichmann was captured and then tried in a court of law, the Israeli government resolves to hunt down and execute the Palestinians they have identified as being responsible for the massacre in Munich. The operation will not only satisfy the thirst for vengeance but is about, in the words of one official, 'fixing the world's attention.' Meir ends the meeting by declaring that Israel must 'Forget peace for now. We have to show them we're strong,' and that 'Every civilisation finds it necessary to negotiate compromises with its own values.'

What follows is the formation of a special secret unit of the Mossad to carry out the mission; its members are Robert (Mathieu Kassovitz), a Belgian bomb maker; Steve (Daniel Craig), a ruthless South African getaway driver; Hans (Hanns Zischler), a German forger; Carl (Ciarán Hinds), the clean-up man; and Avner Kaufman (Eric Bana), the unit's leader and the film's central protagonist. The team's first victim is Wael Zwaiter (Makram Khoury), the supposed head of Black September's Rome-based operations, and who is introduced in the film as an avuncular poet giving a talk to rapturous fans on the streets of Rome after having just authored a translation of *One Thousand and One Nights*. In a sequence that recalls young Vito Corleone's stalking and slaying of Don Fanucci in *The Godfather Part II* (Francis Ford Coppola, 1974), Avner and Robert surreptitiously follow Zwaiter to his apartment door and, after confirming his identity, shoot him to death at close range. Zwaiter is carrying bags of groceries that are pierced by the bullets; the blood that flows from his body blends with milk that flows from the decimated grocery bags, creating a visceral image that accentuates the unpleasant reality of the mission. Just as the killing of Fanucci signified Vito Corleone's transition from penniless peasant to omnipotent mob boss, the killing of Zwaiter signifies the transition of Avner and his colleagues from honourable Mossad agents to conscience-plagued assassins.

Having been profoundly disturbed by having to look Zwaiter in the eye before taking his life, from this point on the group adopts tactics that enable them to maintain a safe distance from their victims. Their second target is Mahmoud Hamshari (Hiam Abbass), a PLO representative based in France whom the Mossad hierarchy posits 'organises for Fatah' – an imprecision that clearly troubles at least one member of the group. The unit plans to blow up Hamshari with a bomb that they will first plant in his home telephone. However, when the time comes to detonate the bomb it is revealed that Hamshari's young daughter is still in the house. Upon discovering the young girl's presence, both Avner and Carl frantically rush to alert their colleagues of the need to momentarily abort the mission, arriving just in time to spare the child's life. The girl soon departs and the plan is then successfully carried out, but the near miss highlights for both the unit and the film's audience the inherent dangers and the moral ambiguity of so-called 'counterterrorist' strikes. The third target, a Fatah representative based in Cyprus named Hussein Al Bashir (Mostéfa Djadjam), is blown up in a Cypriot hotel room. However, the bomb is too powerful and blinds a young Israeli woman who is staying in the adjacent room. The group also takes part in a large-scale raid on a Black September base in Beirut that succeeds in killing innumerable Black September operatives, while also claiming the life of a woman who is either the wife or a lover of a supposed terrorist. Amid all of these executions of members of Black September, the unit also hunts down and kills a Dutch female contract killer who seduces and then murders Carl.

As the body count increases the unit becomes more visibly plagued by questions regarding the morality and the efficacy of their actions. As the group is preparing to board a train to Amsterdam where the will execute the Dutch murderess Robert is so overcome with guilt and self-pity that he backs out of the mission, telling Avner:

> We're Jews, Avner. Jews don't do wrong because our enemies do wrong. We're supposed to be righteous. That's what I was taught, that's Jewish, that's a beautiful thing. That's what I knew. Absolutely. And I think I've lost that, Avner. I've lost that too. That's everything. I've lost everything. My, my soul.

Speaking on a train platform, the characters in this scene are enveloped in a steamy haze and are almost drowned out by the sounds of departing locomotives. Throughout this sequence the audience cannot help but recall the numerous scenes that take place on train platforms in Spielberg's *Schindler's List*. This overt allusion to what Robert Burgoyne calls 'the most consequential, the "jewel in the crown" of Holocaust representation,'[11] has the effect of reminding the audience of the near total annihilation of European Jewry by Nazi Germany, which in turn reaffirms the inherent righteousness of the Jews, who are presented throughout *Munich* as pursuing their new enemies with the utmost trepidation and lament.

Deliberation amongst the group gradually leads to its deterioration. As previously noted, a female contract killer kills Carl after he allows himself to be seduced by her in a hotel bar. Hans is found dead, having been stabbed on a park bench. Rob is killed when a bomb he is working on explodes; in this scene the film is signalling that his own terroristic actions have brought about his demise. Though Avner survives he is left embittered and paranoid, the latter of which is notably signified in a scene where he tears apart his mattress, which he suspects contains a bomb that has been planted by his enemies. Eventually Avner becomes so filled with angst and disillusion that he abandons Israel and relocates his young family to New York.

Figure 5.2 The Mossad hitmen on a steam-soaked platform in *Munich*.

The response to *Munich*

By exploring the crisis of conscience experienced by the various members of the Mossad hit squad, Spielberg, for many, drew a moral equivalence between terrorism and counterterrorism, and thus produced a film that was inherently and vociferously 'anti-Israel'. This attitude is perhaps most notably demonstrated by Leon Wieseltier, who, in a widely acknowledged column in the ostensibly liberal *New Republic*, stated that in *Munich*:

> Palestinians murder, Israelis murder. Palestinians show evidence of a conscience, Israelis show evidence of a conscience. Palestinians suppress their scruples, Israelis suppress their scruples. Palestinians make little speeches about home and blood and soil, Israelis make little speeches about home and blood and soil. Palestinians kill innocents, Israelis kill innocents. All these analogies begin to look ominously like the sin of equivalence, and so it is worth pointing out that the death of innocents was an Israeli mistake but a Palestinian objective.[12]

As I demonstrate later in this chapter, the film lucidly and unequivocally asserts that the death of innocents was only ever the result of Israeli mistakes, while it also positions Palestinians as consciously targeting civilians. Nevertheless, Wieseltier goes on to claim that in the film there are merely two kinds of Israelis – 'cruel Israelis with remorse and cruel Israelis without remorse' – and that ultimately *Munich* 'has no place in its heart for Israel.'[13] Gabriel Schoenfeld, then senior editor of the conservative Jewish-American magazine *Commentary*, deployed similar language in censuring Spielberg for daring to explore the Arab-Israeli conflict in anything even resembling an even-handed manner. Schoenfeld argues that *Munich* demonstrates 'a shocking reluctance to distinguish murderers from their murdered victims – or perhaps not a reluctance at all but rather a deliberate attempt to suggest that all were equally victims.'[14] Schoenfeld goes on to claim that, 'At various junctures, Palestinians press the case both for their methods and for their larger national goals, and in terms that contrast invidiously with the case that is made, or rather not made, for Israeli nationhood.'[15] After having rather tendentiously spelled out his argument through a selectively myopic reading of the film's contrasting representations of its Israeli and Palestinian characters, Schoenfeld contends that the film is a 'blatant attack on Israel in virtually every way, shape, and form,' and the 'most hypocritical film of the year.'[16]

Well-known conservative political pundits such as David Brooks (of the *New York Times*), Michael Medved (of *USA Today*) and Charles Krauthammer (of the *Washington Post*) published similar denunciations of Spielberg's handling of the subject. Brooks claimed that in the film 'the Israelis and the Palestinians are parallel peoples victimized by history and trapped in a cycle of violence,' and thus 'Spielberg allows himself to ignore the core poison that permeates the Middle East, Islamic radicalism.'[17] According to Brooks, Spielberg's film fails to 'admit the existence of evil, as it really exists' and consequently gets 'reality wrong.'[18] Medved similarly condemned the film, claiming that it 'deliberately blurs distinctions between those who commit terrorism and those who combat it.'[19] Meanwhile Krauthammer posited that the film made the case 'for the moral bankruptcy of the Israeli cause.'[20] Perhaps not surprisingly, elements of the Israeli media also denounced Spielberg and *Munich*. Hannah Brown, writing in the *Jerusalem Post*, claimed that *Munich* made earlier films by Spielberg such as *Jaws* (1975) and *E.T. the Extra-Terrestrial* (1982) 'look like Kierkegaard,' before claiming that the film is 'very much an apology for Arab terror groups,' as it finds 'absolute parity between the Israeli Olympic hostages and their PLO murderers.'[21] Also writing in the *Jerusalem Post*, the American political commentator Jonathan Tobin condemned *Munich* for going 'out of its way to portray Palestinian terrorists in a flattering light,' and also the Anti-Defamation League for not opposing the film with the same vigour that it had *The Passion of the Christ* (Mel Gibson, 2004) during the previous year.[22] Criticism of the film and of Spielberg did not come merely from critics and cultural commentators. Ehud Danoch, Israel's consul-general in Los Angeles, lambasted the film as a 'superficial,' 'pretentious,' and 'problematic' work that drew an 'incorrect moral equation' between Mossad agents and Palestinian terrorists.[23] Echoing Danoch, the Zionist Organization of America (ZOA) urged a boycott of *Munich* based on its 'having promoted a moral equivalence between Arab terrorists and Israelis who want to vanquish those terrorists,' and for attempting to 'humanize the Palestinian Arab killers by legitimizing their murder of Jews as their only way to establish a Palestinian state.'[24]

However, the charges proffered by the aforementioned commentators that *Munich* espouses anti-Israel sentiment do not stand up to scrutiny. While promoting the film Spielberg declared in an interview with the German newspaper *Der Spiegel*, 'From the day I started to think politically and to develop my own moral values, from my earliest youth, I have been an ardent defender of Israel. As a Jew I am aware of how important the existence of Israel is for the survival of us all.'[25] In the same interview, Spielberg offered unequivocal support for the Meir administration's response to the Munich massacre, stating the following:

> I believe that Israel's prime minister had to respond to the monstrous provocation of Munich: Jews were being killed in Germany, and that at the Olympic Games [sic]. She could not let an act with such historical implications, such a gross transgression by the Black September movement, go unpunished. Munich was a national trauma for Israel. So in principle I think she [Meir] did the right thing.[26]

Spielberg's belief in the inherent righteousness of Israel's vengeful operation is reflected by his sympathetic construction of the counterterrorists; as noted by critic Jim Emerson, they are 'surely the most humane spy-assassins you've ever stumbled across.'[27] The inherent humanity of the Mossad operatives – and the stark contrast between them and their Palestinian enemies – is lucidly established throughout the film's opening act. Having successfully gained access to the hotel in which the Israeli athletes are staying, the members of Black September appear as figures of unequivocal malevolence, with the camera affirming their collective inhumanity through a series of close-ups that focus not on their faces, but on the loaded AK-47s they hold in their hands. Conversely, Avner is introduced as a loving husband and expectant father. One of the other members of the counterterror unit is a toymaker, while another is an antique dealer. They are characters with whom the film's Western audience can easily empathize and identify. The first scene in which Avner appears, he is shown to be watching the gruesome events unfold on television alongside his pregnant wife and their pet dog. He mentions that he has 'the world's most boring job,' implying the normality of Avner's daily life. He is frequently shown as an enthusiastic cook in what is an affirmation of his common domesticity. However, after he undertakes the mission, Avner eschews his normalcy, and the film centres on him, to quote Spielberg, 'struggling to keep his soul intact.'[28]

Through the presentation of the Israelis as being engaged in a perpetual battle with their psychological demons, the film actually serves to highlight the characters' humanity; to recall Robert's expression of distaste for the job at hand, 'We're Jews, we are supposed to be righteous, and that's beautiful.' Crucially, the film's presentation of the Israelis as being plagued by misgivings constitutes a significant diversion from the film's source material, in which Jonas claims that the Mossad assassins expressed 'absolutely no qualms about anything they did.'[29] In Jonas's recounting Robert expresses no such sentiments, and is no less zealous than every other member of the group in carrying out the mission. In fact, Jonas describes Robert as not only going along on the mission to kill the Dutch assassin, but as being responsible for designing the weapons used to kill her.[30] According to Jonas, the group was plagued not by their respective consciences, but rather by the fear of being killed as easily as they themselves were killing. Jonas claims that they had come to realize, with great anxiety, 'how little trouble it was to set up a hit. How easy it was for a few people, with some money and a little determination, to find and kill a man. With impunity.'[31] Jonas does speak of Avner beginning to have doubts about the propriety of the mission, but only on the basis that fighting terrorism in such a manner was an act of futility, rather than being of dubious morality.[32] Furthermore, it is implied in *Vengeance* that Avner flees Israel and relocates to New York not out of sorrow and disillusionment for having been forced to kill, but out of shame for failing to find and kill all of the targets on the government's list.[33] Here it is also worth noting that Aaron J. Klein, who authored *Striking Back: the 1972 Munich Olympics Massacre and Israel's Deadly Response* (2005),[34] a supposedly more authentic recounting of Operation Wrath of God than Jonas's *Vengeance*, echoed Jonas by claiming in an interview that:

> I spoke and interviewed more than 50 sources, most of them ex-Mossad agents and commanders and leaders. I didn't come across with someone who had doubts. They are very proud of what they did. They are – they still see themselves as the carrier of the sword, the people who did a holy work, a holy job, in this whole apparatus of assassinations. I don't see – I didn't met with anyone who had remorse or second thoughts or – whatsoever [sic].[35]

In an ironic twist that effectively sums up the exasperatingly contentious nature of every aspect of the Arab-Israeli conflict, Spielberg's depiction of morally conflicted Mossad agents – which, as Michelle Goldberg rightfully argues, 'is actually profoundly flattering to Israel' – was a primary source of criticism for those who condemned the film for its supposed 'humanisation of terrorists'.[36] For instance, David Brooks claims, 'The real Israeli fighters tend to be harder and less sympathetic,' rather than the virtuous victim-heroes presented by Spielberg.[37] It is as if, from the viewpoint of conservative critics, a 'fair' representation could only depict the Arabs as being devoid of the qualities of humans, and the Israelis as being devoid of the weaknesses of humans. Michael Medved condemned the film's depiction of Golda Meir making the statement that 'Every civilization finds it necessary to negotiate compromises with its own values,' arguing that 'Meir never made such a statement because she explicitly viewed striking back at terror as upholding – not compromising – civilized values.'[38] Medved instead points to a statement made by Meir on 12 September 1972, a week after the Munich massacre, in which Meir, speaking before the Israeli Knesset, declared:

> From the blood-drenched history of the Jewish nation, we learn that violence which begins with the murder of Jews, ends with the spread of violence and danger to all people, in all nations. We have no choice but to strike at the terrorist organizations wherever we can reach them. That is our obligation to ourselves and to peace.[39]

Tellingly, Medved neglects to mention another of Meir's famous quotations – one that is rather at odds with Medved's portrait of a righteously ruthless leader, and one that speaks to *Munich*'s depiction of guilt-ridden Mossad operatives: 'When peace comes we will perhaps in time be able to forgive the Arabs for killing our sons, but it will be harder for us to forgive them for having forced us to kill their sons.'[40]

In spite of the objections raised by Leon Wieseltier, the film lucidly and unequivocally does assert that the death of innocents was an Israeli mistake and a Palestinian objective. First and foremost, the title of the film is *Munich*, the site of the most notorious act of Arab terrorism in the pre-9/11 age; surely a more appropriate title for a film that is supposedly concerned with the brutality of the Israeli response would have been *Vengeance*, the title of the book upon which the film is based. It is also worth acknowledging that the film begins with the slaughter of Israeli athletes in Munich. As a result, the film unequivocally contextualizes Operation Wrath of God as a direct consequence of the cold-blooded murder of Israeli innocents by Arab terrorists, thus reiterating Rashid Khalidi's claim that American culturally based myths have actively sought to frame the Arab-Israeli conflict as 'one between near equals, and if either party is a victim, it is the Israelis.'⁴¹ This initial establishment of the Israelis as righteous victims signals the film's fidelity to the melodramatic mode of storytelling in which, according to Linda Williams, characters 'acquire moral legitimacy through the public spectacle of their suffering.'⁴² The depiction of the Munich massacre also sends the message that there is no equivalence in the respect for human life held by Israelis and Palestinians; the film juxtaposes images of concerned Israelis clamouring around the television and watching the events of Munich unfold against that of Palestinians watching the same events and passionately and joyously cheering as if they are watching a World Cup football match. Crucially, the Israeli government's immediate response to the massacre – the mass bombing of Palestinian bases in Lebanon and Syria, resulting in what is widely reported as more than 200 casualties – is not depicted, and thus the film spares its audience the unpleasant sight of helpless Arabs dying under a barrage of Israeli bombs.⁴³ There is no spectacle of Arab suffering that imbues the Palestinians with moral legitimacy; instead, the incident is afforded a passing mention at the depicted informal government meeting that follows the massacre, with the number of casualties significantly reduced from 200 to 60, which has the effect of dramatically understating the severity of the response.

As discussed earlier, the Israeli counterterrorist unit encounters a problem when executing its second target due to the unanticipated presence of the man's young daughter in the Parisian apartment that they are about to blow up. However, this is a total invention. Both Jonas's *Vengeance* and Klein's *Striking Back* devote entire chapters to the assassination of Mahmoud Hamshari, and neither mentions his daughter narrowly escaping being killed in the operation.⁴⁴

Figure 5.3 Palestinians cheering the Munich massacre.

The sequence unfolds in a manner that conforms directly to Williams's summation of the classic nick of time rescue that is a fundamental tenet of the melodramatic mode. 'A rapid succession of shots specifying the danger' – in this instance, the potential for an innocent young girl to be blown up by a bomb that is remotely controlled – 'gives the effect of speed,' while the parallel cutting between the young girl, Robert (who has his finger on the trigger), and Avner and Carl (who are each frantically rushing towards Robert in an attempt to prevent him from detonating the bomb) 'prolongs time beyond all possible belief.'[45] As such, 'Actions feel fast, and yet the ultimate duration of the event is retarded ... The effect is to propel events into the future while insisting on the continued reminder of the past pathos of "too late".'[46] The result of this classically executed nick of time rescue is the clear differentiation between the Israelis and the civilian slaughtering murderers of Black September, and the subsequent affirmation of the Israelis' virtue.

The film's depiction of 'collateral damage' that is a result of the operation is also telling. The only time the film depicts the unintended slaying of an Arab comes during the raid on the Black September base in Beirut. In this instance it is the wife or lover of a Black September member who is wielding a machine gun and has just killed a Mossad operative, and she is gunned down alongside her terrorist partner in what appears to be an essentially unavoidable contingency. She is essentially a prop, killed the second she is introduced and only relevant to the narrative due to her having a relationship with a supposed terrorist, and thus she is essentially guilty by association and entirely undeserving of our sympathies. Here it is also worth noting that in *Vengeance* Jonas describes how during the real-life raid in Beirut another innocent Arab woman, one who 'appeared to be a truly innocent bystander, no suggestion having been made, then or later, that she was involved in any way with the Palestinian terrorists,' was killed. Moreover, Jonas mentions that there were reports that a fifteen-year-old boy was also killed during the real-life raid.[47] Conversely, in *Munich* a young Arab boy is saved thanks to the personal intervention of the noble Avner. Finally, and perhaps most significantly, the film – again, unlike the book on which it is based – is completely devoid of any reference to the notorious murder of Moroccan waiter Ahmed Bouchiki, who was gunned down in Lillehammer, Norway, by a Mossad hit squad who had mistaken him for Ali Hassan Salameh, the supposed mastermind of the Munich massacre.[48] The murder of Bouchiki was a major scandal that 'weighed like a millstone on the shoulders of the state of Israel' and resulted in the imprisonment of five Mossad operatives.[49] The absence of any reference to the so-called 'Lillehammer affair' is indicative of the film's commitment to avoid demonizing Israel and instead present the Jewish state as a nation that, unlike its Palestinian adversaries, strenuously avoids civilian casualties in its counterterror operations.

In stark contrast with its aversion to Arab 'collateral damage,' the film contains a sequence in which an innocent Israeli civilian is first humanized, and then severely injured when the operation assassinates Hussein Al Bashir by blowing up his hotel room. The innocent victim is a young Israeli woman who, in the scenes prior to the bomb's detonation, is shown to be blissfully happy as she enjoys her honeymoon with her new husband. Like the aforementioned sequence involving the nick of time rescue of Mahmoud Hamshari's daughter, this melodramatic episode of pathos-infused action is an invention of the film. In Jonas's retelling of the events it is the husband rather than the wife who is the Israeli half of the newlywed couple staying in the next room to the Mossad's target, and neither is blinded or in any other way harmed by the explosion.[50] This subtle alteration of the historical reality is significant, for it reimagines Operation Wrath of God through the prism of the mythic language of America's frontier mythology. As has been discussed in previous chapters, throughout the annals of American history the image of female victimhood has functioned as a symbol for a civilization that was supposedly 'imperiled in the wilderness war.'[51] Furthermore, Hollywood has consistently utilized the captivity narrative of traditional frontier mythology in its stories about Israel for the purpose of constructing Israel as an inherently righteous victim in its ongoing conflict with the Arabs, and to also position Israel as a parallel nation of the United States. With this sequence Spielberg is proffering a variation of that tradition. Like the subjects of the American captivity narrative, the young, beautiful Israeli woman personifies a nation that is positioned as being besieged by dark-skinned savagery. By turning her into a symbol of virtuous suffering, Spielberg is affirming the innocence of the Israeli people, while at the same time reinforcing the notion that, for Israel, the vengeful operation carries with it dire consequences.

The charges of anti-Israel bias levelled by various conservative commentators undoubtedly stem from the film giving voice to the Palestinian cause. The most notable example of this occurs in a fictionalized scene in which one of the Mossad unit's targets articulates to Avner (who is posing as a German member of the Red Army Faction) his people's lack of responsibility for the Holocaust, as well as their unrelenting desire to reclaim their homeland. However, this scene essentially constitutes the film's only attempt to touch on the plight of the Palestinians, and it is easily offset by the aforementioned references to the Holocaust – as well as the frequent flashbacks to the nightmare of Munich – that punctuate the narrative and ultimately proffer justification for Israel's vigorous pursuit of its national security. In an interview with critic Roger Ebert, Spielberg himself stated that he felt that 'there was a justified need to respond to the terrorism in Munich, which is why I keep replaying images of the Munich massacre throughout the movie.'[52] By comparison, the crimes perpetrated by Israelis against Palestinians that motivate the terrorism carried out by the latter are only obliquely referenced rather than explicitly depicted; for instance, in one scene Carl rhetorically asks his colleagues, 'How do you think we got control of the land? By being nice?'

From beginning to end the film is presented from the Israeli perspective, and its focus is the trauma that Israel is forced to endure after having been compelled to compromise its morality in order to defend itself against the scourge of Palestinian terror; from the trauma that is the result of 'being forced to kill' Arab sons, for which Golda Meir could never forgive. There is no individualized representative of the Palestinian people that we see watching television with their wife or cooking dinner for their friends, and with whom we are encouraged to empathize as we do with Avner. Instead, they remain throughout the film little more than terroristic props seen only through the lens of Israeli victimhood. The fact that the film presents terrorists in the form of avuncular scholars and eloquent freedom fighters only serves to imply that all Palestinians, irrespective of their nature or vocation, constitute an existential threat to Israel; indeed, the point is often made throughout the film that the murdered terrorists have been replaced by, to quote the forger Hans, those 'for whom Black September wasn't violent enough,' suggesting a never-ending supply chain of Arab malevolence. While the film was widely denounced in the United States and Israel for 'sympathizing' with and 'humanizing' terrorists, it is, first and foremost, an example of Hollywood's shameful legacy of horribly racist representations of Arabs.[53]

7 September as 11 September

The discourse that surrounded the film upon its release indubitably constituted an instance in which, to borrow a phrase from Miriam Hansen, 'reception takes on a momentum of its own, that is, becomes public in the emphatic sense of the word.'⁵⁴ This discourse engendered an environment in which audiences were invariably conditioned to read the film in relation to the very public debates regarding its supposed framing of the Arab-Israeli conflict. As a result *Munich*'s status as a meditation on the United States' own bellicose adventures in Afghanistan and Iraq launched in the wake of the attacks on the American homeland on 11 September 2001 was effectively suppressed. However, the film is best understood as an allegory of the post-9/11 United States that deploys the image of Israel's counterterrorist campaign to position Americans as virtuous victim-heroes.

Before detailing the ways in which *Munich* speaks to the post-9/11 United States, it must be acknowledged that within the film there are elements that can be seen as undermining any attempt to frame the film as an allegory of contemporary America. For instance, as I have previously noted, the film makes rather forthright pretences towards being interpreted as a literal history. Also, while the film continues the Hollywood tradition established by Charlton Heston and subsequently carried on by Paul Newman and Kirk Douglas of casting iconic American stars as Hebrews,⁵⁵ *Munich* employs a cast of non-American actors as its Israeli counterterrorists (Bana is Australian, Craig is English, Hinds is Irish, Zischler is German, and Kassovitz is French). In featuring an entirely international cast Spielberg puts some distance between the film's American audience and its team of assassins, who thus appear as foreigners, rather than, as in earlier films such as *The Ten Commandments*, *Ben-Hur* and *Exodus*, Americans wearing a thinly veiled disguise. On the one hand, this can be read as Spielberg employing cinematic trickery so as to engender a defence against denunciation from either side of the American political spectrum. On the other hand, the employment of an international cast can be understood as merely the latest evolutionary step in Hollywood's mobilization of Israel as a means of articulating American national identity. As has been discussed in previous chapters, the first wave of Hollywood films to centre on Israel (*The Ten Commandments*, *Ben-Hur* and *Exodus*) presented Hebrew and Israeli characters as proto-Americans. Subsequent films such as *Cast a Giant Shadow*, *Black Sunday* and *The Delta Force* depicted Americans and Israelis as allies in the fight against Arab savagery. In *Munich* the Israelis are a distinct people with their own unique national culture, but they are nonetheless akin to Americans by virtue of their mutual victimhood at the hands of Arab terrorism.

Spielberg's positioning of Israel as a stand-in for the modern-day United States is established at the very beginning of the film. When the film begins the audience is subjected to a blackened screen filled with the names, written in a dull shade of white, of cities that have been the targets of major terrorist attacks. A few seconds pass before the word 'Munich' is illuminated and made to appear more prominent, appearing to the left of the screen; at the exact same time the words 'New York' are positioned towards the centre of the frame. The audience is then taken directly to a depiction of an infamous act of terror committed by Arabs that, like the attacks of 9/11, was captured by television cameras and broadcast live around the world, ultimately becoming among the defining events of its generation.

The film then proceeds to depict an informal meeting of the highest levels of the Israeli government and its military, and it is replete with language that distinctly echoes that of the post-9/11 United States. Golda Meir asserts that, 'They've sworn to destroy us,' essentializing the reductionist 'us and them' rhetoric of George W. Bush, who declared in a State of the Union address on 20 September 2001:

> They hate what they see right here in this chamber: a democratically elected government. Their leaders are self-appointed. They hate our freedoms: our freedom of religion, our freedom of speech, our freedom to vote and assemble and disagree with each other.
>
> They want to overthrow existing governments in many Muslim countries such as Egypt, Saudi Arabia and Jordan. They want to drive Israel out of the Middle East. They want to drive Christians and Jews out of vast regions of Asia and Africa.
>
> These terrorists kill not merely to end lives, but to disrupt and end a way of life. With every atrocity, they hope that America grows fearful, retreating from the world and forsaking our friends. They stand against us because we stand in their way.[56]

Figure 5.4 The opening credits of *Munich*, with 'New York' positioned conspicuously near the centre of the frame.

Meir goes on to state that Israel must 'Forget peace for now. We must show them we're strong.' Such language recalls the jingoistic posturing of Bush who, after 9/11, similarly insisted, 'our country is strong,' and declared that the 'War on Terror' was directed not only at al-Qaeda, but that it would not end, 'until every terrorist group of global reach has been found, stopped and defeated.'[57] Meir then rhetorically asks her cabinet 'tell me what laws protect people like these.' Here Meir's words remind us of those spoken of Bush in the immediate wake of September 11 when he reportedly told Secretary of Defense Donald Rumsfeld, 'I don't care what the international lawyer says, we are going to kick some ass.'[58] Moreover, Meir's dismissal of international law lucidly speaks to the United States government's claim that in the post-9/11 world there emerged a so-called 'new paradigm,' in which 'it is legitimate and legal either to interpret certain core norms of international law as not binding or to consider that the powers of the President under the Constitution to wage a "war" on terrorism supercede international law.'[59] Here it is worth acknowledging that *Munich* was released amid a torrent of intense media scrutiny and public debate pertaining to the Bush administration's numerous violations of United States' constitutional and international law while pursuing the War on Terror, including (but not limited to) torture, prisoner abuse, the suspension of habeas corpus, and extraordinary rendition.[60] Furthermore, in the scene that follows the aforementioned meeting, Avner is recruited to lead the mission and is told by a government official that 'What happened in Munich changes everything,' just as in the wake of 9/11 there was a wealth of commentary asserting that 'everything has changed.'[61]

As noted earlier, Meir ruminates, 'Every civilisation finds it necessary to negotiate compromises with its own morals.' This invention of the film is a clear indication that the story to be told is not one that speaks solely to the Israeli experience.[62] Indeed, *Munich* neglects to touch on a number of subplots detailed in *Vengeance* that are specific to the unique temporality of the operation, and would only serve to dilute its legitimacy as an allegory of the post-9/11 United States. For instance, there is no mention of the unit's slaying of a Russian KGB agent in Athens that would have naturally reminded audiences of the Cold War conflict that defined American foreign policy in the pre-9/11 age.[63] There is also no mention of the outbreak of the Yom Kippur War in 1973, and the subsequent suspension of the operation while Avner and others returned to Israel to fight with their respective military units.[64]

In its final scene *Munich* unambiguously declares its status as a meditation on the implications of America's own War on Terror. Here Avner is met in

New York by his superior Ephraim, played by Geoffrey Rush (yet another non-American actor). Plagued by concerns that he has murdered in cold blood, Avner demands to see evidence that every man killed by him and his men had a direct involvement in the Munich massacre. Ephraim fails to produce such evidence, instead linking all of the operation's victims to other attacks on Israeli citizens. Avner responds with the words, 'If they committed crimes we should have arrested them, like Eichmann.' Ephraim responds by saying, 'If these guys live, Israelis die. Whatever doubts you have, Avner, you know this is true. We are telling them: if you kill us you will never be safe. We'll find you.' Avner asks, 'Did we accomplish anything at all? Every man we killed has been replaced by worse.' Ephraim cynically retorts, 'Why cut my fingernails? They'll grow back.' Avner finishes the conversation by telling Ephraim, 'There's no peace at the end of this. Whatever you believe, you know that's true.' After rebuffing an offer from Avner to 'break bread' together, Ephraim turns his back to him and walks away. At the very end of the scene the camera pulls away from Avner to reveal the then intact World Trade Center towers, over which is superimposed an epilogue that reads, 'Ultimately, *Nine* of the *Eleven* Palestinian men originally targeted for assassination were killed [emphasis added].' To reinforce the point, Spielberg holds on the image of the towers and accentuates the words 'nine' and 'eleven,' unequivocally imparting to his American audience that *this is about us*.[65]

Just as the film is not anti-Israel, it is not anti-America. If we are to understand *Munich* as amplifying the humanity of its Israeli characters, it must necessarily perform the same function for the Americans for whom the said Israelis are effectively standing in. Indeed, Israel/America is presented as a double victim; firstly, as the target of a terrorist attack; and, secondly, as damned for having been compelled to forfeit its position upon the moral high ground through the subsequent launching of the War on Terror. The film does not dare to seriously address the complex myriad of forces that have inspired Arab and Islamic terrorism. For this, audiences had to seek out contemporaneous (and less successful) films that centred on various wars in the Middle East and were populated by morally ambiguous American characters such as *Syriana* (Stephen Gaghan, 2005), *Redacted* (Brian De Palma, 2005) and *Rendition* (Gavin Hood, 2007).[66] Rather, *Munich* presents terrorism as a force of evil that no Israeli (read, no American) can escape, and something that essentially all Arabs partake in. The conflict is thus imagined as a 'savage war' that explicitly draws on American frontier mythology – just as it was in *Exodus, Cast a Giant Shadow* and *Black Sunday* – in which 'coexistence between

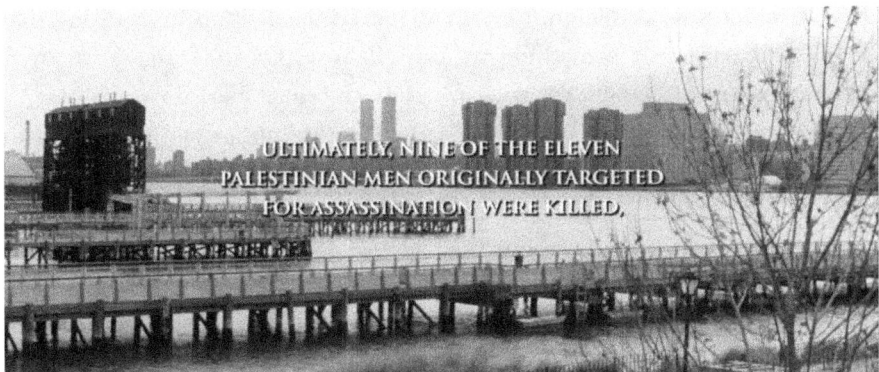

Figure 5.5 The closing shot of *Munich*, against the backdrop of the then intact World Trade Center towers.

primitive natives and civilized Europeans [is] impossible on any basis other than that of subjugation.'[67] Moreover, *Munich* presents government-sanctioned retaliation as a wholly appropriate response – which as noted earlier, Spielberg himself championed in interviews, just as he did the United States' invasion of Iraq.[68] The real tragedy of this cycle of violence, *Munich* argues, is the corrosive effect on the soul of the nation that is forced to retaliate.

Through its affirmation of the United States' virtuous victimhood, *Munich* stands as yet another testament to Spielberg's remarkable ability to effectively satisfy mass desires. Andrew Britton has devoted significant attention to Spielberg's output while lamenting what he refers to as the 'general movement of reaction and conservative reassurance' – what he famously termed 'Reaganite Entertainment' – that pervaded Hollywood in the late 1970s and throughout the 1980s.[69] Similarly, Robert Kolker has posited that, in the cinema of Spielberg, 'images and narratives speak of a place and a way of being in the world (indeed the universe) that viewers find more than just comfortable, but desirable and – within the films – *available*.'[70] This tendency towards wish fulfilment and conservative reassurance is a thread that has essentially run throughout Spielberg's entire body of work. In *Jaws* the white male hero restores the natural (capitalist-driven) order – in this case a beachside community that relies on the tourist dollar for its economic wellbeing – by overcoming his fear of the ocean and destroying a hell-sent man-eating Other. *E.T. the Extra-Terrestrial* is populist escapism in which, in the words of Britton, 'the family has been disrupted by the absence of the father and is cobbled together again through the good offices of a representative of "Otherness," which is conceived of as redemptive and benign.'⁷¹ Robin Wood echoes Britton in asserting that in *E.T.*, 'Otherness is something we can all love and cuddle and cry over, without unduly disturbing the nuclear family and the American Way of Life.'⁷² In *A.I. Artificial Intelligence* (2001) Spielberg serves up a dystopian future in which the human race no longer exists, but where a fantastical interpretation of a long-disintegrated mother–child relationship can nonetheless be restored, upon which the child experiences 'the happiest day of his life.' Spielberg's *War of the Worlds* (2005) presents aliens who are intent on destroying the human race being brought down by a lone male hero who, in the process, is reinstalled as the caring and protective father of his formerly estranged children.⁷³ The tendency even extends to Spielberg's more 'serious' historical event films. In *Saving Private Ryan* Spielberg delivers a breathtakingly visceral depiction of the brutal realities of war, while simultaneously deploying the mythology of the Second World War for the unequivocal celebration of American heroism and valour. Spielberg's slavery epic *Amistad* centres not on the untold millions who suffered the wretched degradations of slavery, but on a relative few captured Africans whose freedom is won thanks to the intervention of great white men (a theme he would later revisit with *Lincoln* [2012]).⁷⁴ Perhaps most notably, *Schindler's List* – which similarly celebrates a lone male hero as the saviour of a besieged people – has also elicited outspoken criticism for what some interpreted as an overly melodramatic representation of the Holocaust. For instance, Claude Lanzmann, director of the acclaimed Holocaust documentary *Shoah* (1985), famously condemned Spielberg for focusing on the Jews who survived rather than on the millions who were killed and thus trivializing the horrors of the Holocaust,⁷⁵ while critic J. Hoberman opined that Spielberg had proven it possible 'to make a feel-good entertainment about the ultimate feel bad experience of the twentieth century.'⁷⁶ In presenting the Holocaust in such a distinctly American fashion, *Schindler's List* was seen as being at the forefront of what Yosefa Loshitzky terms 'the "colonization" of the Holocaust by American culture,' which took place throughout the early-to-mid 1990s.⁷⁷ According to Hansen, this process can be seen as feeding into the United States' perception of self by indicating 'a need for Americans to externalize and project modernity's catastrophic features onto another nation's failure and defeat – so as to salvage modernity the American way.'⁷⁸ With *Munich* Spielberg has similarly appropriated the memory surrounding one of the defining events in Israeli history for the purpose of enunciating for American audiences the notion of the United States as the ultimate locus of innocence and virtue; in this instance, a nation that has its very existence threatened by incorrigible malevolence, and who resents being forced to defend itself as vehemently as it does the assault on its citizenry. However, *Munich* should not be seen as merely a continuation of Spielberg's affinity for satisfying mass desires through the appropriation of Jewish history. Rather, *Munich* carries on the Hollywood tradition established by *The Ten Commandments, Ben-Hur, Exodus, Cast a Giant Shadow, Black Sunday* and *The Delta Force*, of mobilizing images of Israel in aid of constructing and projecting an idealized conception of American national identity.

Conclusion

In *Reel Power: Hollywood Cinema and American Supremacy* (2010) Matthew Alford observes that 'while of course Hollywood is aware of its international markets, it is liable to make films about and for America and Americans, marginalizing the importance of foreigners and foreign perspectives.'[1] Alford's assertion is particularly applicable to Hollywood cinema's disparate representations and invocations of the state of Israel. Each of the films discussed in this study are, at surface level, stories that focus on Israel's struggles against its enemies, both historical and contemporary. However, deeper investigation reveals that *The Ten Commandments*, *Ben-Hur*, *Exodus*, *Cast a Giant Shadow*, *Black Sunday*, *The Delta Force* and *Munich* are all first and foremost *about* and *for* America and Americans.

The Ten Commandments and *Ben-Hur* each present ancient Hebrews engaged in a liberation struggle against oppressive authoritarian rulers. Both films position the ancient Hebrews as clear stand-ins for contemporary Americans, and thus they affirm contemporaneous conceptions of the Cold War conflict as one between 'God's Chosen People' and godless Communism. The conflation of American and Hebrew identity continues in *Exodus*, which presents modern-day Israelis as proto-Americans, and the land of Israel as a 'New Frontier' upon which traditional notions of frontier mythology can be unabashedly celebrated. In *Cast a Giant Shadow* Israel again functions as a New Frontier, though in this instance it is positioned as a damsel in distress ally of the United States and requiring American assistance in its war with the Arabs following the establishment of Israeli statehood. In the late 1970s and 1980s, in films like *Black Sunday* and *The Delta Force*, Israel is now seen as a highly proficient military power that is allied with the United States. However, in this instance, Israel serves as a militaristic model of action for a United States that is attempting to shake off the so-called Vietnam Syndrome, while also still recovering from the social upheaval brought about by the countercultural movements of the previous decade. With *Munich*, Steven Spielberg uses the mythology surrounding Israel's hunt for the perpetrators of the Munich Olympics massacre to reflect upon the United States' own response to the events of 11 September 2001. In this film Israel/America is positioned as a virtuous sufferer; a double victim that was first attacked by vicious terrorists, and then subsequently forced to forgo its moral standards by engaging in counterstrikes against those who wish to bring about its destruction.

Throughout its existence, Israel has been constructed by Hollywood as a nation that is 'like' America. Ancient Hebrews and modern-day Israelis alike have been positioned as being 'like' Americans, be they stand-ins for Americans (as in *The Ten Commandments*, *Ben-Hur*, *Exodus* and *Munich*), or allies of the United States (as in *Cast a Giant Shadow*, *Black Sunday* and *The Delta Force*). This wholly unique relationship of parallelism and alignment has consistently served to articulate idealized conceptions of American identity through the affirmation of dominant ideologies. *The Ten Commandments* and *Ben-Hur* each conflated the ancient Hebrews with modern Americans as a way of championing the notion of American 'chosenness'. *Exodus* presents the birth of Israel as a re-enactment of the settling of America's western frontier, and in so doing celebrates a traditional conception of the United States' frontier mythology. *Cast a Giant Shadow* deploys the outbreak of Arab-Israeli hostilities in order to frame the United States as a benevolent interventionist power. *Black Sunday* and *The Delta Force* both present Israeli militarism as a model of action for a United States weakened by military setbacks in Vietnam and the Middle East. *Munich* invokes Israel's war against Palestinian militants in order to position the modern-day United States as a virtuous victim of Arab terrorism. In each of the aforementioned films we see the explicit valorization of the traditional ideal of the hyper-masculine white American hero, who has been central to popular conceptions of American nationhood since the earliest days of white settlement of the continent.

The unique paralleling of Israel and the United States in the aforementioned films is enabled by the centrality of the ancient Hebrews to early American national identity, and also the development of the special relationship between Israel and the United States. However, it is important to recognize that popular cinema not only reflects the society in which it is produced and exhibited, but that it also plays a role in shaping that society. Popular cinema is particularly central to defining what history *is* within the public consciousness. Hayden

White argues that 'historiophoty' – 'the representation of history and our thought about it in visual images and filmic discourse' – can be just as effective as 'historiography' – 'the representation of history in verbal images and written discourse' – as a means of accurately recounting the past.[2] Indeed, White suggests that 'cinema (and video) are better suited than written discourse to the actual representation of certain kinds of historical phenomena – landscape, scene, atmosphere, complex events such as wars, battles crowds, and emotions.'[3] Robert A. Rosenstone similarly asserts that the modern world is one 'deluged with images,' and as a result, 'the chief source of historical knowledge for the majority of the population ... must surely be the visual media.'[4] We must thus understand Hollywood's construction of Israel as a stand-in for or ally of the United States as also having serious real-world implications in regards to how Americans understand Israel, Israel's Arab neighbours and also the Arab-Israeli conflict. First and foremost, we can see these films as not merely reflecting the special relationship, but as being highly influential in its establishment. Here it is pertinent to acknowledge the words of historian Thomas J. McCormick, who argues, 'the special relationship between the United States and Israel was not a sudden, dramatic development ... but a slow, incremental process nearly two decades in the making.'[5] When the relationship did finally flower, it was not merely a consequence of Israel's astounding success in the Six Day War of 1967 and the United States' subsequent identification of Israel as a formidable partner in the fight against both Communism and Arab nationalism. It was also predicated on the notion that a unique kinship existed between Americans and Israelis, an ideal lent significant cultural capital by Hollywood's various invocations of Israel in the 1950s and early 1960s. The epics of the late 1950s presented the ancient Hebrews as antecedents to modern Americans, as 'God's Chosen People' struggling for liberty against the heathenish forces of oppression. *Exodus* presented Israelis as proto-Americans struggling to make their desert bloom in the face of dark-skinned savagery in a manner that evoked traditional conceptions of the expansion of the American frontier. *Cast a Giant Shadow*, which was released just one year before the consecration of the special relationship, presented Israel as, to borrow a phrase from Israeli historian Ilan Pappé, 'an island of decency in a sea of barbarism.'[6] Here it is significant to note that Israel was framed as being unambiguously aligned with the United States in what is a clear allegory for a war that was a part of the global struggle against Communism. *Black Sunday*, which was released ten years after the consecration of the special relationship, positioned the United States and Israel as united in the fight against Arab terrorism, while *The Delta Force* reiterated the alignment of the United States and Israel nine years later. In *Munich*, Israel's historical fight against Arab terrorism was framed in images and language that deliberately invoked the 'War on Terror' waged by the United States in the wake of 9/11. The accumulative effect of this mode of representation is a reinforcing of the notion that the United States and Israel are united by both culture and religion, and through the sharing of core values and mutual enemies.

The implications for Arabs

According to Michael Rogin there is 'a countersubversive tradition that exists at the core of American politics.'[7] Rogin uses the term countersubversive 'to call attention to the creation of monsters as a continuing feature of American politics by the inflation, stigmatization, and dehumanization of political foes.'[8] Furthermore, Rogin contends:

> The cold war marks the third major moment in the history of countersubversion. In the first moment whites were pitted against peoples of color. In the second Americans were pitted against aliens. In the third, which revolves around mass society and the state, a national-security bureaucracy confronts the invisible agents of a foreign power.[9]

In each of these moments, American identity defined itself through binary opposition to a demonological Other that supposedly threatened the security of the nation. The end of the Cold War necessitated the emergence of a new enemy against which American identity would be constructed. As I detailed in Chapter 5, following the end of the Cold War a wave of big-budget action films emerged in which Arabs and Muslims were cast as demonic figures intent on carrying out attacks on Americans. These films signalled the dawn of a fourth major moment in the history of American countersubversion, one which contains within it elements of each of the previous three. In this moment, Americans are pitted against people who are not only a different colour, but who also adhere to a supposedly archaic, alien religion that inculcates its followers to hate American freedoms. The attacks of 9/11 and the subsequent launching of the War on Terror crystallized the notion of the United States being engaged in a 'Clash of Civilisations' with the Islamic world. Following the attacks Muslims became, in the words of Arun Kundnani, 'an "ideal enemy", a group that is racially and culturally distinct and ideologically hostile.'[10] Indeed, the demonization of Arabs and Muslims has remained one of the defining features of American political life throughout the first two decades of the twenty-first century.[11]

It is important to understand that the emergence of the Muslim as the principal demonological Other in American society is not merely the result of the need to fill the vacuum left by the demise of the Soviet Union. The arrival of this moment has at least, in part, been facilitated by Hollywood's frequent deployment of Israel as a parallel or ally of the United States, and the subsequent demonization of Arabs that has been a natural consequence of this manner of representation. As detailed by Matthew Bernstein, throughout the first few decades of Hollywood film production Arabs were more likely to appear as highly sexualized symbols of exotic Otherness rather than as bloodthirsty savages, 'typically titillating viewers with the thrills of unbridled passion, miscegenation, and wild adventure in a raw and natural setting.'[12] Hollywood's affinity for desert-based adventures replete with skin and sex would persist throughout the following decade, as most notably typified by such immensely successful films as *The Sheik* (George Melford, 1921), its sequel *The Son of the Sheik* (George Fitzmaurice, 1926) and *The Thief of Baghdad* (Raoul Walsh, 1924). This trend would continue through the 1940s and 1950s, as Hollywood studios cynically pumped out low-budget 't and s' movies (short for 'tits and sand') for, as one studio executive put it, 'morons who like this sort of thing.'[13]

The Ten Commandments and *Ben-Hur*, each released during the second half of the 1950s, collectively mark a key moment in the history of American cinematic demonology. Both films contain Orientalist depictions of Middle Eastern peoples while explicitly celebrating Jewish national liberation, at a time in which the establishment of the modern state of Israel was still a relatively recent development. The demonization of Middle Easterners is particularly pronounced in *The Ten Commandments*. As discussed in Chapter 1, Rameses is constructed as an orientalized Other in a manner that facilitates audience identification with the Americanized hyper-masculine Hebrew hero. While this construction was principally informed by the politics of the Cold War, it simultaneously served to frame the burgeoning Arab-Israeli conflict as one being contested by a demonological racial Other, and a people that are fundamentally 'like us.' *The Ten Commandments*' prejudicial framing of the Arab-Israeli conflict was bolstered by the synchronicity between the film's release and the international conflict that arose out of Egypt's nationalization the Suez Canal. Less than one month after the film's theatrical release Israel invaded the Egyptian Sinai, in turn creating another political frame of reference through which audiences could read the film. The mutually determinative relationship that existed between *The Ten Commandments* and the Suez Crisis is evidenced by Bosley Crowther's review of the film for the *New York Times*, which began by pointing out that the film was being screened, 'Against the raw news of modern conflict between Israel and Egypt – a conflict which has its preamble in the Book of Exodus.'[14] Although the Eisenhower Administration refused to provide Israel with military and diplomatic support during the saga, Israel did enjoy widespread support among the American public.[15] In her discussion of the Suez conflict Michelle Mart contends 'images from other contexts helped to strengthen American identification with Israel at the height of this political disagreement between the United States and the Jewish state.'[16] Although Mart doesn't refer to *The Ten Commandments* by name, there can be little doubt that she considers the film to be a primary source of such imagery. Mart contends that one of the primary factors behind Israel's popularity among Americans throughout the first half of the 1950s was that 'Images emphasizing Jewish masculinity and similarity to other American men began to displace the old stereotypes of Jews as weak victims.' As a result, 'Israel and Jews came to be perceived as masculine, ready to fight the Cold War alongside America.' Conversely Arabs were 'increasingly stigmatized as non-Western, undemocratic, racially darker, unmasculine outsiders.'[17] This notion was of course vehemently reinforced by *The Ten Commandments*' hyper-masculine construction of Moses, and his juxtaposition with the effeminized Rameses. The conflict over Suez can thus be seen as functioning in concert with the rhetoric of the Cold War to contribute to the film's construction of a US/Israel, Soviet/Egypt binary, which in turn serves to frame the burgeoning Arab-Israeli conflict in similarly Manichaean terms.[18]

In 1960 the release of *Exodus* signalled a major shift in the representation of Arabs in Hollywood cinema. The relative lack of overt demonization of Arabs in Hollywood films released prior to *Exodus* is attested by the scholarship of Jack Shaheen. Of the sixty-four films that comprise Shaheen's 'Worst List,' which consists of those films that Shaheen identifies as being the most defamatory to Arabs, only a mere nine were produced prior to the release of *Exodus*.[19] However, in the years after the release of *Exodus*, the figure of the Arab would be increasingly positioned by Hollywood as a demonological Other who is fundamentally antithetical to Western civilization. This is a screen image that has persisted, essentially unaltered, through to our present time.[20] This is not to say, of course, that *Exodus* is solely or even primarily responsible for this shift. However, by explicitly transposing onto the Arab the subhuman qualities previously imposed upon Hollywood's Native Americans, *Exodus* nonetheless signals the emergence within American cinema of a new barbarous Other who poses an existential threat to the American way of life, against which can be projected idealized notions of American heroism.

The demonization of Arabs in *Exodus* is not limited to the film's framing of the Arab-Israeli conflict via the traditional language of America's frontier mythology. The film's final act depicts Nazis suddenly and inexplicably appearing to direct the Arab assault on the Israeli settlers. The Arabs' Nazi commandant is said to command '80 Arab stormtroopers' and also refers to plans to 'exterminate' the Jews of Palestine, while Arabs click their heels like SS paladins whenever he exits the room. This is of particular significance, as it further reiterates how *Exodus*'s articulation of frontier mythology radically differs from that which was then prevailing in contemporaneous Hollywood Westerns set in America's past. Merely four years after the release of *Exodus* John Ford would overtly allude to the Nazis while depicting the oppression of the Native Americans in his film *Cheyenne Autumn* (1964).[21] However, in *Exodus*, which transposes the frontier myth onto Israel, it is the Indian-like Arabs who are explicitly aligned with the ultimate symbol of pure evil. This element is completely absent from the novel upon which the film was based, and it is here that the film engages in its most egregious distortion of the real-world contours and conditions of the Arab-Israeli conflict. In the words of Benjamin Beit-Hallahmi, 'The Palestinians ... were not the historical oppressors of the Jews. They did not put Jews into ghettoes and did not force them to wear yellow stars. They did not plan holocausts.'[22] Nevertheless, through the disingenuous aligning of Arabs and Nazis, the Arab assault on Israeli settlers is ultimately positioned as an extension of the Holocaust.[23] In addition to presenting the Arabs as stormtroopers intent on exterminating the Jews, the film underscores this point through dialogue that speaks of the close ties between Haj Amin al-Husseini (the Grand Mufti of Jerusalem) and the Third Reich during the Second World War. Moreover, in the film the character of Dov (Sal Mineo), a young Zionist warrior who is the boyfriend of Karen, the teenage girl slain by the rapacious Arabs, explicitly details the brutalization he suffered as an inmate at the Auschwitz concentration camp (an element that is, again, absent from the novel), while the mise-en-scene of the sequence in which the body of the friendly Palestinian Taha is found swinging from a noose features a conspicuously large red swastika on the wall, apparently painted in blood by the Arabs responsible for his murder. For the film's American audience, the Nazification of the Arabs serves to establish the Arab-Israeli conflict not only as a 'savage war,' but as a lucidly defined Manichaean struggle that is literally for a nation's survival in a manner that mirrors both the Second World War and the contemporaneous Cold War conflict that imagined the world as being divided into two distinct, diametrically opposed spheres.[24] The notion of the Arabs as being aligned with the totalitarian regimes dedicated to the destruction of Western liberal democracies is reiterated when the Nazi officer who commands the Arab assault declares that he does not recognize the decisions of 'a few elderly gentlemen in Flushing Meadows who call themselves the United Nations,' before subsequently telling Taha, 'Since you are a Muslim you cannot recognize them either.' Ironically, it was David Ben-Gurion, Israel's first prime minister, who rejected the authority of the United Nations in a similar fashion to the Nazi character in *Exodus*, declaring that the establishment of the Jewish state was not 'subject to the United Nations resolution of 29 November (1947) – even though the resolution was of great moral and political value – but on our ability here in this country to achieve a decision by force.'[25] Nevertheless, the Muslims' supposed opposition to democratic principles is presented as being in stark contrast to the attitude of the Jewish settlers, which is most lucidly conveyed in the depiction of Barak Canaan and other Israelis listening to a broadcast of the United Nations vote to partition Palestine, where they all declare their faith that 'democracy will prevail,' and that Israel will be granted a portion of the land. Here the film is demonstrating what Shohat and Stam identify as a key tenet of Eurocentrism – namely, the attribution to the West of 'an inherent progress toward democratic institutions.'[26] At a time when Cold War rhetoric effectively reduced the world into a dichotomy consisting of democratic states on one side and authoritarian states on the other, *Exodus* presents Israel as unambiguously conforming to American ideals. Conversely the Arabs are presented as a racial and cultural Other akin to the demonological figure of the savage Native American, while simultaneously being aligned with the undemocratic and inherently evil ideology of Nazism.

Exodus's falsification of history is compounded by its overt glorification of Israeli militant groups. As Tony Shaw details in *Cinematic Terror: A Global History of Terrorism on Film* (2015), the emergence of Paul Newman's Ari Ben Canaan from the Mediterranean Sea at the beginning of the film is 'an iconic moment in cinema' signifying 'a watershed in the representation of cinematic terrorism,' wherein 'a terrorist [was] not only being portrayed as a freedom fighter but as something resembling an eroticized demi-god.'[27]

The film's sanctification of Israeli terror is best epitomized by the manner in which it depicts the bombing of the King David Hotel, which is undoubtedly the most notorious act of terror ever committed by the Irgun (a pre-state Zionist paramilitary organization that was a more aggressive offshoot of the Haganah). The bombing resulted in ninety-one deaths and also injured another forty-six people, causing more casualties than any other subsequent bombing carried out by either side in the Arab-Israeli conflict. The majority of victims were employees of the hotel; by nationality the majority of the victims were Arabs, of which there were forty-one casualties, while the bombing also claimed the lives of seventeen Palestinian Jews.[28] In the film the incident occurs off-screen and thus the horrific consequences are never shown – all the audience witnesses is an explosion in the distance, followed by a medium shot revealing Ari's demonstrable revulsion. Following the explosion the Jewish perpetrators are depicted fleeing the scene, accompanied by a valorizing, grandiose score, as soldiers who speak in what are clearly British accents track their movements. The enterprise and its subsequent aftermath thus frame the bombing as an entirely anti-British, anti-colonial endeavour. Consequently, the deaths of forty-one innocent Arabs are entirely excised from the historical narrative. Instead the bombing is utilized merely as a device to convey the inherent nobility of Ari via his vehement opposition to the terror tactics of the Irgun, and also his valour as a result of his subsequent liberation of his uncle (who is a leader of the Irgun) from the Acre prison after the imperialist British overlords arrest him in the wake of the attack. As detailed by Shaw, the film similarly offers a wholly sanitized depiction of the aforementioned prison break that is absent any reference to the death of innocent civilians, starkly contrasting with the historical record and exemplifying the film's ennobling representation of the Zionist terror campaign.[29]

Crucially, *Exodus* presents Arabs and Israelis as coming into armed conflict only after the declaration of the United Nations vote to partition Palestine. Prior to this point the Arabs, as previously discussed, are either invisible or, as manifested by Taha, seen as embracing the Zionists' civilizing mission. Following the declaration of partition it is said that Arabs have been 'entering the country for days,' thus propagating the notion that the Arabs are invaders rather than a people who have inhabited the area for centuries. Arabs emerge as instigators of the war, when in reality – at least, according to the official *History of the Haganah* – the Palestinians who had arms were 'more concerned with defending their villages or neighbourhoods than with going out to attack the Jewish forces.'[30]

Here the film again signals its fidelity to the classic Western. To quote Peter Homans, in the fundamental clash between Good and Evil that lies at the heart of the classic Western, 'it is the latter who invariably attacks first.'[31] The outbreak of conflict is thus presented as, from the Israeli perspective, a purely defensive war, rather than one that is born out of the dispossession of Arab territories. Through this prejudicial framing of the outbreak of the conflict, the film exemplifies its inherent Eurocentrism, which, as Shohat and Stam claim, 'sanitizes Western history while patronizing and even demonizing the non-West.'[32]

Tellingly, acts of pre-partition Jewish violence that were perpetrated against the Arabs are, like the Arab victims of the King David Hotel bombing, excised from the historical record. For instance, there is no allusion to the terrorism of Zionist leaders such as Vladimir Jabotinsky. Adel Safty details Jabotinsky's terroristic activities in the following terms:

> In July 1938, the so-called Revisionist wing of Zionism led by Vladimir Jabotinsky introduced with deadly perfection the techniques of modern terrorism by placing bombs in crowded public places in Haifa and Jerusalem. The bombing of the Haifa Melon Market alone, on July 26, killed fifty-three Arabs and one Jew. In six separate terrorist attacks of this kind one hundred Arab men, women and children had been killed in the month of July alone.[33]

Exodus also neglects to portray Israeli violence that followed in the wake of the declaration of partition. There is no mention of the operations comprising the Haganah's so-called 'Plan D,' whose objective was, in the words of General Yigael Yadin (then Head of the Operation Branch of the Israeli unified armed forces), 'The destruction of [Arab] villages (by fire, blowing up and mining) – especially of those villages over which we cannot gain [permanent] control …. In the event of resistance – the destruction of the resisting forces and the expulsion of the population beyond the boundaries of the State.'[34] Following the successful implementation of 'Plan D' the Haganah 'had burned, blown up and brought about the total destruction of 350 Arab villages and towns situated in areas assigned to the Jewish state and areas outside it which had been conquered by the Zionist forces.'[35]

In addition to whitewashing from the history an operation 'designed to achieve the destruction of the Palestinian society and the dispersion and expulsion of its population, to ensure the establishment of a Jewish state as a fait accompli,'[36] *Exodus* is devoid of even a hint of the well documented rhetoric that emanated from the early Zionist leadership that explicitly advocated the expulsion of the region's Arab population, of which 'Plan D' can be rightly understood as a clear manifestation. There is no echo of Chaim Weizmann notoriously stating that the Zionist aim was to make Palestine 'as Jewish as England is English'.[37] Nor is there any allusion to the words of Ben-Gurion, Weizmann's successor as the undisputed leader of the Zionist movement, who claimed, 'I am for compulsory transfer [of the Arab population]; I don't see anything immoral in it'.[38] Conversely, in *Exodus*, the Zionist leadership, as embodied by Ari and Barak Canaan, articulates a Jewish dream of living side-by-side in peace and harmony with their Arab neighbours – a dream that is shattered by Nazi-fuelled Arab belligerence. By rewriting Israel's history so as to render it a faithful re-enactment of the United States' own national mythology, *Exodus* presents violence as being something that is either committed by Israelis against the occupying British, or committed against Israelis by the savage natives.

Cast a Giant Shadow serves as yet another example of how Hollywood has consistently served to frame the Arab-Israeli conflict as an inherently Manichaean conflict contested by lucidly defined paradigms of good and evil. As I argued in Chapter 3, *Cast a Giant Shadow* primarily functions to valorize American interventionism, which, within the confines of the film's narrative, is largely predicated on the notion of Israel's abject vulnerability. This is established throughout the film's opening sequence in which Marcus is approached by the Haganah, and is emphatically reinforced by the film's deployment of the rape/rescue trope. The film also depicts a US battalion liberating a Nazi death camp at the end of the Second World War in what is an overt allusion to the history of Jewish suffering. The dialogue is also replete with references to the futility of Israel's plight. A Pentagon official refers to Israel as 'a pipsqueak nation' which is sure to be 'blown off the map'. Marcus's wife, in an unsuccessful attempt to discourage Marcus from going to Palestine, tells him, 'They don't stand a chance. They'll be dying by the thousands, and you with them.' Marcus tells the American general played by John Wayne that the Israelis are surrounded by millions of Arabs who want to 'push them into the Mediterranean,' and that all the Israelis want is 'a little patch of dirt.' When Marcus implores the Israelis to 'at least die standing up' he is told by a Haganah soldier that 'Sometimes we do,' as the camera cuts to the corpse of an Israeli woman who is tied up and splayed on the side of a burning bus. In direct contrast to the film's sympathetic depiction of the Israelis, *Cast a Giant Shadow* presents the region's Arabs as marauding savages diametrically opposed to Western civilization.

The Ten Commandments, *Ben-Hur*, *Exodus* and *Cast a Giant Shadow* each constitute key moments in the development of the Arab as the United States' principal demonological Other. By explicitly positioning Middle Eastern characters as either strange Oriental Others or savages akin to Hollywood Indians, each film established Middle Easterners as fundamentally antithetical to American society. In so doing, these films laid the groundwork for the eventual popularization of the image of Arabs as terrorists intent on destroying American civilization. This image would first emerge cinematically in *Black Sunday*. As Stephen Prince details in *Firestorm: American Film in the Age of Terrorism* (2009), prior to the 1980s, terrorism was a concept rarely broached by Hollywood films. When it was touched upon, it most notably appeared in two distinct types of films; the outlandish James Bond series; and the disaster genre, in which the perpetrators were generally psychopathic Americans, which had the effect of depoliticizing the terror plot.[39] *Black Sunday* was thus a landmark film, serving as 'the first prominent disaster spectacle that was also explicitly and emphatically about terrorism.'[40] Furthermore, by presenting Israel and the United States as aligned in the fight against Arab terror, it was the first film that responded to the development of the special relationship in the late 1960s. Crucially, *Black Sunday* eschewed the absurdity of the James Bond films. Instead, the film strives for the illusion of verisimilitude. For instance, for the film's climax, which takes place during the Super Bowl, John Frankenheimer filmed Robert Shaw and Fritz Weaver on the sidelines during the actual Super Bowl of 1975, and this footage is intercut with footage of the game. Frankenheimer even cast the winner of the *National Enquirer* Jimmy Carter look-alike contest to play the recently elected president.[41] Through its conflation of fantasy and reality, *Black Sunday* presents the Arab attack on American soil as something that could conceivably happen. As a result, Arabs are consecrated as not merely the enemy of Israel, but also that of the United States.

This notion is reaffirmed by *The Delta Force*, which positions Arab terrorists as attacking Israelis and American Jews alike. Like *The Ten Commandments*, *Ben-Hur*, *Exodus* and *Cast a Giant Shadow* before them, *Black Sunday* and *The Delta Force* each constitute key moments in the evolution of the countersubversive tradition that has remained central to American political life. Whereas the earlier films depicted Arabs as the enemy of people that were 'like' Americans, *Black Sunday* and *The Delta Force* showed Arabs attacking Americans. Crucially, the motive behind the Arab characters' hatred for Americans was the support proffered to Israel by the US government. This positioning of the Arab as a demonological anti-American Other can be seen as foreshadowing the emergence of the Middle Easterner as the United States' principal ideological antagonist as the Cold War came to its end.

As I have demonstrated, throughout its history Hollywood has mobilized the image of Israel for the purpose of enunciating a glorified conception of Americanism, and this deployment of Israel has had significant ramifications for Americans, Israelis and particularly for the Arab world. The countersubversive tradition that has been historically central to the establishment of American political identity required a new enemy in the wake of the collapse of the Soviet Union, and Hollywood's consistent deployment of Israel as a parallel nation and later, as an ally of the United States, meant that there was a ready-made enemy to step into the void. Decades before Arab terrorists ever posed a legitimate threat to American society, fictional Arab terrorists were attacking proto-Americans in films like *Exodus* and *Cast a Giant Shadow*. In 1977, almost a quarter of a century before the attacks of 9/11, *Black Sunday* brought Arab terror to the American homeland as a means of juxtaposing Israeli military might and American weakness in the wake of the loss in Vietnam. By the time the Cold War was finally over, American audiences had already consumed countless images of demonic Arabs, with many of the primordial examples of these images coming out of Hollywood's various invocations of Israel. This is the unfortunate legacy of Hollywood's deployment of Israel as a parallel nation for the purpose of articulating an idealized notion of American national identity.

Notes

Introduction

1. Robert Burgoyne, *Film Nation: Hollywood Looks at U.S. History* (Minneapolis: University of Minnesota Press, 1997), 6.
2. Ibid., 2–3.
3. Edward Buscombe, ed., *The BFI Companion to the Western: New Edition* (London: Andre Deutsch Limited, 1993), 24.
4. Richard Slotkin, *Regeneration through Violence: The Mythology of the American Frontier, 1600–1860* (Connecticut: Wesleyan University Press, 1973), 189.
5. Richard Slotkin, *Gunfighter Nation: The Myth of the Frontier in Twentieth-Century America* (New York: University of Oklahoma Press, 1998), 313–28, 520–32.
6. See Michael Rogin, '"The Sword Became a Flashing Vision": D.W. Griffith's *The Birth of a Nation*', in *Ronald Reagan, the Movie: And Other Episodes in Political Demonology* (Berkeley: University of California Press, 1987), 190–235.
7. See Tony Shaw, *Hollywood's Cold War* (Edinburgh: Edinburgh University Press, 2007), 42–65.
8. See Lina Khatib, *Filming the Modern Middle East: Politics in the Cinemas of Hollywood and the Arab World* (New York: I.B. Tauris, 2006).
9. Tim Jon Semmerling, *'Evil' Arabs in American Popular Film: Orientalist Fear* (Texas: University of Texas Press, 2006).
10. Edward Said, *Orientalism*, Rev. ed. (New York: Vintage Books, 1994).
11. Ibid., 300.
12. Burgoyne, *Film Nation*, 3.
13. For an extended discussion of early Puritan mythology see Slotkin, *Regeneration through Violence*, 37–42.
14. For an extended discussion of Winthrop's sermon see Edmund S. Morgan, 'John Winthrop's "Modell of Christian Charity" in a Wider Context', *Huntington Library Quarterly* 50, no. 2 (Spring 1987): 145–51.
15. Eran Shalev, *American Zion: The Old Testament as a Political Text from the Revolution to the Civil War* (New Haven: Yale University Press, 2013), 1.
16. Michael B. Oren, *Power, Faith, and Fantasy: America in the Middle East 1776 to the Present* (New York: W. W. Norton, 2007), 85.
17. Lester C. Olson, *Benjamin Franklin's Vision of American Community: A Study in Rhetorical Iconology* (Columbia: University of South Carolina Press, 2004), 234.

18 Ibid.
19 Peter Grose, *Israel in the Mind of America* (New York: Alfred A Knopf, 1983), 5.
20 For an extended discussion of American attitudes towards the establishment of a Jewish state in Mandatory Palestine in the immediate aftermath of the Second World War see Eytan Gilboa, *American Public Opinion of Israel and the Arab-Israeli Conflict* (Massachusetts: Lexington Books, 1987), 16–18.
21 Quoted in Adel Safty, *Might Over Right: How the Zionists Took Over Palestine* (Reading: Garnet Publishing, 2009), 149.
22 Ibid., 166.
23 Quoted in Michael T. Benson, *Harry S. Truman and the Founding of Israel* (Connecticut: Praeger Publishers, 1997), 190.
24 Douglas Little, *American Orientalism: The United States and the Middle East since 1945*, 3rd ed. (Chapel Hill: University of North Carolina Press, 2008), 87–8.
25 For an extended discussion of Eisenhower's response to the Suez Crisis see Melani McAlister, *Epic Encounters: Culture, Media, & U.S. Interests in the Middle East since 1945*, Rev. ed. (Berkeley: University of California Press, 2005), 80–1.
26 Little, *American Orientalism*, 93.
27 Gilboa, *American Public Opinion toward Israel and the Arab-Israeli Conflict*, 34. For an extended discussion of the American public's response to the Suez Crisis, see pages 27–39.
28 Will Herberg, *Protestant-Catholic-Jew: An Essay in American Religious Sociology* (Chicago: The University of Chicago Press, 1955), 87.
29 Quoted in Steven L. Spiegel, *The Other Arab-Israeli Conflict: Making America's Middle East Policy, from Truman to Reagan* (Chicago: University of Chicago Press, 1985), 123.
30 See Lester D. Friedman, *Hollywood's Image of the Jew* (New York: Frederick Ungar Publishing, 1982); Patricia Erens, *The Jew in American Cinema* (Bloomington: Indiana University Press, 1984); Omer Bartov, *The 'Jew' in Cinema: From the Golem to Don't Touch My Holocaust* (Indiana: Indiana University Press, 2005); Nathan Abrams, *The New Jew in Film: Exploring Jewishness and Judaism in Contemporary Cinema* (New Jersey: Rutgers University Press, 2012).
31 By the end of the 1960s both *The Ten Commandments* and *Ben-Hur* were among *Variety*'s all-time top 5 domestic 'Box office Champs'. See Tino Balio, *United Artists, Volume 2, 1951–1978: The Company that Changed the Film Industry* (Madison: The University of Wisconsin Press, 2009), 126.
32 See Maria Wyke, *Projecting the Past: Ancient Rome, Cinema and History* (New York: Routledge, 1997).
33 Martin M. Winkler, 'The Roman Empire in American Cinema after 1945', in *Imperial Projections: Ancient Rome in Modern Popular Culture*, ed. Sandra R. Joshel,

Margaret Malamud, and Donald T. McGuire (Maryland: Johns Hopkins University Press, 2005), 50–76.

34 Sumiko Higashi, 'Antimodernism as Historical Representation in a Consumer Culture: Cecil B. DeMille's *The Ten Commandments*, 1923, 1956, 1993', in *The Persistence of History: Cinema, Television, and the Modern Event*, ed. Vivian Sobchack (New York: Routledge, 1996), 91–112.

35 Lew Wallace, *Ben-Hur: A Tale of the Christ* (Raleigh, NC: Generic NL Freebook Publisher, n.d.), doi: 1086058.

36 Amy Lifson, '*Ben Hur*: The Book That Shook the World', *Humanities* 30, no. 6 (November/December 2009), accessed 29 November 2012, http://www.neh.gov/humanities/2009/novemberdecember/feature/ben-hur.

37 See *The Ten Commandments* (Cecil B. DeMille, 1923) and *Ben-Hur: A Tale of the Christ* (Fred Niblo, 1925).

38 Leon Uris, *Exodus* (New York: Doubleday & Company, 1958).

39 See McAlister, *Epic Encounters*, 159.

40 Quoted in ibid.

41 Shawn Levy, *Paul Newman: A Life* (London: Aurum Press, 2009), 166.

42 Ted Berkman, *Cast a Giant Shadow* (New York: Pocket Books, Inc., 1963).

43 Director Melville Shavelson lamented that the public agreed with more critical reviewers 'by staying away in droves'. See Melville Shavelson, *How to Make a Jewish Movie* (New Jersey: Prentice-Hall, Inc., 1971), 169–70.

44 Eric Bentley, *Theatre of War: Comments on 32 Occasions* (New York: Viking Press, 1972), 311.

45 Thomas Harris, *Black Sunday* (New York: G.P. Putnam's Sons, 1975).

46 George Jonas, *Vengeance*, Rev. ed. (London: Harper Perennial, 2006).

Chapter 1

1 See Sheldon Hall and Stephen Neale, *Epics, Spectacles, and Blockbusters: A Hollywood History* (Detroit: Wayne State University Press, 2010), 160–1.

2 For figures pertaining to *The Ten Commandment*'s box office performance see Box Office Mojo, 'All Time Box Office Adjusted for Ticket Price Inflation', Boxofficemojo.com, accessed 11 May 2015, http://www.boxofficemojo.com/alltime/adjusted.htm.

3 Steven Cohan, *Masked Men: Masculinity and the Movies in the Fifties* (Bloomington: Indiana University Press, 1997), 122.

4 See Hall and Neale, *Epics, Spectacles, and Blockbusters*, 162.

5 In the historical drama film *Frost/Nixon* (Ron Howard, 2008), which depicts the series of interviews given by former president Richard Nixon to journalist David Frost in

the aftermath of Nixon's resignation, when Nixon is informed that the enterprise will cost $2,000,000 Nixon retorts, 'Jesus, I didn't realise we were making *Ben-Hur*'.
6   Maria Wyke, *Projecting the Past: Ancient Rome, Cinema and History* (New York: Routledge, 1997), 23.
7   Martin M. Winkler, 'The Roman Empire in American Cinema after 1945', in *Imperial Projections: Ancient Rome in Modern Popular Culture*, ed. Sandra R. Joshel, Margaret Malamud, and Donald T. McGuire (Maryland: Johns Hopkins University Press, 2005), 53.
8   Sumiko Higashi, 'Antimodernism as Historical Representation in a Consumer Culture: Cecil B. DeMille's *The Ten Commandments*, 1923, 1956, 1993', in *The Persistence of History: Cinema, Television, and the Modern Event*, ed. Vivian Sobchack (New York: Routledge, 1996), 101.
9   Rick Altman, *The American Film Musical* (Bloomington & Indianapolis: Indiana University Press, 1987), 2.
10 Harry Truman, 'Truman Doctrine – President Harry S. Truman's Address before a Joint Session of Congress', 12 March 1947, Avalon Project, accessed 12 October2013, http://avalon.law.yale.edu/20th_century/trudoc.asp.
11 Melvyn P. Leffler, *A Preponderance of Power: National Security, the Truman Administration, and the Cold War* (California: University of Stanford Press, 1992), 145–6. The Monroe Doctrine asserted American dominance of the Western Hemisphere by stating that 'the American continents, by the free and independent condition which they have assumed and maintain, are henceforth not to be considered as subjects for future colonization by any European powers'. Quoted in Gretchen Murphy, *Hemispheric Imaginings: The Monroe Doctrine and Narratives of U.S. Empire* (Durham: Duke University Press, 2004), 4.
12 Douglas T. Miller and Marion Nowak, *The Fifties: The Way We Really Were* (New York: Doubleday & Company, Inc., 1977), 92.
13 See Michelle Mart, *Eye on Israel: How America Came to View Israel as an Ally* (Albany: State University of New York Press, 2006), 85.
14 Eric R. Crouse, 'Popular Cold Warriors: Conservative Protestants, Communism, and Culture in Early Cold War America', *Journal of Religion and Popular Culture* 2 (Fall 2002), accessed 14 May 2012, http://www.usask.ca/relst/jrpc/popcoldwarprint.html.
15 'President Sees Editors: Tells Them Communism Can Be Beaten through Religion', *New York Times*, 10 April 1953.
16 Quoted in Margaret Malamud, 'Cold War Romans', *Arion* 14, no. 3 (Winter 2007): 124.
17 Crouse, *Popular Cold Warriors*.
18 Quoted in Miller and Nowak, *The Fifties*, 92.
19 Quoted in Stephen J. Whitfield, *The Culture of the Cold War*, 2nd ed. (Baltimore: Johns Hopkins University Press, 1996), 68.
20 Tony Shaw, *Hollywood's Cold War* (Edinburgh: Edinburgh University Press, 2007), 4.

21 Ibid., 2–3.
22 Quoted in Tony Shaw and Denise J. Youngblood, *Cinematic Cold War: The American and Soviet Struggle for Hearts and Minds* (Lawrence: University Press of Kansas, 2010), 26.
23 Ibid., 21.
24 Ibid., 26.
25 Shaw, *Hollywood's Cold War*, 115.
26 Quoted in Larry Ceplair and Steven Englund, *The Inquisition in Hollywood: Politics in the Film Community 1930–1960* (New York: Anchor Press/Double Day, 1980), 211.
27 Shaw, *Hollywood's Cold War*, 114.
28 See Ceplair and Englund, *The Inquisition in Hollywood*, 368.
29 Harry S. Truman Library & Museum, 'A Report to the National Security Council – NSC 68', 12 April 1950, accessed 14 November 2015, http://www.trumanlibrary.org/whistlestop/study_collections/coldwar/documents/pdf/10-1.pdf.
30 Stanley Corkin, *Cowboys as Cold Warriors: The Western as U.S. History* (Philadelphia: Temple University Press, 2004), 159.
31 Here it is also worth noting that months after the release of *The Ten Commandments* Brynner would play the role of a Russian general in the film *Anastasia* (Anatole Litvak, 1956).
32 See Cohan, *Masked Men*, 132.
33 Ibid.
34 For an extended discussion on newsreel footage of the liberation of Nazi concentration camps and its airing in the United States, see Jeffrey Shandler, 'The Testimony of Images: The Allied Liberation of Nazi Concentration Camps in American Newsreels', in *Why Didn't the Press Shout?: American & International Journalism during the Holocaust*, ed. Robert Moses Shapiro (New York: Yeshiva University Press, 2003), 109–25.
35 Les K. Adler and Thomas G. Paterson, 'Red Fascism: The Merger of Nazi Germany and Soviet Russia in the American Image of Totalitarianism, 1930s–1950s', *The American Historical Review* 75, no. 4 (April 1970): 1046.
36 See ibid., 1046.
37 See ibid., 1053.
38 Harry S. Truman Library & Museum, 'The President's Special Conference with the Association of Radio News Analysts', 13 May 1947, accessed 13 April 2014, http://www.trumanlibrary.org/publicpapers/index.php?pid=2155.
39 Siegfried Kracauer, 'National Types as Hollywood Presents Them', *The Public Opinion Quarterly* 13, no. 1 (Spring 1949): 58.
40 Ibid., 68.
41 Quoted in Higashi, 'Antimodernism as Historical Representation in a Consumer Culture', 101.

42 Shaw, *Hollywood's Cold War*, 199.
43 Ibid., 102.
44 Quoted in Higashi, 'Antimodernism as Historical Representation in a Consumer Culture', 102.
45 James Powers, '"The Ten Commandments": Read THR's 1956 Review', *Hollywood Reporter*, 5 October 1956, accessed 11 October 2015, http://www.hollywoodreporter.com/news/ten-commandments-read-thrs-1956-754677.
46 See Cohan, *Masked Men*, 125.
47 Shaw, *Hollywood's Cold War*, 121.
48 Michael Wood, *America in the Movies: Or 'Santa Maria, It Had Slipped My Mind'* (New York: Delta Publishing, 1975), 187.
49 See Marc Vernet, 'Wings of the Desert; or, the Invisible Superimpositions', *Velvet Light Trap: A Critical Journal of Film and Television* 91, no. 28 (September 1991): 65–72.
50 Lester D. Friedman, *Hollywood's Image of the Jew* (New York: Frederick Ungar Publishing, 1982), 146.
51 Bruce Babington and Peter William Evans, *Biblical Epics: Sacred Narrative in the Hollywood Cinema* (Manchester: Manchester University Press, 1993), 35.
52 Ibid.
53 See Michael T. Benson, *Harry S. Truman and the Founding of Israel* (Connecticut: Praeger Publishers, 1997), 34.
54 For an extended discussion see Michelle Mart, 'The "Christianization" of Israel and Jews in 1950s America', *Religion and American Culture: A Journal of Interpretation* 14, no. 1 (Winter 2004): 109–47.
55 Melani McAlister, *Epic Encounters: Culture, Media, & U.S. Interests in the Middle East since 1945*, Rev. ed. (Berkeley: University of California Press, 2005), 163.
56 Mart, 'The "Christianization" of Israel and Jews in 1950s America', 115–16.
57 See ibid., 121–6.
58 Exod. 1:9–10.
59 Matt. 2:16–18.
60 Exod. 2:11–15.
61 Melanie J. Wright, *Religion and Film: An Introduction* (New York: I.B. Tauris, 2007), 63.
62 'The Ten Commandments', *Variety*, 10 October 1956.
63 Mart, *Eye on Israel*, 99.
64 Alan Nadel, 'God's Law and the Wide Screen: *The Ten Commandments* as Cold War "Epic"', *Publications of the Modern Language Association of America* (*PMLA*) 108, no. 3 (May 1993): 424–5.
65 See Winkler, 'The Roman Empire in American Cinema after 1945', 67.
66 For an extended discussion of the Hitler Myth see Ian Kershaw, *The 'Hitler Myth': Image and Reality in the Third Reich* (Oxford: Clarendon Press, 1987).

67　See Martin M. Winkler, *The Roman Salute: Cinema, History, Ideology* (Columbus: Ohio State University Press, 2009).
68　In 1947 Wyler, alongside like-minded colleagues Philip Dunne and John Huston, formed the Committee for the First Amendment, which worked to forestall censorship and helped support directors who had been subpoenaed by HUAC. Wyler also co-founded the Committee for the First Amendment, which would become Hollywood's foremost liberal voice of opposition to HUAC. Moreover, Wyler donated to the legal fund of the so-called 'Hollywood Ten' and also wrote to parole boards on their behalf. For an extended discussion see Sarah Kozloff, 'Wyler's Wars', *Film History* 20, no. 4 (2008): 463–5.
69　Ibid., 465.
70　See ibid., 456.
71　See ibid., 457.
72　Winkler, 'The Roman Empire in American Cinema after 1945', 50.
73　Quoted in Norman G. Finkelstein, *Image and Reality of the Israel-Palestine Conflict* (London: Verso, 1995), 14.
74　Lew Wallace, *Ben-Hur: A Tale of the Christ* (Raleigh, NC: Generic NL Freebook Publisher, n.d.), doi: 1086058. 389.
75　Ibid., 419.
76　Rupert Wilkinson, *American Tough: The Tough-Guy Tradition and American Character* (Westport: Greenwood Press, 1984), 8.
77　Ibid., 9.
78　Mart, *Eye on Israel*, 65.
79　Paul Breines, *Tough Jews: Political Fantasies and the Moral Dilemma of American Jewry* (New York: Basic Books, 1990), ix.
80　Ibid., 54.
81　Katherine Orrison details in the film's DVD commentary track that DeMille insisted that all of the blue-eyed actors wear brown contact lenses to help achieve the Middle Eastern look appropriate for Egyptians and Israelites – with the exception of Heston and Yvonne De Carlo, who plays Moses's wife Sephora. See Katherine Orrison, 'Commentary', *The Ten Commandments*, special collector's ed., DVD, directed by Cecil B. DeMille (Paramount, 2004).
82　Quoted in Emilie Raymond, *From My Cold, Dead Hands: Charlton Heston and American Politics* (Kentucky: The University of Kentucky Press, 2006), 25–6.
83　Vincent Canby, 'For De Mille, Moses' Egypt Was Really America', *New York Times*, 25 March 1984.
84　Cohan, *Masked Men*, 148.
85　Wilkinson, *American Tough*, 7.
86　Breines, *Tough Jews*, ix.

87 See Chapter 8 in Charles Hilliard, *The Cross, the Sword, the Dollar* (New York: North River Press, 1951), 64–74. See McAlister, *Epic Encounters*, 43–83 for an extended discussion of Hilliard's concept of 'benevolent supremacy' and the manner in which it informed the Hollywood epics of the 1950s.
88 Mart, *Eye on Israel*, 65.
89 Cohan, *Masked Men*, 149. Here it is important to note that Cohan, while acknowledging the 'feminizing implications' of Brynner's/Rameses's spectacularity, asserts that '*The Ten Commandments* never loses sight of Brynner's maleness'. Cohan devotes significant attention to the Brynner's status as a virile symbol of male sexuality; see 150–5.
90 Ibid., 154.
91 Ibid.
92 Leo Braudy, *The World in a Frame: What We See in Films* (New York: Anchor Press/ Doubleday, 1976), 208.
93 For an extended discussion of Rudolph Valentino's screen-image, see Miriam Hansen, *Babel and Babylon: Spectatorship in American Silent Film* (Massachusetts: Harvard University Press, 1991), 254–68.
94 Cohan, *Masked Men*, 150.
95 Edward Said, *Orientalism*, Rev. ed. (New York: Vintage Books, 1994).
96 Ibid., 206.
97 Ibid., 300.
98 See Wallace, *Ben-Hur*, 62.
99 Hansen, *Babel and Babylon*, 254.
100 See Wallace, *Ben-Hur*, 79.
101 Wilkinson, *American Tough*, 7.
102 Ibid.
103 Wallace, *Ben-Hur*, 123.
104 Wood, *America in the Movies*, 173.
105 Wilkinson, *American Tough*, 7.
106 Vito Russo, *The Celluloid Closet: Homosexuality in the Movies*, Rev. ed. (New York: Harper & Row, 1987), 76–7.
107 John D'Emilio, 'The Homosexual Menace: The Politics of Sexuality in Cold War America', in *Making Trouble: Essays on Gay History, Politics, and the University* (New York: Routledge, 1992), 57–73.
108 Cohan, *Masked Men*, ix.
109 Ibid., xv.
110 Peter Biskind, *Seeing Is Believing: How Hollywood Taught Us to Stop Worrying and Love the Fifties* (New York: Pantheon Books, 1983), 257.
111 Cohan., *Masked Men*, 122–63.

112 Cohan devotes significant attention to the new wave of Method actors. See Chapter 6 of *Masked Men*, 'Why Boys Are Not Men', 201–63.
113 Ibid., 151.
114 Ibid., 252.
115 Ibid., 260.
116 See Richard Dyer, *Stars*, New ed. (London: BFI Publishing, 1998). See also Richard Dyer, *Heavenly Bodies: Film Stars and Society*, 2nd ed. (London: Routledge, 2004).
117 Patricia White, *Uninvited: Classical Hollywood Cinema and Lesbian Representability* (Indiana: Indiana University Press, 1999), 197.
118 Ibid.
119 Raymond, *From My Cold, Dead* Hands, 4.
120 Ibid.
121 Michel Mourlet, 'In Defence of Violence', in *Stardom: Industry of Desire*, ed. Christine Gledhill (London: Routledge, 1991), 234.
122 Ibid.
123 Dyer, *Heavenly* Bodies, 2.
124 Raymond, *From My Cold, Dead Hands*, 5.
125 Edgar Morin, *The Stars*, trans. Richard Howard (New York: Grove Press, Inc., 1960), 38.
126 Raymond, *From My Cold, Dead Hands*, 5.
127 Dyer, *Heavenly Bodies*, 2–3.
128 Ibid.
129 See the episodes *Eenie, Meenie, Miney, MURDER!* (Jeff Melman, 2001) and *A Poorly Executed Plan* (Jeff Melman, 2001).

Chapter 2

1 Tino Balio, *Hollywood in the Age of Television* (London: Unwin Hyman, 1990), 3.
2 Steven Cohan, *Masked Men: Masculinity and the Movies in the Fifties* (Bloomington: Indiana University Press, 1997), 126.
3 Matthew M. Silver, *Our Exodus: Leon Uris and the Americanization of Israel's Founding Story* (Detroit: Wayne State University Press, 2010), 58.
4 See Melani McAlister, *Epic Encounters: Culture, Media, & U.S. Interests in the Middle East since 1945*, Rev. ed. (Berkeley: University of California Press, 2005), 159.
5 Ibid., 86.
6 Quoted in Silver, *Our Exodus*, 87.

7   Ira B. Nadel, *Leon Uris: Life of a Best Seller* (Austin: University of Texas Press, 2010), 116.
8   Quoted in Silver, *Our Exodus*, 202.
9   Ibid., 204.
10 Ibid., 203–4.
11 Ibid., 204.
12 Shawn Levy, *Paul Newman: A Life* (London: Aurum Press, 2009), 166.
13 Silver, *Our Exodus*, 204.
14 Silver, *Our Exodus*, 133. See 141–6 for an extended discussion of the film's similarities with the classical Hollywood Western.
15 Lester D. Friedman, *Hollywood's Image of the Jew* (New York: Frederick Ungar Publishing Co., 1982), 192.
16 Omer Bartov, *The 'Jew' in Cinema: From The Golem to Don't Touch My Holocaust* (Indiana: Indiana University Press, 2005), 198.
17 Friedman, *Hollywood's Image of the Jew*, 173.
18 Bartov, *The 'Jew' in Cinema*, 189.
19 Amy Kaplan, 'Zionism as Anticolonialism: The Case of *Exodus*', *American Literary History* 25, no. 4 (Winter 2013): 871.
20 John O'Sullivan, 'Annexation', *The United States Magazine and Democratic Review* 17, no. 1 (July–August 1845): 6.
21 Anders Stephanson, *Manifest Destiny: American Expansionism and the Empire of Right* (New York: Hill and Wang, 1995), 43.
22 See Frederick Jackson Turner, 'The Significance of the Frontier in American History', in *The Frontier in American History* (New York: Holt, Rinehart and Winston, Inc., 1962), 1–38.
23 Ibid., 38.
24 This quote comes from the entry for the term 'Frontier', authored by Edward Countryman, in Edward Buscombe, ed., *The BFI Companion to the Western: New Edition* (London: Andre Deutsch Limited, 1993), 124.
25 This identification of the core tenets of the Western comes from Jim Kitses, *Horizons West: Anthony Mann, Budd Boetticher, Sam Peckinpah: Studies of Authorship within the Western* (London: Thames & Hudson, 1969), 8.
26 Jim Kitses, 'The Western: Ideology and Archetype', in *Focus on the Western*, ed. Jack Nachbar (Englewood Cliffs: Prentice-Hall Inc., 1974), 64.
27 Richard Slotkin, *Gunfighter Nation: The Myth of the Frontier in Twentieth-Century America* (New York: University of Oklahoma Press, 1998), 231.
28 Buscombe, *The BFI Companion to the Western*, 24.
29 Ibid., 38.
30 See Slotkin, *Gunfighter Nation*, 259.

31 Ibid., 256.
32 Ibid., 278.
33 Ibid., 279.
34 Ibid., 313–46.
35 These statistics come from Buscombe, *The BFI Companion to the Western*, 427.
36 Slotkin, *Gunfighter Nation*, 383. For an extended discussion of the political and ideological underpinnings of the gunfighter Western, see 379–404.
37 Ibid., 365.
38 Ibid., 366–78.
39 John H. Lenihan, *Showdown: Confronting Modern America in the Western Film* (Chicago: University of Illinois Press, 1980), 23–81.
40 Thomas Cripps, *Making Movies Black: The Hollywood Message Movie from World War II to the Civil Rights Era* (New York: Oxford University Press, 1993), 281–3.
41 See Edward Buscombe, *'Injuns!': Native Americans in the Movies* (Cornwall: Reaktion Books, 2006), 99.
42 John G. Cawelti, *Adventure, Mystery, and Romance: Formula Stories as Art and Popular Culture* (Chicago: University of Chicago Press, 1976), 247.
43 Thomas Schatz, *Hollywood Genres: Formulas, Filmmaking, and the Studio System* (Philadelphia: Temple University Press, 1981), 21.
44 Ibid., 47.
45 Ella Shohat and Robert Stam, *Unthinking Eurocentrism: Multiculturalism and the Media* (London: Routledge, 1994), 116.
46 See Tom Ryan, *Otto Preminger Films Exodus* (New York: Random House, 1960), 7.
47 Shohat and Stam, *Unthinking Eurocentrism*, 120.
48 According to the two *Books of Kings* from the Hebrew Bible, in which the Battle of Megiddo in 609 BC is recounted, Ari should be saying 'Josiah', rather than 'Joshua'.
49 Shohat and Stam, *Unthinking Eurocentrism*, 119–20.
50 Schatz, *Hollywood Genres*, 24–5.
51 Ibid., 26.
52 Ibid.
53 Douglas Pye, 'Introduction: Criticism and the Western', in *The Movie Book of the Western*, ed. Ian Cameron and Douglas Pye (London: Studio Vista, 1996), 13.
54 See Richard Slotkin, *Regeneration through Violence: The Mythology of the American Frontier, 1600–1860* (Connecticut: Wesleyan University Press, 1973).
55 Ibid., 313.
56 Peter Homans, 'Puritanism Revisited: An Analysis of the Contemporary Screen-Image Western', in *Focus on the Western*, ed. Jack Nachbar (Englewood Cliffs: Prentice-Hall Inc., 1974), 84.
57 Tony Shaw, *Cinematic Terror: A Global History of Terrorism on Film* (New York: Bloomsbury Publishing, 2015), 62.

58 Nadel, *Leon Uris*, 96.
59 Ibid., 109.
60 Ibid., 100. Uris originally named the character Avi, rather than Ari.
61 Paul Breines, *Tough Jews: Political Fantasies and the Moral Dilemma of American Jewry* (New York: Basic Books, 1990), 54.
62 Bartov, *The 'Jew' in Cinema*, 189.
63 Leon Uris, *Exodus* (London: Corgi, 1961), 177.
64 See Mary Ann Doane, 'The Close-Up: Scale and Detail in the Cinema', *Differences: A Journal of Feminist Cultural Studies* 14, no. 3 (2003): 89–111.
65 Ibid., 94–6.
66 Yosefa Loshitzky, *Identity Politics on the Israeli Screen* (Austin: University of Texas Press, 2001), 6.
67 Adel Safty, *Might Over Right: How the Zionists Took Over Palestine* (Reading: Garnet Publishing, 2009).
68 *Exodus* is here echoing the Biblical and historical epics of the period, which frequently cast British actors as malevolent tyrants in opposition to heroic Americans whose characters yearned for freedom from oppression. Michael Wood breaks down the ideological implications of this ubiquitous casting practice in the following terms; 'The heroes are American: Robert Taylor, Kirk Douglas, Charlton Heston, Stephen Boyd. But then these are military men, or slaves, or Jews, and the *other* men, the ruling class, are again invariably English: Peter Ustinov, Alec Guinness, Laurence Olivier, Christopher Plummer. I don't mean to suggest that this pattern is intentional, merely that it reveals some interesting assumptions, since it clearly hints at a famous old transatlantic story: The English have manners and purity while the Americans have life; the decadent English, like the rotten Romans they so often portray, have a wonderful past while the energetic Americans, like the Christians and Jews in these stories, are promised a fabulous tomorrow'. See Michael Wood, *America in the Movies: Or 'Santa Maria, It Had Slipped My Mind'* (New York: Delta Publishing, 1975), 183–4.
69 Rupert Wilkinson, *American Tough: The Tough-Guy Tradition and American Character* (Westport: Greenwood Press, 1984), 95–6.
70 Levy, *Paul Newman*, 200.
71 Friedman writes, 'Ari is a fighter who resembles John Wayne more than he does George Sidney'. See Friedman, *Hollywood's Image of the Jew*, 192.
72 The name 'Fremont' can also be seen as an invocation of American frontier mythology. As Silver points out, Fremont Street was the setting for the legendary Gunfight at O.K. Corral. Not coincidentally, Uris authored the screenplay to the film *Gunfight at the O.K. Corral* (John Sturges, 1959), which was released just one year prior to the publishing of *Exodus*. See Silver, *Our Exodus*, 84.

73. The term 'special relationship' originally referred to the extremely close political, cultural, economic and military relations between the United States and Great Britain. For an extended discussion see Duncan Andrew Campbell, *Unlikely Allies: Britain, America and the Victorian Origins of the Special Relationship* (London: Hambledon Continuum, 2007).
74. For an extended discussion of the general decline of overt anti-Semitism in American society during this period see McAlister, *Epic Encounters*, 163.
75. See Chapter 8 in Charles Hilliard, *The Cross, the Sword, the Dollar* (New York: North River Press, 1951), 64–74. For an extended discussion of Hilliard's concept of 'benevolent supremacy', see McAlister, *Epic Encounters*, 43–83.
76. As will be detailed extensively in the following chapter, the United States' vision of itself as the world's defender of liberty and protector of weaker nations manifested itself most notably in American military intervention in Southeast Asia.
77. Robert A. Lovett, Truman's Secretary of Defense, wrote in a memorandum dated 17 May 1948, 'My protests against the precipitate action and warnings as to consequences with the Arab world appear to have been outweighed by considerations unknown to me, but I can only conclude that the President's political advisers having failed last Wednesday afternoon to make the President a father of the new state, have determined at least to make him the midwife'. Quoted in Douglas Little, *American Orientalism: the United States and the Middle East since 1945*, 3rd ed. (Chapel Hill: University of North Carolina Press, 2008), 87.
78. Notable pre-*Exodus* Westerns which either centre on the Civil War or the effects of its aftermath include *They Died with Their Boots On* (Raoul Walsh, 1941), and the John Ford films *Fort Apache* (1948), *She Wore a Yellow Ribbon* (1949), *Rio Grande* (1950), *The Searchers* (1956) and *The Horse Soldiers* (1959).
79. Pye, 'Introduction: Criticism and the Western', 14.
80. Robert Warshow, 'Movie Chronicle: The Westerner', in *Focus on the Western*, ed. Jack Nachbar (Englewood Cliffs: Prentice-Hall Inc., 1974), 46.
81. André Bazin, 'The Western: Or the American Film Par Excellence', in *What Is Cinema? Vol. II*, trans. Hugh Gray (Berkeley: University of California Press, 1971), 143.
82. Safty, *Might Over Right*, 168.
83. For an extended discussion of the so-called 'Myth of the Garden' and its centrality to nineteenth-century American thought see Henry Nash Smith, *Virgin Land: The American West as Symbol and Myth* (Cambridge: Harvard University Press, 1950), 121–260.
84. Shohat and Stam, *Unthinking Eurocentrism*, 119.
85. For an extended discussion of the legacy of white men playing Native Americans in Hollywood Westerns see Ralph E. Friar and Natasha A. Friar, 'White Man Speaks with Split Tongue, Forked Tongue, Tongue of Snake', in *The Pretend Indians: Images of Native Americans in the Movies*, ed. Gretchen M. Bataille and Charles L. P. Silet (Ames: The Iowa State University Press, 1980), 92–7.

86   Loshitzky, *Identity Politics on the Israeli Screen*, 8.
87   Silver identifies Taha as being akin to an 'honorable but weak Indian chief'. See Silver, *Our Exodus*, 142–4.
88   Uris, *Exodus*, 537.
89   See Shohat and Stam, *Unthinking Eurocentrism*, 115–16.
90   Slotkin, *Gunfighter Nation*, 621.
91   Slotkin, *Regeneration through Violence*, 202.
92   Ibid., 95.
93   Richard Slotkin, *The Fatal Environment: The Myth of the Frontier in the Age of Industrialization 1800–1890* (New York: Atheneum, 1985), 80.
94   Smith, *Virgin Land*, 103.
95   Ibid., 104.
96   For an extended discussion of the concept of 'savage war', see Slotkin, *Gunfighter Nation*, 12.
97   Miriam Hansen, '"*Schindler's List*" Is Not "*Shoah*": The Second Commandment, Popular Modernism, and Public Memory', *Critical Inquiry* 22, no. 2 (1996): 293.
98   Michael Rogin, 'Preface', in *Ronald Reagan, the Movie: And Other Episodes in Political Demonology* (Berkeley: University of California Press, 1987), xviii. For an extended discussion of the film by Rogin, see '"The Sword Became a Flashing Vision": D.W. Griffith's *The Birth of a Nation*', in *Ronald Reagan, the Movie: And Other Episodes in Political Demonology* (Berkeley: University of California Press, 1987), 190–235.
99   See Slotkin, *Gunfighter Nation*, 468–9; Richard Maltby, 'A Better Sense of History: John Ford and the Indians', in *The Movie Book of the Western*, ed. Ian Cameron and Douglas Pye (London: Studio Vista, 1996), 42; Patrick McGee, *From Shane to Kill Bill: Rethinking the Western* (Massachusetts: Blackwell Publishing, 2007), 99–100; Peter Lehman, 'Texas 1868/America 1956: *The Searchers*', in *Close Viewings: An Anthology of New Film Criticism*, ed. Peter Lehman (Tallahassee: The Florida State University Press, 1990), 387–415; Robert B. Pippin, *Hollywood Westerns and American Myth: The Importance of Howard Hawks and John Ford for Political Philosophy* (New Haven: Yale University Press, 2010), 110–22.
100 Lehman, 'Texas 1868/America 1956', 404.
101 Douglas Pye, 'Double Vision: Miscegenation and Point of View in *The Searchers*', in *The Movie Book of the Western*, ed. Ian Cameron and Douglas Pye (London: Studio Vista, 1996), 229.
102 Pye notes that this presentation of the US Cavalry is radically different from those of Ford's earlier films, and can be seen as a microcosm of the shifting attitudes regarding the United States' traditional national mythology. See ibid., 232.
103 Shohat and Stam, *Unthinking Eurocentrism*, 119.
104 For an extended discussion of 'genre memory', see Caryl Emerson and Gary Saul Emerson, *Mikhail Bakhtin: Creation of a Prosaics* (California: Stanford University Press, 1990), 271–305.

105 Turner, 'The Significance of the Frontier in American History', 3.
106 Slotkin, *Gunfighter Nation*, 14.
107 Ibid., 12.

Chapter 3

1 Richard Slotkin, *Gunfighter Nation: The Myth of the Frontier in Twentieth-Century America* (New York: University of Oklahoma Press, 1998), 10.
2 Ibid., 313–46.
3 Ibid., 4.
4 Ted Berkman, *Cast a Giant Shadow* (New York: Pocket Books, Inc., 1963).
5 Melville Shavelson, *How to Make a Jewish Movie* (New Jersey: Prentice-Hall, Inc., 1971), 169–70.
6 Lawrence H. Suid, *Guts & Glory: The Making of the American Military Image in Film*, Rev., exp. ed. (Lexington: The University Press of Kentucky, 2002), 129.
7 For an extended discussion of John Wayne's personal politics see Emanuel Levy, *John Wayne: Prophet of an American Way of Life* (New Jersey: The Scarecrow Press, Inc., 1988); Garry Wills, *John Wayne: The Politics of Celebrity* (London: Faber and Faber, 1997); Michael Munn, *John Wayne: The Man behind the Myth* (London: Robson Books, 2004); Randy Roberts, *John Wayne: American* (New York: Free Press, 1995).
8 Slotkin, *Gunfighter Nation*, 518–19.
9 Ibid., 518.
10 Levy, *John Wayne*, vii.
11 Ibid., 19.
12 See Wills, *John Wayne*.
13 'Texian' is an archaic term formerly applied to residents of Texas up until the mid-1800s. See Herbert Fletcher, *Handbook of Texas Online*, s.v. 'TEXIAN', 15 June 2010, accessed 14 December 2015, http://www.tshaonline.org/handbook/online/articles/pft05.
14 Eric Bentley, *Theatre of War: Comments on 32 Occasions* (New York: Viking Press, 1972), 311.
15 Ismail Xavier, *Allegories of Underdevelopment: Aesthetics and Politics in Modern Brazilian Cinema* (Minneapolis: University of Minnesota Press, 1997), 16.
16 John F. Kennedy, 'Democratic National Convention Nomination Acceptance Address – "The New Frontier"', 15 July 1960, American Rhetoric, accessed 13 April 2013, http://www.americanrhetoric.com/speeches/jfk1960dnc.htm.
17 For an extended discussion of the ideological underpinnings of the New Frontier presidency, see Bruce Miroff, *Pragmatic Illusions: The Presidential Politics of John*

F. Kennedy (New York: David McKay Company Inc., 1976) and Herbert S. Parmet, *JFK: The Presidency of John F. Kennedy* (New York: The Dial Press, 1983).
18. John F. Kennedy, 'Inaugural Address', 20 January 1961, American Rhetoric, accessed 18 April 2013, http://www.americanrhetoric.com/speeches/jfkinaugural.htm.
19. See Stanley Karnow, *Vietnam: A History* Rev. ed. (New York: Penguin, 1997), 264–5.
20. See ibid., 270.
21. Ibid., 380–92.
22. See George McTurnan Kahin, *Intervention: How America Became Involved in Vietnam* (New York: Alfred A. Knopf, 1986), 287.
23. Ibid., 357.
24. Ibid., 238.
25. Slotkin, *Gunfighter Nation*, 410.
26. Ibid., 474–86.
27. Michael Coyne, *The Crowded Prairie: American National Identity in the Hollywood Western* (London: I.B. Tauris, 1997), 105–6.
28. Stanley Corkin, *Cowboys as Cold Warriors: The Western as U.S. History* (Philadelphia: Temple University Press, 2004), 279.
29. Kennedy, 'Inaugural Address'.
30. Slotkin, *Gunfighter Nation*, 523–4.
31. Ibid., 410.
32. Ibid., 485–6.
33. See Berkman, *Cast a Giant Shadow*, 126–31.
34. See ibid., 54.
35. Kennedy, 'Inaugural Address'.
36. Corkin, *Cowboys as Cold Warriors*, 181.
37. See Nachman Ben-Yahuda, *The Masada Myth: Collective Memory and Mythmaking in Israel* (Madison: University of Wisconsin Press, 1995).
38. Rupert Wilkinson, *American Tough: The Tough-Guy Tradition and American Character* (Westport: Greenwood Press, 1984), 7.
39. Ibid.
40. Quoted in Patricia Erens, *The Jew in American Cinema* (Bloomington: Indiana University Press, 1984), 292.
41. Ibid.
42. Peter Homans, 'Puritanism Revisited: An Analysis of the Contemporary Screen-Image Western', in *Focus on the Western*, ed. Jack Nachbar (Englewood Cliffs: Prentice-Hall Inc., 1974), 87.
43. The cycle is generally understood to have begun with *The Gunfighter* (Henry King, 1950). Subsequent major films that followed in the wake of *The Gunfighter* include *Shane* (George Stevens, 1953) and *High Noon* (Fred Zinnemann, 1952). Lesser known films of this ilk that were produced during this period include *Man*

without a Star (King Vidor, 1955), *The Tall T* (Budd Boetticher, 1957), *The Proud Rebel* (Michael Curtiz, 1958), *At Gunpoint* (Alfred L. Werker, 1955), *Johnny Concho* (Don McGuire, 1956), *Man from Del Rio* (Harry Horner, 1956), *Fury at Showdown* (Gerd Oswald, 1957), *Gun for a Coward* (Abner Biberman, 1957) *Gun Glory* (Roy Rowland, 1957), and *The Last of the Fast Guns* (George Sherman, 1958).

44 Slotkin, *Gunfighter Nation*, 379–81.
45 Ibid., 400.
46 Ibid.
47 Ibid.
48 For an extended discussion of Douglas's role in 'breaking the blacklist' see Kirk Douglas, *I Am Spartacus!: Making a Film, Breaking the Blacklist* (New York: Open Road Integrated Media, 2012).
49 Leo Braudy, *The World in a Frame: What We See in Films* (New York: Anchor Press/Doubleday, 1976), 208.
50 Leonard Mustazza, 'Introduction', in *Frank Sinatra and Popular Culture: Essays on an American Icon*, ed. Leonard Mustazza (Connecticut: Praeger, 1998), 6.
51 See Wilkinson, *American* Tough, 87.
52 Shavelson, *How to Make a Jewish Movie*, 169–70.
53 Kennedy, 'Inaugural Address'.
54 '*Cast a Giant Shadow* review', *Time*, 15 April 1966, 66.
55 See Shavelson, *How to Make a Jewish Movie*, 18.
56 Ibid.
57 Ibid., 12.
58 Ibid., 22.
59 Ibid.
60 Kirk Douglas, *The Ragman's Son: An Autobiography* (London: Simon & Schuster, 1988), 382.
61 Roberts, *John Wayne*, 525.
62 Munn, *John Wayne*, 275–6.
63 Shavelson, *How to Make a Jewish Movie*, 231.
64 Corkin, *Cowboys as Cold Warriors*, 179.
65 Levy, *John Wayne*, 314.
66 Ibid.
67 Ibid.
68 For an extended discussion of the 'domino theory' see Frank Ninkovich, *Modernity and Power: A History of the Domino Theory in the Twentieth Century* (Chicago: University of Chicago, 1994).
69 Ibid., 288–9.
70 Andrew Martin, *Receptions of War: Vietnam in American Culture* (Norman: University of Oklahoma Press, 1993), 107.

71 Quoted in Suid, *Guts and Glory*, 248.
72 Ibid.
73 Levy, *John Wayne*, 319.
74 Ibid., 281.
75 Quoted in Julian Smith, *Looking Away: Hollywood and Vietnam* (New York: Charles Scribner's Sons, 1975), 129.
76 John Belton, *American Cinema/American Culture*, 4th ed. (New York: McGraw-Hill, 2013), 260.
77 Quoted in Suid, *Guts and Glory*, 254.
78 Ibid., 254–5.
79 For figures pertaining to *The Green Berets*' box office performance, see The Numbers, 'The Green Berets (1968)', The-numbers.com, accessed 13 May 2013, http://www.the-numbers.com/movies/1968/00232.php.
80 Bentley, *Theatre of War*, 311.
81 Rashid Khalidi, 'The United States and the Palestinians, 1977–2012: Three Key Moments', *Journal of Palestine Studies* 42, no. 4 (2013): 62.
82 Slotkin, *Gunfighter Nation*, 12.
83 Edward Said, *Orientalism*, Rev. ed. (New York: Vintage Books, 1994), 286.
84 For an extended discussion of 'genre memory', see Caryl Emerson and Gary Saul Emerson, *Mikhail Bakhtin: Creation of a Prosaics* (California: Stanford University Press, 1990), 271–305.
85 Slotkin, *Gunfighter Nation*, 15.
86 Following the discovery of the dead Vietnamese girl, Wayne doubles down by describing in detail a similar incident in which a woman died after being raped by 40 Viet Cong soldiers.
87 Ella Shohat, 'Gender and Culture of Empire: Toward a Feminist Ethnography of the Cinema', *Quarterly Review of Film and Video* 13, no. 1 (1991): 45–84.
88 Ibid., 49.

Chapter 4

1 For an extended discussion of the New Hollywood revolution, see Peter Biskind, *Easy Riders, Raging Bulls: How the Sex 'n' Drugs 'n' Rock 'n' Roll Generation Saved Hollywood* (London: Bloomsbury Publishing, 1999).
2 David A. Cook, *Lost Illusions: American Cinema in the Shadow of Watergate and Vietnam 1970–1979* (Berkeley: University of California Press, 2000), 251.
3 As of January 2016, *Airport* remains among the top 50 grossing films of all time (after adjusting for inflation). For figures pertaining to *Airport*'s box office

performance see Box Office Mojo, 'Airport (1970)', Boxofficemojo.com, accessed 30 May 2015, http://www.boxofficemojo.com/movies/?id=airport.htm.

4   For an extended discussion of the proliferation of international terrorist incidents throughout the 1970s see Gérard Chaliand and Arnaud Blin, 'From 1968 to Radical Islam', in *The History of Terrorism: From Antiquity to ISIS*, Updated ed., ed. Gérard Chaliand and Arnaud Blin (Oakland: University of California Press, 2016), 221–54.

5   Melani McAlister, *Epic Encounters: Culture, Media, & U.S. Interests in the Middle East since 1945*, Rev. ed. (Berkeley: University of California Press, 2005), 187–92.

6   Tony Shaw, *Cinematic Terror: A Global History of Terrorism on Film* (New York: Bloomsbury Publishing, 2015), 139. See pages 139–43 for Shaw's analysis of *The Delta Force*.

7   Bernard Drew, 'John Frankenheimer: His Rise and Fall', *American Film* 2, no. 5 (1977): 8.

8   See ibid; Aljean Harmetz, 'Frankenheimer Rides a Blimp to a Big, Fat Comeback', *New York Times*, 10 April 1977; G. D. Engle, 'An Interview with John Frankenheimer', *Film Criticism* 1, no. 2 (1977): 2–14.

9   See Drew, 'John Frankenheimer', 16; 'The "Black Sunday" Blimp Goes Up: Will It Soar – Or Crash?' *Chicago Daily News*, 12–13 March 1977.

10 For figures pertaining to *Black Sunday*'s box office performance see Box Office Mojo, 'Black Sunday (1977)', Boxofficemojo.com, accessed 23 October 2013, http://www.boxofficemojo.com/movies/?id=blacksunday.htm.

11 See Stephen Prince, *Firestorm: American Film in the Age of Terrorism* (New York: Columbia University Press, 2009).

12 See Lina Khatib, *Filming the Modern Middle East: Politics in the Cinemas of Hollywood and the Arab World* (New York: I.B. Tauris, 2006); Tim Jon Semmerling, *'Evil' Arabs in American Popular Film: Orientalist Fear* (Texas: University of Texas Press, 2006).

13 Not insignificantly, *Black Sunday* depicts an aircraft as the deliverer of destruction – a fact that doubtlessly fuelled post-9/11 interest in the film.

14 Corey K. Creekmur, 'John Frankenheimer's "War on Terror"', in *A Little Solitaire: John Frankenheimer and American Film*, ed. Murray Pomerance and R. Barton Palmer (New Brunswick: Rutgers University Press, 2011), 104.

15 Ibid.

16 Prince, *Firestorm*, 25–8.

17 Semmerling, *'Evil' Arabs in American Popular Film*, 93–123.

18 Ibid., 122.

19 Vincent Canby, 'Terror over the Super Bowl', *New York Times*, 1 April 1977.

20 For an authoritative discussion of the Baader-Meinhof group see Jillian Becker, *Hitler's Children: The Story of the Baader-Meinhof Terrorist Group* (London: Michael Joseph, 1977).

21 Harmetz, 'Frankenheimer Rides a Blimp to a Big, Fat Comeback', 10 April 1977.
22 Engle, 'An Interview with John Frankenheimer', 9.
23 Stephen Farber, 'Robert Evans's Rise from Grade-B Actor to A-Plus Producer', *New York Times*, 15 August 1976.
24 Harmetz, 'Frankenheimer Rides a Blimp to a Big Fat Comeback', 10 April 1977.
25 See John E. Mueller, *War, Presidents and Public Opinion* (New York: John Wiley & Sons, Inc., 1973), 85–7.
26 Stanley Karnow, *Vietnam: A History*, Rev. ed. (New York: Penguin, 1997), 559.
27 Ibid.
28 Ibid., 536–81.
29 Daniel C. Hallin, *The 'Uncensored War': The Media and Vietnam* (New York: Oxford University Press, 1986), 168–74.
30 Karnow, *Vietnam*, 558–61.
31 Kim McQuaid, *The Anxious Years: America in the Vietnam-Watergate Era* (New York: Basic Books, Inc., 1989), 17.
32 For an extended discussion of the My Lai massacre, see Seymour M. Hersh, *My Lai 4: A Report on the Massacre and Its Aftermath* (New York: Random House, 1970).
33 Quoted in ibid., 141.
34 'The Clamor over Calley: Who Shares the Guilt?' *Time*, 12 April 1971, 19.
35 Mueller, *War, Presidents and Public Opinion*, 95–8.
36 Richard Nixon, 'Address to the Nation on the Situation in Southeast Asia', 30 April, 1970, EdWeb, accessed 20 October 2013, http://www.edwebproject.org/sideshow/resources/nixon.430speech.html.
37 Ibid.
38 For an extended discussion of the Vietnam Syndrome, see Geoff Simons, *Vietnam Syndrome: Impact on US Foreign Policy* (New York: St. Martin's Press, 1998).
39 Quoted in Karnow, *Vietnam*, 16.
40 See Robert Bly, 'The Vietnam War and the Erosion of Male Confidence', in *The Vietnam Reader*, ed. Walter Capps (New York: Routledge, 1991), 82–6.
41 Ibid., 82.
42 Michael Kimmel, *Manhood in America: A Cultural History* (New York: The Free Press, 1996), 270–1.
43 Ibid., 272.
44 Keith Beattie, *The Scar That Binds: American Culture and the Vietnam War*, (New York: New York University Press, 1998), 23.
45 Ruth R. Wisse, *The Schlemiel as Modern Hero* (Chicago: The University of Chicago Press, 1971), 72.
46 For an extended discussion of the events that precipitated the Six Day War, see Michael Oren, *Six Days of War: June 1967 and the Making of the Modern Middle East* (New York: Oxford University Press, 2002), 1–32.

47 Michael Oren, *Power, Faith, and Fantasy: America in the Middle East 1776 to the Present* (New York: W. W. Norton, 2007), 526.
48 Oren, *Six Days of War*, 313.
49 See Michael W. Sulieman, 'The American Mass Media and the June Conflict', in *The Arab-Israeli Confrontation of June 1967: An Arab Perspective*, ed. Ibrahim Abu-Lughod (Evanston: Northwestern University Press, 1970), 138.
50 Janice Monti Belkaoui, 'Images of Arabs and Israelis in the Prestige Press, 1966–1974', *Journalism Quarterly* 55, no. 4 (Winter 1978): 732–8.
51 Eytan Gilboa, *American Public Opinion of Israel and the Arab-Israeli Conflict* (Massachusetts: Lexington Books, 1987), 49.
52 Quoted in Oren, *Six Days of War*, 307–9.
53 'The Three-Day Blitz from Gaza to Suez', *U.S. News & World Report*, 19 June 1967, 33.
54 McAlister, *Epic Encounters*, 157.
55 Oren, *Power, Faith, and Fantasy*, 527.
56 Quoted in Douglas Little, *American Orientalism: The United States and the Middle East since 1945*, 3rd ed. (Chapel Hill: University of North Carolina Press, 2008), 32.
57 For an extended discussion of Operation Thunderbolt, see Edgar O'Ballance, *Language of Violence: The Blood Politics of Terrorism* (San Rafael: Presidio Press, 1979), 239–58.
58 Quoted in Terrence Smith, 'Israelis Return with 103 Rescued in Uganda Raid', *New York Times*, 5 July 1976.
59 Quoted in Kathleen Teltsch, 'Rescue by Israel Acclaimed by U.S. at Debate in U.N.', *New York Times*, 13 July 1976.
60 'A Legend is Born', *New York Times*, 6 July 1976.
61 Fran Starr, 'Israel's Entebbe Raid is Cheered as a Gutsy Performance', *Chicago Tribune*, 7 July 1976.
62 Paul Breines, *Tough Jews: Political Fantasies and the Moral Dilemma of American Jewry* (New York: Basic Books, 1990), 5.
63 James Burnham, 'Reflections on Entebbe', *National Review*, 6 August 1976, 834.
64 'Will "Hot Pursuit" Stop Terrorism?' & 'When U.S. Rescue Mission Fizzled', *U.S. News & World Report*, 19 July 1976, 30–2.
65 McAlister, *Epic Encounters*, 187.
66 Susan Jeffords, *The Remasculinization of America: Gender and the Vietnam War* (Bloomington: Indiana University Press, 1989), 5.
67 For an extended discussion of the ways in which these films construct the ideal of American victimhood see Beattie, *The Scar That Binds*; Gilbert Adair, *Vietnam on Film: From the Green Berets to Apocalypse Now* (London: Proteus, 1981); Edwin A. Martini, *Invisible Enemies: The American War on Vietnam, 1975–2000* (Amherst: University of Massachusetts Press, 2007), 46–77.

68 Quoted in Martini, *Invisible Enemies*, 45–6. For an extended discussion on the ideal of the United States as the war's true victim see Beattie, *The Scar That Binds*, 11–57.
69 This scene implies the alignment of Black September with North Vietnamese Communists, in turn framing the Arab-Israeli conflict as an extension of the Cold War.
70 Nixon, 'Address to the Nation on the Situation in Southeast Asia', 30 April 1970.
71 Semmerling, *'Evil' Arabs in American Popular Film*, 96.
72 For an extended discussion of the POW/MIA myth, see H. Bruce Franklin, *M.I.A., or, Mythmaking in America* (New York: Lawrence Hill Books, 1992).
73 For an extended discussion on the 'stabbed-in-the-back' myth, see Beattie, *The Scar That Binds*, 21–2; Jeffords, *The Remasculinization of America*, 122–3.
74 As noted by Beattie, when cultural productions invoke the malady of impotence it generally functions to symbolize 'a loss of power [and/or] psychic trauma'. See Beattie, *The Scar That Binds*, 17–21.
75 Semmerling, *'Evil' Arabs in American Popular Film*, 104.
76 Michael Rogin, 'Kiss Me Deadly: Communism, Motherhood, and Cold War Movies', in *Ronald Reagan, the Movie: And Other Episodes in Political Demonology* (California: University of California Press, 1987), 236–71; Rebecca Bell-Metereau, 'Stealth, Sexuality, and Cult Status in *The Manchurian Candidate* and *Seconds*', in *A Little Solitaire: John Frankenheimer and American Film*, ed. Murray Pomerance and R. Barton Palmer (New Brunswick: Rutgers University Press, 2011), 48–61.
77 Philip Wylie, *Generation of Vipers* (Illinois: Dalkey Archive Press, [1942] 1996), 194–217.
78 Kimmel, *Manhood in America*, 261–90.
79 Bell-Metereau, 'Stealth, Sexuality, and Cult Status in *The Manchurian Candidate* and *Seconds*', 52.
80 Ibid.
81 Rogin, 'Kiss Me Deadly', 252.
82 Here it is worth noting that Lansbury played a similarly domineering mother in *All Fall Down*, another film directed by Frankenheimer that was released in 1962.
83 The term 'Backlash' is borrowed from the book of the same title by Susan Faludi, in which she argues for the existence of a media-driven campaign against the social gains made by women throughout the 1970s. See Susan Faludi, *Backlash: The Undeclared War against Women* (London: Vintage, 1992).
84 Rupert Wilkinson, *American Tough: The Tough-Guy Tradition and American Character* (Westport: Greenwood Press, 1984), 87.
85 Charles Higham and Joel Greenberg, 'John Frankenheimer (1969)', in *John Frankenheimer: Interviews, Essays, and Profiles*, ed. Stephen B. Armstrong (Plymouth: Scarecrow Press, 2013), 28.
86 Harmetz, 'Frankenheimer Rides a Blimp to a Big, Fat Comeback', 10 April 1977.

87 Semmerling also identifies Kabakov as a modern-day incarnation of 'the man who knows Indians'. See Semmerling, *'Evil' Arabs in American Popular Film*, 110.
88 Richard Slotkin, *Gunfighter Nation: The Myth of the Frontier in Twentieth-Century America* (New York: University of Oklahoma Press, 1998), 16.
89 Ibid., 14.
90 The first three films in the Dirty Harry series were all released in the six years prior to the release of *Black Sunday*; see *Dirty Harry* (Don Siegel, 1971), *Magnum Force* (Ted Post, 1973), and *The Enforcer* (James Fargo, 1976).
91 The novel also features a love interest for Kabakov who assists him in foiling the terrorist plot (she provides some advice in relation to criminal profiling and also puts him in touch with acquaintances of hers that help him uncover clues as to the identity of the terrorists).
92 Slotkin, *Gunfighter Nation*, 400.
93 For figures pertaining to *The Delta Force*'s box office performance see Box Office Mojo, 'The Delta Force (1986)', Boxofficemojo.com, accessed 25 October 2013, http://www.boxofficemojo.com/movies/?id=deltaforce.htm.
94 See Robert Fisk, *Pity the Nation: Lebanon at War*, 3rd ed. (New York: Oxford University Press, 2001), 605–8; Bethami A. Dobkin, *Tales of Terror: Television News and the Construction of the Terrorist Threat* (New York: Praeger, 1992), 65.
95 Shaw, *Cinematic Terror*, 140.
96 See, for example, Vincent Canby, 'Chuck Norris: The Public Has Made Him a Star', *New York Times*, 12 May 1985; Judy Klemesrud, 'Chuck Norris – Strong, Silent and Popular', *New York Times*, 1 September 1985.
97 The inherent toughness of the Marvin persona is memorably asserted in Quentin Tarantino's *Reservoir Dogs* (1992) where, following a quarrel between the hyper-violent gangsters Mr. Blonde (Michael Madsen) and Mr. White (Harvey Keitel), Mr. Blonde remarks to Mr. White, 'I bet you're a big Lee Marvin fan. Me too, I love that guy'.
98 See Yvonne Tasker, *Spectacular Bodies: Gender, Genre and the Action Cinema* (London: Routledge, 1993).
99 See Andrew Britton, 'Blissing Out: The Politics of Reaganite Entertainment (1986)', in *Britton on Film: The Complete Film Criticism of Andrew Britton*, ed. Barry Keith Grant (Michigan: Wayne State University Press, 2009), 97–154.
100 Ibid., 97.
101 Robert Kolker, *A Cinema of Loneliness*, 4th ed. (New York: Oxford University Press, 2011), 282.
102 Ibid., 284.
103 Ibid., 283.
104 John Orman, *Comparing Presidential Behavior: Carter, Reagan, and the Macho Presidential Style* (New York: Greenwood Press, 1987), 17, 95.

105 John Mihalic, 'Hair on the President's Chest', *Wall Street Journal*, 11 May 1984.
106 Orman, *Comparing Presidential Behavior*, 18.
107 For an example of Reagan being marketed to the public as a cowboy see Roger Rosenblatt, 'Out of the Past, Fresh Choices for the Future: Invoking Old Values, Ronald Reagan Must Make Them Work for the '80s', *Time*, 5 January 1981, 10–23.
108 Ronald Reagan, 'Inaugural Address', 20 January 1981, The American Presidency Project, accessed 25 October 2013, http://www.presidency.ucsb.edu/ws/?pid=43130.
109 Ronald Reagan, 'Address to the National Association of Evangelicals', 8 March 1983, Voices of Democracy, accessed 25 October 2013, http://voicesofdemocracy.umd.edu/reagan-evil-empire-speech-text/.
110 For Carter's characterization of Vietnam as a 'mistake', see 'The Second Carter-Ford Presidential Debate', 6 October 1976, Commission on Presidential Debates, accessed 25 October2013, http://www.debates.org/index.php?page=october-6-1976-debate-transcript.
111 For Reagan's characterization of Vietnam as a 'noble cause', see Ronald Reagan, 'Address to the Veterans of Foreign Wars Convention in Chicago', 18 August 1980, The American Presidency Project, accessed 25 October 2013, http://www.presidency.ucsb.edu/ws/?pid=85202. See also Ronald Reagan, 'Remarks at Dedication Ceremonies for the Vietnam Veterans Memorial Statue', 11 November 1984, The American Presidency Project, accessed 25 October 2013, http://www.presidency.ucsb.edu/ws/?pid=39414.
112 Kolker, *A Cinema of Loneliness*, 280.
113 Michael Rogin, 'Ronald Reagan, the Movie', in *Ronald Reagan, the Movie: And Other Episodes in Political Demonology* (California: University of California Press, 1987), 7.
114 Tasker, *Spectacular Bodies*, 92.
115 Ibid.
116 Ibid., 93.
117 Jeffords, *The Remasculinization of America*, 126–36.
118 Kolker, *A Cinema of Loneliness*, 287.
119 For an extended discussion of Operation Eagle Claw, see Charles G. Cogan, 'Desert One and Its Disorders', *The Journal of Military History* 67, no. 1 (January 2003): 201–16.
120 See 'Debacle in the Desert', *Time*, 5 May 1980, 12–25.
121 Kolker, *A Cinema of Loneliness*, 284.
122 Ibid., 285–9.
123 Devoted cinephiles are perhaps more likely to identify Lee Marvin's Anderson as the surrogate of Reagan than they are Richard Crenna's Trautman, as a consequence of the respective film careers of Marvin and Reagan being indelibly

linked due to their both starring in *The Killers* (Don Siegel, 1964). Marvin, receiving top billing for the first time in his career, played an assassin employed by a crime boss played by Reagan, who was making his final appearance in a theatrically released film. In an unfortunate irony, *The Delta Force* represented the final performance of Marvin's career.

124   Ibid., 285.
125   Jeffords, *The Remasculinization of America*, 130–38.
126   Kolker, *A Cinema of Loneliness*, 282.
127   Britton, 'Blissing Out', 114.
128   Kolker, *A Cinema of Loneliness*, 283.
129   In addition to borrowing elements of its plot, *The Delta Force* features a number of actors who also appear in *Mivtsa Yonatan*, including Shaike Ophir, Assi Dayan, Richard Selano, Yitshak Aloni and Yehuda Efroni. Furthermore, the casting of Martin Balsam as a passenger further bolsters the film's bonds to the Entebbe raid, as he also appeared as a passenger on the hijacked plane in the TV movie *Raid on Entebbe*.

Chapter 5

1   Robert Kolker, *A Cinema of Loneliness*, 4th ed. (New York: Oxford University Press, 2011), 290.
2   Michael Rogin, 'Preface', in *Ronald Reagan, the Movie: And Other Episodes in Political Demonology* (Berkeley: University of California Press, 1987), xiii.
3   Ibid., xix.
4   Michael Rogin, 'American Political Demonology: A Retrospective', in *Ronald Reagan, the Movie: And Other Episodes in Political Demonology* (Berkeley: University of California Press, 1987), 296.
5   See, for example, the films *Black Hawk Down* (Ridley Scott, 2001), *United 93* (Paul Greengrass, 2006), *The Kingdom* (Peter Berg, 2007), *Iron Man* (Jon Favreau, 2008), *Body of Lies* (Ridley Scott, 2008), *The Hurt Locker* (Kathryn Bigelow, 2008) and *American Sniper* (Clint Eastwood, 2014). Similarly themed television programmes produced during this period include *24* (2001–2010), *Sleeper Cell* (2005–2006) and *Homeland* (2011–2015).
6   George Jonas, *Vengeance*, Rev. ed. (London: Harper Perennial, 2006).
7   For figures pertaining to *Munich*'s box office performance see Box Office Mojo, 'Munich (2005)', Boxofficemojo.com, accessed 12 May 2015, http://www.boxofficemojo.com/movies/?id=munich.htm.
8   The notion of Spielberg as a public historian has been further bolstered in recent years with the release of *Lincoln* (2012), which centres on Lincoln's struggle to have the Thirteenth Amendment to the United States Constitution passed by the United

States House of Representatives. In the 29 November 2012 edition of the *New York Times* Philip Zelikow, Professor of History at the University of Virginia, published a piece titled 'Steven Spielberg, Historian', in which he claimed that the speculations within *Lincoln* 'actually advance the way historians will continue this subject'.
9. Linda Williams, 'Why I Did Not Want to Write This Essay', *Signs* 30, no. 1 (Autumn 2004): 1269.
10. Hannah Arendt, *Eichmann in Jerusalem: A Report on the Banality of Evil*, Rev. ed. (New York: Penguin Books, 2006), 279.
11. Robert Burgoyne, *The Hollywood Historical Film* (Massachusetts: Blackwell Publishing, 2008), 101.
12. Leon Wieseltier, 'Hits', *New Republic*, 19 December 2005, 38.
13. Ibid.
14. Gabriel Schoenfeld, 'Spielberg's "Munich"', *Commentary*, 1 February 2006, accessed 1 May 2014, https://www.commentarymagazine.com/article/spielberg's-'munich'/.
15. Ibid.
16. Ibid.
17. David Brooks, 'What "Munich" Left Out', *New York Times*, 11 December 2005.
18. Ibid.
19. Michael Medved, '"Munich" Distorts History', *USA Today*, 1 October 2006, accessed 2 May 2014, http://usatoday30.usatoday.com/news/opinion/editorials/2006-01-10-munich_x.htm.
20. Charles Krauthammer, '"Munich," the Travesty', *Washington Post*, 13 January 2006, accessed 2 May 2014, http://www.washingtonpost.com/wp-dyn/content/article/2006/01/12/AR2006011201541.html.
21. Hannah Brown, 'Munich: Portentous and preachy', *Jerusalem Post*, 19 January 2006, accessed 1 May 2014, http://www.jpost.com/Arts-and-Culture/Entertainment/Munich-Portentous-and-preachy.
22. Jonathan Tobin, 'Worth getting upset about', *Jerusalem Post*, 29 December 2005, accessed 2 May 2014, http://www.jpost.com/Business/Worth-getting-upset-about.
23. Gary Younge, 'Israeli consul attacks Spielberg's Munich as "problematic"', *Guardian*, 12 December 2005, accessed 1 May 2014, http://www.theguardian.com/world/2005/dec/12/israel.filmnews.
24. Morton A. Klein, 'ZOA: Don't See Spielberg's "Munich" Unless You Like Humanizing Terrorists & Dehumanizing Israelis', *Zionist Organization of America*, 27 December 2005, accessed 2 May 2014, http://zoa.org/2005/12/102082-zoa-dont-see-spielbergs-munich-unless-you-like-humanizing-terrorists-dehumanizing-israelis/#ixzz38mEGcIDt.
25. 'SPIEGEL Interview with Steven Spielberg: I Would Die for Israel', *Der Spiegel*, 26 January 2006, accessed 3 May 2014, http://www.spiegel.de/international/spiegel/spiegel-interview-with-steven-spielberg-i-would-die-for-israel-a-397378.html.

26　Ibid.
27　Jim Emerson, 'Spy vs. Spy: The Morality of Munich', *RogerEbert.com*, 14 December 2005, accessed 2 May 2014, http://www.rogerebert.com/scanners/spy-vs-spy-the-morality-of-munich.
28　Richard Schickel, 'Spielberg Takes on Terror', *Time*, 4 December 2005, accessed 5 May 2014, http://content.time.com/time/subscriber/article/0,33009,1137679-1,00.html.
29　Jonas, *Vengeance*, 335.
30　Ibid., 262–3.
31　Ibid., 200.
32　Ibid., 216.
33　Ibid., 309–11.
34　Aaron J. Klein, *Striking Back: The 1972 Munich Olympics Massacre and Israel's Deadly Response* (New York: Random House, 2005).
35　Michele Norris, 'Interview: Aaron Klein Discusses "Striking Back," A Look at the Munich Killings, Aftermath', *All Things Considered*, 22 December 2005, accessed 4 May 2014, http://www.npr.org/programs/atc/transcripts/2005/dec/051222.siegel.html.
36　Michelle Goldberg, 'The War on Munich', *Salon*, 20 December 2005, accessed 2 May 2014, http://www.salon.com/2005/12/20/munich_3/.
37　Brooks, 'What "Munich" Left Out', 11 December 2005.
38　Medved, '"Munich" Distorts History', 1 October 2006.
39　Ibid.
40　Marie Syrkin, *Golda Meir Speaks Out* (London: Weidenfeld and Nicolson, 1973), 242.
41　Rashid Khalidi, 'The United States and the Palestinians, 1977–2012: Three Key Moments', *Journal of Palestine Studies* 42, no. 4 (Summer 2013): 62.
42　Linda Williams, *Playing the Race Card: Melodramas of Black and White from Uncle Tom to O.J. Simpson* (Princeton: Princeton University Press, 2001), 44.
43　In regards to the bombing of Palestinian bases in Lebanon and Syria, Klein writes: 'At 1550 hours, on Friday, September 8, on the eve of the Jewish New Year, two dozen fighter jets from the Ramat David base in northern Israel struck deep in Lebanese and Syrian territory. It was the IDF's most devastating attack in two years – air force planes bombed eleven Palestinian bases, including one just five miles from Damascus, killing two hundred terrorists and eleven Lebanese civilians. Hundreds more, both terrorists and civilians, were injured. But the dead and injured had no connection with Black September of the massacre in Munich'. See Klein, *Striking Back*, 94.
44　See Jonas, *Vengeance*, 144–57; Klein, *Striking Back*, 129–34.
45　Williams, *Playing the Race Card*, 33.
46　Ibid.
47　Jonas, *Vengeance*, 184–5.

48 Ibid., 219–20. Jonas refers to the incident but attributes it to another Mossad hit squad operating under the umbrella of Operation Wrath of God. See also Klein, *Striking Back*, 184–98.
49 Klein, *Striking Back*, 197.
50 In *Vengeance* the victim's name is reported as being Abad al-Chir; see Jonas, *Vengeance*, 158–66. Klein makes no mention of a newlywed couple in his discussion of the assassination of Al Bashir (who, in *Striking Back*, is referred to as Hussain Abu-Khair); see Klein, *Striking Back*, 135–41.
51 Richard Slotkin, *Gunfighter Nation: The Myth of the Frontier in Twentieth-Century America* (New York: University of Oklahoma Press, 1998), 14.
52 Roger Ebert, 'I Knew I Would Lose Friends over This Film', *Sunday Telegraph*, 1 January 2006, accessed 3 May 2014, http://www.telegraph.co.uk/news/worldnews/1506765/I-knew-I-would-lose-friends-over-this-film.html.
53 For an extended discussion of the history of Hollywood's demonological representations of Arabs, see Tim Jon Semmerling, *'Evil' Arabs in American Popular Film: Orientalist Fear* (Texas: University of Texas Press, 2006); Jack Shaheen, *Guilty: Hollywood's Verdict on Arabs after 9/11* (Massachusetts: Olive Branch Press, 2008); Jack Shaheen, *Reel Bad Arabs: How Hollywood Vilifies a People* (New York: Olive Branch Press, 2001).
54 Miriam Hansen, '*Schindler's List* Is Not *Shoah*: Second Commandment, Popular Modernism, and Public Memory', in *Spielberg's Holocaust: Critical Perspectives on* Schindler's List, ed. Yosefa Loshitzky (Bloomington: Indiana University Press, 1997), 79.
55 At the time of *Munich*'s release in 2005 Eric Bana was best known in the United States for his role as an American soldier in Ridley Scott's 2001 film *Black Hawk Down*, and as the leader of the Trojan forces in the big-budget mythical epic *Troy* (Wolfgang Peterson, 2003). Moreover, a mere two months prior to the release of *Munich* it was announced that Daniel Craig would be assuming the role of James Bond for the foreseeable future.
56 Quoted in Chris Abbott, *21 Speeches That Shaped Our World: The People and Ideas That Changed the Way We Think* (London: Rider, 2010), 125.
57 Ibid.
58 Richard Clarke, *Against All Enemies: Inside America's War on Terror* (New York: The Free Press, 2004), 24.
59 Stephen P. Marks, 'International Law and the "War on Terrorism": Post 9/11 Responses by the United States and Asia Pacific Countries', *Asia Pacific Law Review* 14, no. 1 (2006): 59.
60 For an extended discussion of the United States' circumvention of domestic and international law in its prosecution of the War on Terror, see Martin Henn, *Under*

the Color of Law: The Bush Administration's Subversion of U.S. Constitutional and International Law in the War on Terror (Lanham: Lexington Books, 2010); Seymour M. Hersh, *Chain of Command: The Road from 9/11 to Abu Ghraib* (London: Penguin Books, 2004).

61 For an extended discussion of the pervasiveness of the notion that 'everything changed' in the wake of the events of 11 September 2001, see Douglas Kellner, 'September 11, Social Theory and Democratic Politics', *Theory, Culture & Society* 19, no. 3 (August 2002): 147–59.

62 In *Vengeance* Meir is described as making comments similar to those she makes in this scene upon first meeting Avner and offering him the position to lead the team. See Jonas, *Vengeance*, 70.

63 Ibid., 182–97.

64 Ibid., 215–28.

65 Here it is worth nothing that in the ending of the HBO miniseries *Sword of Gideon* (Michael Anderson, 1986), which is a far more faithful adaptation of Jonas's book, Avner and Ephraim are depicted as clashing in a non-descript New York café in scenes that totally avoid the heavy-handed symbolism of the denouement of *Munich*. *Sword of Gideon* instead ends with an epilogue that details Avner's eventual return to Israel to fight in the Yom Kippur War. This ending serves to position the film as one that is fundamentally about Israel, as opposed to one that is an appropriation of Israeli history for the purpose of expressing uniquely American anxieties.

66 For an extended discussion of these and other consciously post-9/11 films, see Douglas Kellner, *Cinema Wars: Hollywood Film and Politics in the Bush-Cheney Era* (West Sussex: Wiley-Blackwell, 2010).

67 Slotkin, *Gunfighter Nation*, 12.

68 Joseph McBride, *Steven Spielberg: A Biography*, 3rd ed. (London: Faber and Faber Limited, 1997), 501.

69 Andrew Britton, 'Blissing Out: The Politics of Reaganite Entertainment (1986)', in *Britton on Film: The Complete Film Criticism of Andrew Britton*, ed. Barry Keith Grant (Michigan: Wayne State University Press, 2009), 97. See also Robin Wood, *Hollywood from Vietnam to Reagan* (New York: Columbia University Press, 1986), 162–88.

70 Kolker, *A Cinema of Loneliness*, 274.

71 Britton, 'Blissing Out', 147.

72 Wood, *Hollywood from Vietnam to Reagan*, 180.

73 For an extended discussion on the inherent conservatism of *War of the Worlds*, see Lester D. Friedman, *Citizen Spielberg* (Chicago: University of Illinois Press, 2006), 151–5.

74 Jesse Lemisch, 'Film: Black Agency in the Amistad Uprising: Or, You've Taken Our Cinque and Gone', *Souls: A Critical Journal of Black Politics, Culture, and Society* 1, no. 1 (1999): 57–70.

75 Claude Lanzmann, 'Schindler's List Is an Impossible Story', *Approaches to the Humanities*, Spring 2007, accessed 8 May 2014, http://www.phil.uu.nl/~rob/2007/hum291/lanzmannschindler.shtml.
76 J. Hoberman, 'Spielberg's Oskar', *Village Voice*, 21 December 1993, 63.
77 Yosefa Loshitzky, 'Introduction', in *Spielberg's Holocaust: Critical Perspectives on Schindler's List*, ed. Yosefa Loshitzky (Bloomington: Indiana University Press, 1997), 4.
78 Hansen, *Schindler's List* Is Not *Shoah*, 99.

Conclusion

1 Matthew Alford, *Reel Power: Hollywood Cinema and American Supremacy* (London: Pluto Press, 2010), 5.
2 Hayden White, 'Historiography and Historiophoty', *The American Historical Review* 93, no. 5 (December 1988): 1193.
3 Ibid.
4 Robert A. Rosenstone, 'History in Images/History in Words: Reflections on the Possibility of Really Putting History onto Film', *The American Historical Review* 93, no. 5 (December 1988): 1174.
5 Thomas J. McCormick, *America's Half-Century: United States Foreign Policy in the Cold War*, 2nd ed. (Baltimore: The Johns Hopkins Press, 1995), 11–12.
6 Ilan Pappé, 'The Israeli Fallacy Is Over', *Pravda.ru*, 19 February 2011, accessed 17 September 2012, http://english.pravda.ru/opinion/columnists/19-02-2011/116945-The_Israeli_fallacy_is_over-0/.
7 Michael Rogin, 'American Political Demonology: A Retrospective', in *Ronald Reagan, the Movie: And Other Episodes in Political Demonology* (Berkeley: University of California Press, 1987), 274.
8 Michael Rogin, 'Preface', in *Ronald Reagan, the Movie: And Other Episodes in Political Demonology* (Berkeley: University of California Press, 1987), xiii.
9 Michael Rogin, 'Political Repression in the United States', in *Ronald Reagan, the Movie: And Other Episodes in Political Demonology* (Berkeley: University of California Press, 1987), 68.
10 Arun Kundnani, *The Muslims Are Coming!: Islamophobia, Extremism, and the Domestic War on Terror* (London: Verso, 2014), 18.
11 For an extended discussion of the ways in which Arabs and Muslims have been demonized in the wake of the 9/11 attacks, see ibid., 40–77.
12 Matthew Bernstein, 'Introduction', in *Visions of the East: Orientalism in Film*, ed. Matthew Bernstein and Gaylyn Studlar (London: I.B. Tauris, 1997), 3.
13 Quoted in ibid., 11.

14 Bosley Crowther, 'Screen: "The Ten Commandments": De Mille's Production Opens at Criterion', *New York Times*, 9 November 1956.
15 For a detailed breakdown of American attitudes regarding Israel and Egypt during and immediately after the Suez-Sinai crisis see Eytan Gilboa, *American Public Opinion of Israel and the Arab-Israeli Conflict* (Massachusetts: Lexington Books, 1987), 29–31.
16 Michelle Mart, *Eye on Israel: How America Came to View Israel as an Ally* (Albany: State University of New York Press, 2006), 151.
17 Ibid., 57.
18 Ironically, members of the real Egyptian army play Rameses's soldiers. As detailed in the film's DVD commentary by Katherine Orrison, the film was made with enthusiastic co-operation of the Egyptian government; Nasser was a fan of DeMille based on what he considered a favourable depiction of the Muslim legend Saladin in DeMille's *The Crusades* (1935). Thus, the Egyptians chasing the Hebrews as they make their escape from Egypt serves as a cinematic playing out of the familiar refrain of the Arabs' desire to 'drive the Israelis into the sea.' See Katherine Orrison, 'Commentary', *The Ten Commandments*, special collector's ed., DVD, directed by Cecil B. DeMille (Paramount, 2004).
19 Jack Shaheen, *Reel Bad Arabs: How Hollywood Vilifies a People* (New York: Olive Branch Press, 2001), 550–1.
20 In addition to *Reel Bad Arabs,* see also Shaheen's *The TV Arab* (Ohio: Bowling Green State University Popular Press, 1984), and *Guilty: Hollywood's Verdict on Arabs after 9/11* (Massachusetts: Olive Branch Press, 2008).
21 Philip French argues that in *Cheyenne Autumn* the comparison is made between the genocide of the Native Americans and the Nazi Holocaust of the Jews through the performance of Karl Malden as Captain Wessells, a German commandant in charge of a military prison in which the Cheyenne are incarcerated under truly wretched conditions. See Philip French, 'The Indian in the Western Movie', in *The Pretend Indians: Images of Native Americans in the Movies*, ed. Gretchen M. Bataille and Charles L. P. Silet (Ames: The Iowa State University Press, 1980), 104–5.
22 Quoted in Adel Safty, *Might Over Right: How the Zionists Took Over Palestine* (Reading: Garnet Publishing, 2009), x.
23 For an extended discussion of how in contemporary times 'the Holocaust saturates Israeli consciousness' and is exploited 'to justify the violence of the state', see Jacqueline Rose, *The Question of Zion* (Carlton: Melbourne University Press, 2005), 141–3.
24 As discussed in Chapter 1, throughout the collective conscience of post–Second World War America, there existed a casual and deliberate conflation of Nazi and Communist ideologies under the inclusive rubric of 'totalitarianism', to which the

United States was diametrically opposed. See Les K. Adler and Thomas G. Paterson, 'Red Fascism: The Merger of Nazi Germany and Soviet Russia in the American Image of Totalitarianism, 1930s–1950s', *The American Historical Review* 75, no. 4 (April 1970): 1046–64.

25 Quoted in Safty, *Might Over Right*, 176.
26 Ella Shohat and Robert Stam, *Unthinking Eurocentrism: Multiculturalism and the Media* (London: Routledge, 1994), 2. Here it is worth noting that contemporaneous Hollywood Westerns often featured similarly overt celebrations of democratic process; see, for instance, the statehood convention sequence in *The Man Who Shot Liberty Valance* (John Ford, 1962).
27 Tony Shaw, *Cinematic Terror: A Global History of Terrorism on Film* (New York: Bloomsbury Publishing, 2015), 62.
28 For an extended discussion of the bombing of the King David Hotel see Thurston Clarke, *By Blood and Fire: The Attack on the King David Hotel* (London: Hutchinson Group, 1981).
29 Shaw, *Cinematic Terror*, 75.
30 Quoted in Safty, *Might Over Right*, 177.
31 Peter Homans, 'Puritanism Revisited: An Analysis of the Contemporary Screen-Image Western', in *Focus on the Western*, ed. Jack Nachbar (New Jersey: Prentice-Hall, 1974), 86.
32 Shohat and Stam, *Unthinking Eurocentrism*, 3.
33 Safty, *Might Over Right*, 125.
34 Quoted in ibid., 185.
35 Ibid., 190.
36 Ibid., 186.
37 Ibid., 180.
38 Ibid.
39 Stephen Prince, *Firestorm: American Film in the Age of Terrorism* (New York: Columbia University Press, 2009), 23. A notable example of American terrorists in pre-1980s Hollywood cinema is the suicidal passenger played by Van Heflin in *Airport* (George Seaton, 1970).
40 Ibid., 25.
41 See 'The "Black Sunday" Blimp Goes Up: Will It Soar – Or Crash?' *Chicago Daily News*, 12–13 March 1977.

Bibliography

Books and journal articles

Abbott, Chris. *21 Speeches That Shaped Our World: The People and Ideas That Changed the Way We Think*. London: Rider, 2010.

Abrams, Nathan. *The New Jew in Film: Exploring Jewishness and Judaism in Contemporary Cinema*. New Jersey: Rutgers University Press, 2012.

Adair, Gilbert. *Vietnam on Film: From The Green Berets to Apocalypse Now*. London: Proteus, 1981.

Adler, Les K. and Thomas G. Paterson. 'Red Fascism: The Merger of Nazi Germany and Soviet Russia in the American Image of Totalitarianism, 1930s–1950s'. *The American Historical Review* 75, no. 4 (April 1970): 1046–64.

Alford, Matthew. *Reel Power: Hollywood Cinema and American Supremacy*. London: Pluto Press, 2010.

Altman, Rick. *The American Film Musical*. Bloomington & Indianapolis: Indiana University Press, 1987.

Anderson, Benedict. *Imagined Communities: Reflections on the Origin and Spread of Nationalism*, Rev. ed. London: Verso, 1991.

Arendt, Hannah. *Eichmann in Jerusalem: A Report on the Banality of Evil*. Rev. ed. New York: Penguin Books, 2006.

Babington, Bruce and Peter William Evans. *Biblical Epics: Sacred Narrative in the Hollywood Cinema*. Manchester: Manchester University Press, 1993.

Balio, Tino. *Hollywood in the Age of Television*. London: Unwin Hyman, 1990.

Balio, Tino. *United Artists, Volume 2, 1951–1978: The Company That Changed the Film Industry*. Madison: The University of Wisconsin Press, 2009.

Bartov, Omer. *The 'Jew' in Cinema: From The Golem to Don't Touch My Holocaust*. Indiana: Indiana University Press, 2005.

Bazin, André. 'The Western: Or the American Film Par Excellence'. In *What Is Cinema? Vol. II*, translated by Hugh Gray, 140–8. Berkeley: University of California Press, 1971.

Beattie, Keith. *The Scar That Binds: American Culture and the Vietnam War*. New York: New York University Press, 1998.

Becker, Jillian. *Hitler's Children: The Story of the Baader-Meinhof Terrorist Group*. London: Michael Joseph, 1977.

Bell-Metereau, Rebecca. 'Stealth, Sexuality, and Cult Status in *The Manchurian Candidate* and *Seconds*'. In *A Little Solitaire: John Frankenheimer and American Film*, edited by Murray Pomerance and R. Barton Palmer, 48–61. New Brunswick: Rutgers University Press, 2011.

Belton, John. *American Cinema/American Culture*. 4th ed. New York: McGraw-Hill, 2013.
Ben-Yahuda, Nachman. *The Masada Myth: Collective Memory and Mythmaking in Israel*. Madison: University of Wisconsin Press, 1995.
Benson, Michael T. *Harry S. Truman and the Founding of Israel*. Connecticut: Praeger Publishers, 1997.
Bentley, Eric. *Theatre of War: Comments on 32 Occasions*. New York: Viking Press, 1972.
Berkman, Ted. *Cast a Giant Shadow*. New York: Pocket Books, Inc., 1963.
Bernstein, Matthew. 'Introduction'. In *Visions of the East: Orientalism in Film*, edited by Matthew Bernstein and Gaylyn Studlar, 1–18. London: I.B. Tauris, 1997.
Biskind, Peter. *Seeing Is Believing: How Hollywood Taught Us to Stop Worrying and Love the Fifties*. New York: Pantheon Books, 1983.
Biskind, Peter. *Easy Riders, Raging Bulls: How the Sex 'N' Drugs 'N' Rock 'N' Roll Generation Saved Hollywood*. London: Bloomsbury Publishing, 1999.
Bly, Robert. 'The Vietnam War and the Erosion of Male Confidence'. In *The Vietnam Reader*, edited by Walter Capps, 82–6. New York: Routledge, 1991.
Braudy, Leo. *The World in a Frame: What We See in Films*. New York: Anchor Press/Doubleday, 1976.
Breines, Paul. *Tough Jews: Political Fantasies and the Moral Dilemma of American Jewry*. New York: Basic Books, 1990.
Britton, Andrew. 'Blissing Out: The Politics of Reaganite Entertainment (1986)'. In *Britton on Film: The Complete Film Criticism of Andrew Britton*, edited by Barry Keith Grant, 97–154. Michigan: Wayne State University Press, 2009.
Burgoyne, Robert. *Film Nation: Hollywood Looks at U.S. History*. Minneapolis: University of Minnesota Press, 1997.
Burgoyne, Robert. *The Hollywood Historical Film*. Massachusetts: Blackwell Publishing, 2008.
Buscombe, Edward, ed. *The BFI Companion to the Western: New Edition*. London: Andre Deutsch Limited, 1993.
Buscombe, Edward. *'Injuns!': Native Americans in the Movies*. Cornwall: Reaktion Books, 2006.
Campbell, Duncan Andrew. *Unlikely Allies: Britain, America and the Victorian Origins of the Special Relationship*. London: Hambledon Continuum, 2007.
Cawelti, John G. *Adventure, Mystery, and Romance: Formula Stories as Art and Popular Culture*. Chicago: University of Chicago Press, 1976.
Ceplair, Larry and Steven Englund. *The Inquisition in Hollywood: Politics in the Film Community 1930–1960*. New York: Anchor Press/Double Day, 1980.
Chaliand, Gérard and Arnaud Blin. 'From 1968 to Radical Islam'. In *The History of Terrorism: From Antiquity to ISIS*. Updated ed., edited by Gérard Chaliand and Arnaud Blin, 221–54. Oakland: University of California Press, 2016.
Clarke, Richard. *Against All Enemies: Inside America's War on Terror*. New York: The Free Press, 2004.

Clarke, Thurston. *By Blood and Fire: The Attack on the King David Hotel*. London: Hutchinson Group, 1981.
Cogan, Charles G. 'Desert One and Its Disorders'. *The Journal of Military History* 67, no. 1 (January 2003): 201–16.
Cohan, Steven. *Masked Men: Masculinity and the Movies in the Fifties*. Bloomington: Indiana University Press, 1997.
Cook, David A. *Lost Illusions: American Cinema in the Shadow of Watergate and Vietnam 1970–1979*. Berkeley: University of California Press, 2000.
Corkin, Stanley. *Cowboys as Cold Warriors: The Western as U.S. History*. Philadelphia: Temple University Press, 2004.
Coyne, Michael. *The Crowded Prairie: American National Identity in the Hollywood Western*. London: I.B. Tauris, 1997.
Creekmur, Corey K. 'John Frankenheimer's "War on Terror"'. In *A Little Solitaire: John Frankenheimer and American Film*, edited by Murray Pomerance and R. Barton Palmer, 103–16. New Brunswick: Rutgers University Press, 2011.
Cripps, Thomas. *Making Movies Black: The Hollywood Message Movie from World War II to the Civil Rights Era*. New York: Oxford University Press, 1993.
D'Emilio, John. 'The Homosexual Menace: The Politics of Sexuality in Cold War America'. In *Making Trouble: Essays on Gay History, Politics, and the University*, 57–73. New York: Routledge, 1992.
Davis, Moshe. *America and the Holy Land*. Wesport: Praeger, 1995.
Doane, Mary Ann. 'The Close-Up: Scale and Detail in the Cinema'. *Differences: A Journal of Feminist Cultural Studies* 14, no. 3 (2003): 89–111.
Dobkin, Bethami A. *Tales of Terror: Television News and the Construction of the Terrorist Threat*. New York: Praeger, 1992.
Douglas, Kirk. *The Ragman's Son: An Autobiography*. London: Simon & Schuster, 1988.
Douglas, Kirk. *I Am Spartacus!: Making a Film, Breaking the Blacklist*. New York: Open Road Integrated Media, 2012.
Drew, Bernard. 'John Frankenheimer: His Rise and Fall'. *American Film* 2, no. 5 (1997): 8–16.
Dyer, Richard. *Stars*. New ed. London: BFI Publishing, 1998.
Dyer, Richard.. *Heavenly Bodies: Film Stars and Society*. 2nd ed. London: Routledge, 2004.
Emerson, Caryl and Gary Saul Emerson. *Mikhail Bakhtin: Creation of a Prosaics*. California: Stanford University Press, 1990.
Engle, G. D. 'An Interview with John Frankenheimer'. *Film Criticism* 1, no. 2 (1977): 2–14.
Erens, Patricia. *The Jew in American Cinema*. Bloomington: Indiana University Press, 1984.
Faludi, Susan. *Backlash: The Undeclared War against Women*. London: Vintage, 1992.
Finkelstein, Norman G. *Image and Reality of the Israel-Palestine Conflict*. London: Verso, 1995.
Fisk, Robert. *Pity the Nation: Lebanon at War*. 3rd ed. New York: Oxford University Press, 2001.

Franklin, H. Bruce. *M.I.A., or, Mythmaking in America*. New York: Lawrence Hill Books, 1992.

French, Philip. 'The Indian in the Western Movie'. In *The Pretend Indians: Images of Native Americans in the Movies*, edited by Gretchen M. Bataille and Charles L. P. Silet, 98–105. Ames: The Iowa State University Press, 1980.

Friar, Ralph E. and Natasha A. Friar. 'White Man Speaks with Split Tongue, Forked Tongue, Tongue of Snake'. In *The Pretend Indians: Images of Native Americans in the Movies*, edited by Gretchen M. Bataille and Charles L. P. Silet, 92–7. Ames: The Iowa State University Press, 1980.

Friedman, Lester D. *Hollywood's Image of the Jew*. New York: Frederick Ungar Publishing, 1982.

Friedman, Lester D. *Citizen Spielberg*. Chicago: University of Illinois Press, 2006.

Gilboa, Eytan. *American Public Opinion of Israel and the Arab-Israeli Conflict*. Massachusetts: Lexington Books, 1987.

Grose, Peter. *Israel in the Mind of America*. New York: Alfred A Knopf, 1983.

Hall, Sheldon and Stephen Neale. *Epics, Spectacles, and Blockbusters: A Hollywood History*. Detroit: Wayne State University Press, 2010.

Hallin, Daniel C. *The 'Uncensored War': The Media and Vietnam*. New York: Oxford University Press, 1986.

Hansen, Miriam. *Babel and Babylon: Spectatorship in American Silent Film*. Massachusetts: Harvard University Press, 1991.

Hansen, Miriam. '*Schindler's List* Is Not *Shoah*: Second Commandment, Popular Modernism, and Public Memory'. In *Spielberg's Holocaust: Critical Perspectives on* Schindler's List, edited by Yosefa Loshitzky, 77–103. Bloomington: Indiana University Press, 1997.

Harris, Thomas. *Black Sunday*. New York: G.P. Putnam's Sons, 1975.

Henn, Martin. *Under the Color of Law: The Bush Administration's Subversion of U.S. Constitutional and International Law in the War on Terror*. Lanham: Lexington Books, 2010.

Herberg, Will. *Protestant-Catholic-Jew: An Essay in American Religious Sociology*. Chicago: The University of Chicago Press, 1955.

Hersh, Seymour M. *My Lai 4: A Report on the Massacre and Its Aftermath*. New York: Random House, 1970.

Hersh, Seymour M. *Chain of Command: The Road from 9/11 to Abu Ghraib*. London: Penguin Books, 2004.

Higashi, Sumiko. 'Antimodernism as Historical Representation in a Consumer Culture: Cecil B. DeMille's *The Ten Commandments*, 1923, 1956, 1993'. In *The Persistence of History: Cinema, Television, and the Modern Event*, edited by Vivian Sobchack, 91–112. New York: Routledge, 1996.

Higham, Charles and Joel Greenberg. 'John Frankenheimer (1969)'. In *John Frankenheimer: Interviews, Essays, and Profiles*, edited by Stephen B. Armstrong, 19–31. Plymouth: Scarecrow Press, 2013.

Hilliard, Charles. *The Cross, the Sword, the Dollar*. New York: North River Press, 1951.

Homans, Peter. 'Puritanism Revisited: An Analysis of the Contemporary Screen-Image Western'. In *Focus on the Western*, edited by Jack Nachbar, 84–92. New Jersey: Prentice-Hall, 1974.

Jeffords, Susan. *The Remasculinization of America: Gender and the Vietnam War*. Bloomington: Indiana University Press, 1989.

Jonas, George. *Vengeance*. Rev. ed. London: Harper Perennial, 2006.

Kaplan, Amy. 'Zionism as Anticolonialism: The Case of *Exodus*'. *American Literary History* 25, no. 4 (Winter 2013): 870–95.

Karnow, Stanley. *Vietnam: A History*. Rev. ed. New York: Penguin, 1997.

Kellner, Douglas. 'September 11, Social Theory and Democratic Politics'. *Theory, Culture & Society* 19, no. 3 (August 2002): 147–59.

Kellner, Douglas. *Cinema Wars: Hollywood Film and Politics in the Bush-Cheney Era*. West Sussex: Wiley-Blackwell, 2010.

Kershaw, Ian. *The 'Hitler Myth': Image and Reality in the Third Reich*. Oxford: Clarendon Press, 1987.

Khalidi, Rashid. 'The United States and the Palestinians, 1977–2012: Three Key Moments'. *Journal of Palestine Studies* 42, no. 4 (Summer 2013): 61–72.

Khatib, Lina. *Filming the Modern Middle East: Politics in the Cinemas of Hollywood and the Arab World*. New York: I.B. Tauris, 2006.

Kimmel, Michael. *Manhood in America: A Cultural History*. New York: The Free Press, 1996.

Kitses, Jim. *Horizons West: Anthony Mann, Budd Boetticher, Sam Peckinpah: Studies of Authorship within the Western*. London: Thames & Hudson, 1969.

Kitses, Jim. 'The Western: Ideology and Archetype'. In *Focus on the Western*, edited by Jack Nachbar, 64–72. Englewood Cliffs: Prentice-Hall Inc., 1974.

Klein, Aaron J. *Striking Back: The 1972 Munich Olympics Massacre and Israel's Deadly Response*. New York: Random House, 2005.

Kolker, Robert. *A Cinema of Loneliness*. 4th ed. New York: Oxford University Press, 2011.

Kozloff, Sarah. 'Wyler's Wars'. *Film History* 20, no. 4 (2008): 456–73.

Kracauer, Siegfried. 'National Types as Hollywood Presents Them'. *The Public Opinion Quarterly* 13, no. 1 (Spring 1949): 53–72.

Kundnani, Arun. *The Muslims Are Coming!: Islamophobia, Extremism, and the Domestic War on Terror*. London: Verso, 2014.

Leffler, Melvyn P. *A Preponderance of Power: National Security, the Truman Administration, and the Cold War*. California: University of Stanford Press, 1992.

Lehman, Peter. 'Texas 1868/America 1956: *The Searchers*'. In *Close Viewings: An Anthology of New Film Criticism*, edited by Peter Lehman, 387–415. Tallahassee: The Florida State University Press, 1990.

Lemisch, Jesse. 'Film: Black Agency in the Amistad Uprising: Or, You've Taken Our Cinque and Gone'. *Souls: A Critical Journal of Black Politics, Culture, and Society* 1, no. 1 (1999): 57–70.
Lenihan, John H. *Showdown: Confronting Modern America in the Western Film*. Chicago: University of Illinois Press, 1980.
Levy, Emanuel. *Prophet of an American Way of Life*. New Jersey: The Scarecrow Press, Inc., 1988.
Levy, Shawn. *Paul Newman: A Life*. London: Aurum Press, 2009.
Little, Douglas. *American Orientalism: the United States and the Middle East since 1945*. 3rd ed. Chapel Hill: University of North Carolina Press, 2008.
Loshitzky, Yosefa. 'Introduction'. In *Spielberg's Holocaust: Critical Perspectives on Schindler's List*, edited by Yosefa Loshitzky, 1–17. Bloomington: Indiana University Press, 1997.
Loshitzky, Yosefa. *Identity Politics on the Israeli Screen*. Austin: University of Texas Press, 2001.
McAlister, Melani. *Epic Encounters: Culture, Media, & U.S. Interests in the Middle East since 1945*. Rev. ed. Berkeley: University of California Press, 2005.
McBride, Joseph. *Steven Spielberg: A Biography*. 3rd ed. London: Faber and Faber Limited, 1997.
McCormick, Thomas J. *America's Half-Century: United States Foreign Policy in the Cold War*. 2nd ed. Baltimore: The Johns Hopkins Press, 1995.
McGee, Patrick. *From Shane to Kill Bill: Rethinking the Western*. Massachusetts: Blackwell Publishing, 2007.
McQuaid, Kim. *The Anxious Years: America in the Vietnam-Watergate Era*. New York: Basic Books, Inc., 1989.
McTurnan Kahin, George. *Intervention: How America Became Involved in Vietnam*. New York: Alfred A. Knopf, 1986.
Malamud, Margaret. 'Cold War Romans'. *Arion* 14, no. 3 (Winter 2007): 121–54.
Maltby, Richard. 'A Better Sense of History: John Ford and the Indians'. In *The Movie Book of the Western*, edited by Ian Cameron and Douglas Pye, 34–49. London: Studio Vista, 1996.
Maltby, Richard.. *Hollywood Cinema*. 2nd ed. Massachusetts: Blackwell Publishing, 2003.
Marks, Stephen P. 'International Law and the "War on Terrorism": Post 9/11 Responses by the United States and Asia Pacific Countries'. *Asia Pacific Law Review* 14, no. 1 (2006): 59.
Mart, Michelle. 'The 'Christianization' of Israel and Jews in 1950s America'. *Religion and American Culture: A Journal of Interpretation* 14, no. 1 (Winter 2004): 109–47.
Mart, Michelle. *Eye on Israel: How America Came to View Israel as an Ally*. Albany: State University of New York Press, 2006.

Martin, Andrew. *Receptions of War: Vietnam in American Culture*. Norman: University of Oklahoma Press, 1993.

Martini, Edwin A. *Invisible Enemies: The American War on Vietnam, 1975–2000*. Amherst: University of Massachusetts Press, 2007.

Miller, Douglas T. and Marion Nowak. *The Fifties: The Way We Really Were*. New York: Doubleday & Company, Inc., 1977.

Miroff, Bruce. *Pragmatic Illusions: The Presidential Politics of John F. Kennedy*. New York: David McKay Company Inc., 1976.

Monti-Belkaoui, Janice. 'Images of Arabs and Israelis in the Prestige Press, 1966–1974'. *Journalism Quarterly* 55, no. 4 (Winter 1978): 732–8.

Morgan, Edmund S. 'John Winthrop's "Modell of Christian Charity" in a Wider Context'. *Huntington Library Quarterly* 50, no. 2 (Spring 1987): 145–51.

Morin, Edgar. *The Stars*. Translated by Richard Howard. New York: Grove Press, Inc., 1960.

Mourlet, Michel. 'In Defence of Violence'. In *Stardom: Industry of Desire*, edited by Christine Gledhill, 233–6. London: Routledge, 1991.

Mueller, John E. *War, Presidents and Public Opinion*. New York: John Wiley & Sons, Inc., 1973.

Munn, Michael. *John Wayne: The Man Behind the Myth*. London: Robson Books, 2004.

Murphy, Gretchen. *Hemispheric Imaginings: The Monroe Doctrine and Narratives of U.S. Empire*. Durham: Duke University Press, 2004.

Mustazza, Leonard. 'Introduction'. In *Frank Sinatra and Popular Culture: Essays on an American Icon*, edited by Leonard Mustazza, 1–19. Connecticut: Praeger, 1998.

Nadel, Alan. 'God's Law and the Wide Screen: *The Ten Commandments* as Cold War "Epic"'. *Publications of the Modern Language Association of America (PMLA)* 108, no. 3 (May 1993): 415–30.

Nadel, Ira B. *Leon Uris: Life of a Best Seller*. Austin: University of Texas Press, 2010.

Ninkovich, Frank. *Modernity and Power: A History of the Domino Theory in the Twentieth Century* (Chicago: University of Chicago, 1994).

O'Ballance, Edgar. *Language of Violence: The Blood Politics of Terrorism*. San Rafael: Presidio Press, 1979.

O'Sullivan, John. 'Annexation'. *The United States Magazine and Democratic Review* 17, no. 1 (July–August 1845): 5–10.

Olson, Lester C. *Benjamin Franklin's Vision of American Community: A Study in Rhetorical Iconology*. Columbia: University of South Carolina Press, 2004.

Oren, Michael B. *Six Days of War: June 1967 and the Making of the Modern Middle East*. New York: Oxford University Press, 2002.

Oren, Michael B. *Power, Faith, and Fantasy: America in the Middle East 1776 to the Present*. New York: W. W. Norton, 2007.

Orman, John. *Comparing Presidential Behavior: Carter, Reagan, and the Macho Presidential Style*. New York: Greenwood Press, 1987.

Parmet, Herbert S. *JFK: The Presidency of John F. Kennedy*. New York: The Dial Press, 1983.
Pippin, Robert B. *Hollywood Westerns and American Myth: The Importance of Howard Hawks and John Ford for Political Philosophy*. New Haven: Yale University Press, 2010.
Prince, Stephen. *Firestorm: American Film in the Age of Terrorism*. New York: Columbia University Press, 2009.
Pye, Douglas. 'Double Vision: Miscegenation and Point of View in *The Searchers*'. In *The Movie Book of the Western*, edited by Ian Cameron and Douglas Pye, 229–35. London: Studio Vista, 1996.
Pye, Douglas. 'Introduction: Criticism and the Western'. In *The Movie Book of the Western*, edited by Ian Cameron and Douglas Pye, 9–21. London: Studio Vista, 1996.
Raymond, Emilie. *From My Cold, Dead Hands: Charlton Heston and American Politics*. Kentucky: The University of Kentucky Press, 2006.
Roberts, Randy. *John Wayne: American*. New York: Free Press, 1995.
Rogin, Michael. 'American Political Demonology: A Retrospective'. In *Ronald Reagan, the Movie: And Other Episodes in Political Demonology*, 272–300. Berkeley: University of California Press, 1987.
Rogin, Michael. 'Kiss Me Deadly: Communism, Motherhood, and Cold War Movies'. In *Ronald Reagan, the Movie: And Other Episodes in Political Demonology*, 236–71. Berkeley: University of California Press, 1987.
Rogin, Michael. 'Political Repression in the United States'. In *Ronald Reagan, the Movie: And Other Episodes in Political Demonology*, 44–80. Berkeley: University of California Press, 1987.
Rogin, Michael. 'Preface'. In *Ronald Reagan, the Movie: And Other Episodes in Political Demonology*, xiii–xx. Berkeley: University of California Press, 1987.
Rogin, Michael. '*Ronald Reagan*, the Movie'. In *Ronald Reagan, the Movie: And Other Episodes in Political Demonology*, 1–43. Berkeley: University of California Press, 1987.
Rogin, Michael. '"The Sword Became a Flashing Vision": D.W. Griffith's *The Birth of a Nation*'. In *Ronald Reagan, the Movie: And Other Episodes in Political Demonology*, 190–235. Berkeley: University of California Press, 1987.
Rose, Jacqueline. *The Question of Zion*. Carlton: Melbourne University Press, 2005.
Rosenstone, Robert A. 'History in Images/History in Words: Reflections on the Possibility of Really Putting History onto Film'. *The American Historical Review* 93, no. 5 (December 1988): 1173–85.
Russo, Vito. *The Celluloid Closet: Homosexuality in the Movies*. Rev. ed. New York: Harper & Row, 1987.
Ryan, Tom. *Otto Preminger Films Exodus*. New York: Random House, 1960.
Safty, Adel. *Might Over Right: How the Zionists Took Over Palestine*. Reading: Garnet Publishing, 2009.
Said, Edward. *Orientalism*. Rev. ed. New York: Vintage Books, 1994.

Schatz, Thomas. *Hollywood Genres: Formulas, Filmmaking, and the Studio System*. Philadelphia: Temple University Press, 1981.

Semmerling, Tim Jon. *'Evil' Arabs in American Popular Film: Orientalist Fear*. Texas: University of Texas Press, 2006.

Shaheen, Jack. *The TV Arab*. Ohio: Bowling Green State University Popular Press, 1984.

Shaheen, Jack. *Reel Bad Arabs: How Hollywood Vilifies a People*. New York: Olive Branch Press, 2001.

Shaheen, Jack. *Guilty: Hollywood's Verdict on Arabs After 9/11*. Massachusetts: Olive Branch Press, 2008.

Shalev, Eran. *American Zion: The Old Testament as a Political Text from the Revolution to the Civil War*. New Haven: Yale University Press, 2013.

Shandler, Jeffrey. 'The Testimony of Images: The Allied Liberation of Nazi Concentration Camps in American Newsreels'. In *Why Didn't the Press Shout?: American & International Journalism during the Holocaust*, edited by Robert Moses Shapiro, 109–25. New York: Yeshiva University Press, 2003.

Shavelson, Melville. *How to Make a Jewish Movie*. New Jersey: Prentice-Hall, Inc., 1971.

Shaw, Tony. *Hollywood's Cold War*. Edinburgh: Edinburgh University Press, 2007.

Shaw, Tony. *Cinematic Terror: A Global History of Terrorism on Film*. New York: Bloomsbury Publishing, 2015.

Shaw, Tony and Denise J. Youngblood. *Cinematic Cold War: The American and Soviet Struggle for Hearts and Minds*. Kansas: University Press of Kansas, 2010.

Shohat, Ella. 'Gender and Culture of Empire: Toward a Feminist Ethnography of the Cinema'. *Quarterly Review of Film and Video* 13, no. 1 (1991): 45–84.

Shohat, Ella and Robert Stam. *Unthinking Eurocentrism: Multiculturalism and the Media*. London: Routledge, 1994.

Silver, Matthew M. *Our Exodus: Leon Uris and the Americanization of Israel's Founding Story*. Detroit: Wayne State University Press, 2010.

Simons, Geoff. *Vietnam Syndrome: Impact on US Foreign Policy*. New York: St. Martin's Press, 1998.

Slotkin, Richard. *Regeneration through Violence: The Mythology of the American Frontier, 1600–1860*. Connecticut: Wesleyan University Press, 1973.

Slotkin, Richard. *The Fatal Environment: The Myth of the Frontier in the Age of Industrialization 1800–1890*. New York: Atheneum, 1985.

Slotkin, Richard. *Gunfighter Nation: The Myth of the Frontier in Twentieth-Century America*. New York: University of Oklahoma Press, 1998.

Smith, Henry Nash. *Virgin Land: The American West as Symbol and Myth*. Cambridge: Harvard University Press, 1950.

Smith, Julian. *Looking Away: Hollywood and Vietnam*. New York: Charles Scribner's Sons, 1975.

Spiegel, Steven L. *The Other Arab-Israeli Conflict: Making America's Middle East Policy, from Truman to Reagan*. Chicago: University of Chicago Press, 1985.

Stephanson, Anders. *Manifest Destiny: American Expansionism and the Empire of Right*. New York: Hill and Wang, 1995.
Suid, Lawrence H. *Guts & Glory: The Making of the American Military Image in Film*. Rev., exp. ed. Lexington: The University Press of Kentucky, 2002.
Sulieman, Michael W. 'The American Mass Media and the June Conflict'. In *The Arab-Israeli Confrontation of June 1967: An Arab Perspective*, edited by Ibrahim Abu-Lughod, 138–54. Evanston: Northwestern University Press, 1970.
Syrkin, Marie. *Golda Meir Speaks Out*. London: Weidenfeld and Nicolson, 1973.
Tasker, Yvonne. *Spectacular Bodies: Gender, Genre and the Action Cinema*. London: Routledge, 1993.
Turner, Frederick Jackson. 'The Significance of the Frontier in American History'. In *The Frontier in American History*, 1–38. New York: Holt, Rinehart and Winston, Inc., 1962.
Uris, Leon. *Exodus*. New York: Doubleday & Company, 1958.
Vernet, Marc. 'Wings of the Desert; or, the Invisible Superimpositions'. *Velvet Light Trap: A Critical Journal of Film and Television* 91, no. 28 (September 1991): 65–72.
Wallace, Lew. *Ben-Hur: A Tale of the Christ*. Raleigh, NC: Generic NL Freebook Publisher, n.d. doi: 1086058.
Warshow, Robert. 'Movie Chronicle: The Westerner'. In *Focus on the Western*, edited by Jack Nachbar, 45–56. New Jersey: Prentice-Hall, 1974.
White, Hayden. 'Historiography and Historiophoty'. *The American Historical Review* 93, no. 5 (December 1988): 1193–9.
White, Patricia. *Uninvited: Classical Hollywood Cinema and Lesbian Representability*. Indiana: Indiana University Press, 1999.
Whitfield, Stephen J. *The Culture of the Cold War*. 2nd ed. Baltimore: Johns Hopkins University Press, 1996.
Wilkinson, Rupert. *American Tough: The Tough-Guy Tradition and American Character*. Westport: Greenwood Press, 1984.
Williams, Linda. *Playing the Race Card: Melodramas of Black and White from Uncle Tom to O.J. Simpson*. Princeton: Princeton University Press, 2001.
Williams, Linda. 'Why I Did Not Want to Write This Essay'. *Signs* 30, no. 1 (Autumn 2004): 1264–72.
Wills, Garry. *John Wayne: The Politics of Celebrity*. London: Faber and Faber, 1997.
Winkler, Martin M. 'The Roman Empire in American Cinema after 1945'. In *Imperial Projections: Ancient Rome in Modern Popular Culture*, edited by Sandra R. Joshel, Margaret Malamud, and Donald T. McGuire, 50–76. Maryland: Johns Hopkins University Press, 2005.
Winkler, Martin M. *The Roman Salute: Cinema, History, Ideology*. Columbus: Ohio State University Press, 2009.
Wisse, Ruth R. *The Schlemiel as Modern Hero*. Chicago: The University of Chicago Press, 1971.

Wood, Michael. *America In the Movies: Or 'Santa Maria, It Had Slipped My Mind'*. New York: Delta Publishing, 1975.

Wood, Robin. *Hollywood from Vietnam to Reagan*. New York: Columbia University Press, 1986.

Wright, Melanie J. *Religion and Film: An Introduction*. New York: I.B. Tauris, 2007.

Wyke, Maria. *Projecting the Past: Ancient Rome, Cinema and History*. New York: Routledge, 1997.

Wylie, Philip. *Generation of Vipers*. Illinois: Dalkey Archive Press, [1942] 1996.

Xavier, Ismail. *Allegories of Underdevelopment: Aesthetics and Politics in Modern Brazilian Cinema*. Minneapolis: University of Minnesota Press, 1997.

Newspaper and magazine articles (print)

'The "Black Sunday" Blimp Goes Up: Will it Soar – or Crash?' *Chicago Daily News*, 12–13 March 1977.

Brooks, David. 'What "Munich" Left Out'. *New York Times*, 11 December 2005.

Burnham, James. 'Reflections on Entebbe'. *National Review*, 6 August 1976, 834.

Canby, Vincent. 'Terror Over the Super Bowl'. *New York Times*, 1 April 1977.

Canby, Vincent. 'For De Mille, Moses' Egypt Was Really America'. *New York Times*, 25 March 1984.

Canby, Vincent. 'Chuck Norris: The Public Has Made Him a Star'. *New York Times*, 12 May 1985.

'*Cast a Giant Shadow* review'. *Time*, 15 April 1966, 66.

'The Clamor Over Calley: Who Shares the Guilt?' *Time*, 12 April 1971, 19.

Crowther, Bosley. 'Screen: "The Ten Commandments": De Mille's Production Opens at Criterion'. *New York Times*, 9 November 1956.

'Debacle in the Desert'. *Time*, 5 May 1980, 12–25.

Farber, Stephen. 'Robert Evans's Rise from Grade-B Actor to A-Plus Producer'. *New York Times*, 15 August 1976.

Harmetz, Aljean. 'Frankenheimer Rides a Blimp to a Big, Fat Comeback'. *New York Times*, 10 April 1977.

Hoberman, J. 'Spielberg's Oskar'. *Village Voice*, 21 December 1993, 63.

Klemesrud, Judy. 'Chuck Norris – Strong, Silent and Popular'. *New York Times*, 1 September 1985.

'A Legend Is Born'. *New York Times*, 6 July 1976.

Mihalic, John. 'Hair on the President's Chest'. *Wall Street Journal*, 11 May 1984.

'President Sees Editors: Tells Them Communism Can Be Beaten through Religion'. *New York Times*, 10 April 1953.

Rosenblatt, Roger. 'Out of the Past, Fresh Choices for the Future: Invoking Old Values, Ronald Reagan Must Make Them Work for the '80s'. *Time*, 5 January 1981, 10–23.
Smith, Terrence. 'Israelis Return with 103 Rescued in Uganda Raid'. *New York Times*, 5 July 1976.
Starr, Fran. 'Israel's Entebbe Raid Is Cheered as a Gutsy Performance'. *Chicago Tribune*, 7 July 1976.
Teltsch, Kathleen. 'Rescue by Israel Acclaimed by U.S. at Debate in U.N.' *New York Times*, 13 July 1976.
'The Ten Commandments'. *Variety*, 10 October 1956.
'The Three-Day Blitz from Gaza to Suez'. *U.S. News & World Report*, 19 June 1967, 33–6.
'When U.S. Rescue Mission Fizzled'. *U.S. News & World Report*, 19 July 1976, 30–2.
Wieseltier, Leon. 'Hits'. *New Republic*, 19 December 2005, 38.
'Will "Hot Pursuit" Stop Terrorism?' *U.S. News & World Report*, 19 July 1976, 30–2.
Zelikow, Philip. 'Steven Spielberg, Historian'. *New York Times*, 29 November 2012.

Online sources

Box Office Mojo. 'Black Sunday (1977)'. Boxofficemojo.com. Accessed 23 October 2013. http://www.boxofficemojo.com/movies/?id=blacksunday.htm.
Box Office Mojo. 'The Delta Force (1986)'. Boxofficemojo.com. Accessed 25 October 2013. http://www.boxofficemojo.com/movies/?id=deltaforce.htm.
Box Office Mojo. 'All Time Box Office Adjusted for Ticket Price Inflation'. Boxofficemjojo.com. Accessed 11 May 2015. http://www.boxofficemojo.com/alltime/adjusted.htm.
Box Office Mojo. 'Munich (2005)'. Boxofficemojo.com. Accessed 12 May 2015. http://www.boxofficemojo.com/movies/?id=munich.htm.
Box Office Mojo. 'Airport (1970)'. Boxofficemojo.com. Accessed 30 May 2015. http://www.boxofficemojo.com/movies/?id=airport.htm.
Brown, Hannah. 'Munich: Portentous and preachy'. *Jerusalem Post*, 19 January 2006. Accessed 1 May 2014. http://www.jpost.com/Arts-and-Culture/Entertainment/Munich-Portentous-and-preachy.
Crouse, Eric R. 'Popular Cold Warriors: Conservative Protestants, Communism, and Culture in Early Cold War America'. *Journal of Religion and Popular Culture* 2 (Fall 2002). Accessed 14 May 2012. http://www.usask.ca/relst/jrpc/popcoldwarprint.html.
Ebert, Roger. 'I Knew I Would Lose Friends over This Film'. *Sunday Telegraph*, 1 January 2006. Accessed 3 May 2014. http://www.telegraph.co.uk/news/worldnews/1506765/I-knew-I-would-lose-friends-over-this-film.html.
Emerson, Jim. 'Spy vs. Spy: The Morality of Munich'. *RogerEbert.com*. 14 December 2005. Accessed 2 May 2014. http://www.rogerebert.com/scanners/spy-vs-spy-the-morality-of-munich.

Fletcher, Herbert. 'TEXIAN'. *Handbook of Texas Online*. 15 June 2010. Accessed 14 December 2015. http://www.tshaonline.org/handbook/online/articles/pft05.

Goldberg, Michelle. 'The War on Munich'. *Salon*, 20 December 2005. Accessed 2 May 2014. http://www.salon.com/2005/12/20/munich_3/.

Kennedy, John F. 'Democratic National Convention Nomination Acceptance Address – "The New Frontier"'. 15 July 1960. American Rhetoric. Accessed 13 April 2013. http://www.americanrhetoric.com/speeches/jfk1960dnc.htm

Kennedy, John F. 'Inaugural Address'. 20 January 1961. American Rhetoric. Accessed 18 April 2013. http://www.americanrhetoric.com/speeches/jfkinaugural.htm.

Klein, Morton A. 'ZOA: Don't See Spielberg's "Munich" Unless You Like Humanizing Terrorists & Dehumanizing Israelis'. *Zionist Organization of America*, 27 December2005. Accessed 2 May 2014. http://zoa.org/2005/12/102082-zoa-dont-see-spielbergs-munich-unless-you-like-humanizing-terrorists-dehumanizing-israelis/#ixzz38mEGcIDt.

Krauthammer, Charles. '"Munich," the Travesty'. *Washington Post*, 13 January 2006. Accessed 2 May 2014. http://www.washingtonpost.com/wp-dyn/content/article/2006/01/12/AR2006011201541.html.

Lanzmann, Claude. 'Schindler's List is an Impossible Story'. *Approaches to the Humanities*, Spring 2007. Accessed 8 May 2014. http://www.phil.uu.nl/~rob/2007/hum291/lanzmannschindler.shtml.

Lifson, Amy. '*Ben Hur*: The Book that Shook the World'. *Humanities* 30, no. 6 (November/December 2009). Accessed 29 November 2012. http://www.neh.gov/humanities/2009/novemberdecember/feature/ben-hur.

Medved, Michael. '"Munich" Distorts History'. *USA Today*, 1 October 2006. Accessed 2 May 2014. http://usatoday30.usatoday.com/news/opinion/editorials/2006-01-10-munich_x.htm.

Nixon, Richard. 'Address to the Nation on the Situation in Southeast Asia'. 30 April 1970. EdWeb. Accessed 20 October 2013. http://www.edwebproject.org/sideshow/resources/nixon.430speech.html.

Norris, Michele. 'Interview: Aaron Klein Discusses "Striking Back," A Look At The Munich Killings, Aftermath'. *All Things Considered*. 22 December 2005. Accessed 4 May 2014. http://www.npr.org/programs/atc/transcripts/2005/dec/051222.siegel.html.

The Numbers. 'The Green Berets (1968)'. The-numbers.com. Accessed 13 May 2013. http://www.the-numbers.com/movies/1968/00232.php.

Pappé, Ilan. 'The Israeli fallacy is over'. *Pravda.ru*, 19 February 2011. Accessed 17 September 2012. http://english.pravda.ru/opinion/columnists/19-02-2011/116945-The_Israeli_fallacy_is_over-0/.

Powers, James. '"The Ten Commandments": Read THR's 1956 Review'. *Hollywood Reporter*. 5 October 1956. Accessed 11 October 2015. http://www.hollywoodreporter.com/news/ten-commandments-read-thrs-1956-754677.

'The President's Special Conference With the Association of Radio News Analysts'. 13 May 1947. Harry S. Truman Library & Museum. Accessed 13 April 2014. http://www.trumanlibrary.org/publicpapers/index.php?pid=2155.

Reagan, Ronald. 'Address to the Veterans of Foreign Wars Convention in Chicago'. 18 August 1980. The American Presidency Project. Accessed 25 October 2013. http://www.presidency.ucsb.edu/ws/?pid=85202.

Reagan, Ronald. 'Inaugural Address'. 20 January 1981. The American Presidency Project. Accessed 25 October 2013. http://www.presidency.ucsb.edu/ws/?pid=43130.

Reagan, Ronald. 'Address to the National Association of Evangelicals'. 8 March 1983. Voices of Democracy. Accessed 25 October 2013. http://voicesofdemocracy.umd.edu/reagan-evil-empire-speech-text/.

Reagan, Ronald. 'Remarks at Dedication Ceremonies for the Vietnam Veterans Memorial Statue'. 11 November 1984. The American Presidency Project. Accessed 25 October 2013. http://www.presidency.ucsb.edu/ws/?pid=39414.

'A Report to the National Security Council – NSC 68'. 12 April 1950. Harry S. Truman Library & Museum. Accessed 14 November 2015. http://www.trumanlibrary.org/whistlestop/study_collections/coldwar/documents/pdf/10-1.pdf.

'The Second Carter-Ford Presidential Debate'. 6 October 1976. Commission on Presidential Debates. Accessed 25 October 2013. http://www.debates.org/index.php?page=october-6-1976-debate-transcript.

Schickel, Richard. 'Spielberg Takes on Terror'. *Time*, 4 December 2005. Accessed 5 May 2014. http://content.time.com/time/subscriber/article/0,33009,1137679-1,00.html.

Schoenfeld, Gabriel. 'Spielberg's "Munich"'. *Commentary*, 1 February 2006. Accessed 1 May 2014. https://www.commentarymagazine.com/article/spielbergs-"munich"/.

'"SPIEGEL Interview with Steven Spielberg": I Would Die For Israel'. *Der Spiegel*, 26 January 2006. Accessed 3 May 2014. http://www.spiegel.de/international/spiegel/spiegel-interview-with-steven-spielberg-i-would-die-for-israel-a-397378.html.

Tobin, Jonathan. 'Worth Getting Ppset About'. *Jerusalem Post*, 29 December 2005. Accessed 2 May 2014. http://www.jpost.com/Business/Worth-getting-upset-about.

Truman, Harry. 'Truman Doctrine – President Harry S. Truman's Address Before a Joint Session of Congress'. 12 March 1947. Avalon Project. Accessed 12 October 2013. http://avalon.law.yale.edu/20th_century/trudoc.asp.

Younge, Gary. 'Israeli Consul Attacks Spielberg's Munich as "Problematic"'. *Guardian*, 12 December 2005. Accessed 1 May 2014. http://www.theguardian.com/world/2005/dec/12/israel.filmnews.

Films cited

A.I. Artificial Intelligence (Steven Spielberg, 2001)
Airport (George Seaton, 1970)

The Alamo (John Wayne, 1960)
All Fall Down (John Frankenheimer, 1962)
American Sniper (Clint Eastwood, 2014)
Amistad (Steven Spielberg, 1997)
Anastasia (Anatole Litvak, 1956)
Apache (Robert Aldrich, 1954)
The Bad Man (Richard Thorpe, 1941)
Bataan (Tay Garnett, 1943)
Ben-Hur: A Tale of the Christ (Fred Niblo, 1925)
Ben-Hur (William Wyler, 1959)
The Big Country (William Wyler, 1958)
The Birth of a Nation (D.W. Griffith, 1915)
Black Hawk Down (Ridley Scott, 2001)
Black Sunday (John Frankenheimer, 1977)
Body of Lies (Ridley Scott, 2008)
Bonnie and Clyde (Arthur Penn, 1967)
Bowling for Columbine (Michael Moore, 2002)
Broken Arrow (Delmer Daves, 1950)
Butch Cassidy and the Sundance Kid (George Roy Hill, 1969)
Cast a Giant Shadow (Melville Shavelson, 1966)
Champion (Mark Robson, 1949)
Cheyenne Autumn (John Ford, 1964)
Cleopatra (Cecil B. DeMille, 1934)
Code of Silence (Andrew Davis, 1985)
Coming Home (Hal Ashby, 1978)
Cool Hand Luke (Stuart Rosenberg, 1967)
The Cowboys (Mark Rydell, 1972)
The Crusades (Cecil B. DeMille, 1935)
The Deer Hunter (Michael Cimino, 1978)
The Delta Force (Menahem Golan, 1986)
Devil's Doorway (Anthony Mann, 1950)
Dirty Harry (Don Siegel, 1971)
Double Indemnity (Billy Wilder, 1944)
Drums Along the Mohawk (John Ford, 1939)
Earthquake (Mark Robson, 1974)
East of Eden (Elia Kazan, 1955)
Easy Rider (Dennis Hopper, 1969)
El Cid (Anthony Mann, 1961)
The Enforcer (James Fargo, 1976)
E.T. the Extra-Terrestrial (Steven Spielberg, 1982)
Executive Decision (Stuart Baird, 1996)

Exodus (Otto Preminger, 1960)
Fail-Safe (Sidney Lumet, 1964)
First Blood (Ted Kotcheff, 1982)
Fort Apache (John Ford, 1948)
Frost/Nixon (Ron Howard, 2008)
Fury at Showdown (Gerd Oswald, 1957)
Giant (George Stevens, 1956)
The Godfather Part II (Francis Ford Coppola, 1974)
Gone with the Wind (Victor Fleming, 1939)
The Graduate (Mike Nichols, 1967)
The Great Train Robbery (Edwin S. Porter, 1903)
The Greatest Story Ever Told (George Stevens, 1965)
The Green Berets (John Wayne, 1968)
Gun for a Coward (Abner Biberman, 1957)
Gun Glory (Roy Rowland, 1957)
Gunfight at the O.K. Corral (John Sturges, 1959)
The Gunfighter (Henry King, 1950)
At Gunpoint (Alfred L. Werker, 1955)
Hang 'Em High (Ted Post, 1968)
Hearts and Minds (Peter Davis, 1974)
Hell Night (Tom DeSimone, 1981)
From Here to Eternity (George Stevens, 1953)
High Noon (Fred Zinnemann, 1952)
The Horse Soldiers (John Ford, 1959)
How the West Was Won (John Ford, Henry Hathaway, and George Marshall, 1963)
Hud (Martin Ritt, 1963)
The Hurt Locker (Kathryn Bigelow, 2008)
The Hustler (Robert Resson, 1961)
Intolerance (D.W. Griffith, 1916)
Invasion U.S.A. (Joseph Zito, 1985)
Iron Man (Jon Favreau, 2008)
Jaws (Steven Spielberg, 1975)
Johnny Concho (Don McGuire, 1956)
Judgment at Nuremburg (Stanley Kramer, 1961)
Khartoum (Basil Dearden, 1966)
The Killers (Don Siegel, 1964)
The King and I (Walter Lang, 1956)
The Kingdom (Peter Berg, 2007)
The Last of the Fast Guns (George Sherman, 1958)
The Last Outpost (Lewis R. Foster, 1951)
Last Train from Gun Hill (John Sturges, 1959)

Law and Order (Nathan Juran, 1953)
The Left Handed Gun (Arthur Penn, 1958)
Lincoln (Steven Spielberg, 2012)
Little Big Man (Arthur Penn, 1970)
Lonely Are the Brave (David Miller, 1962)
The Longest Day (Ken Annakin, Andrew Marton, and Bernhard Wicki, 1962)
The Magnificent Seven (John Sturges, 1960)
Magnum Force (Ted Post, 1973)
Man from Del Rio (Harry Horner, 1956)
The Man Who Shot Liberty Valance (John Ford, 1962)
Man without a Star (King Vidor, 1955)
The Manchurian Candidate (John Frankenheimer, 1962)
Marathon Man (John Schlesinger, 1976)
Midnight Cowboy (John Schlesinger, 1969)
The Misfits (John Huston, 1961)
Miss V. from Moscow (Albert Herman, 1942)
Missing in Action (Joseph Zito, 1984)
Missing in Action 2: The Beginning (Lance Hool, 1985)
Mission to Moscow (Michael Curtiz, 1943)
Mivtsa Yonatan (Menahem Golan, 1977)
Munich (Steven Spielberg, 2005)
My Darling Clementine (John Ford, 1946)
My Son John (Leo McCarey, 1952)
The North Star (Lewis Milestone, 1943)
Northwest Passage (King Vidor, 1940)
On the Waterfront (Elia Kazan, 1954)
Operation, Burma! (Raoul Walsh, 1945)
The Outlaw Josey Wales (Clint Eastwood, 1976)
The Passion of the Christ (Mel Gibson, 2004)
Paths of Glory (Stanley Kubrick, 1957)
The Pawnbroker (Sidney Lumet, 1964)
A Place in the Sun (George Stevens, 1951)
Planet of the Apes (Franklin J. Schaffner, 1968)
The Poseidon Adventure (Ronald Neame, 1972)
The Postman Always Rings Twice (Fritz Lang, 1946)
The Prodigal (Richard Thorpe, 1955)
The Proud Rebel (Michael Curtiz, 1958)
Quo Vadis (Mervyn LeRoy, 1951)
Raiders of the Lost Ark (Steven Spielberg, 1981)
Raid on Entebbe (Irvin Kershner, 1977)
Rambo: First Blood Part II (George P. Cosmatos, 1985)

Rebel Without a Cause (Nicholas Ray, 1955)
Redacted (Brian De Palma, 2005)
Red River (Howard Hawks, 1948)
Rendition (Gavin Hood, 2007)
Reservoir Dogs (Quentin Tarantino, 1992)
Rio Grande (John Ford, 1950)
Rolling Thunder (John Flynn, 1977)
Samson & Delilah (Cecil B. DeMille, 1949)
Saving Private Ryan (Steven Spielberg, 1998)
Schindler's List (Steven Spielberg, 1993)
The Searchers (John Ford, 1956)
Seven Samurai (Akira Kurosawa, 1954)
Shane (George Stevens, 1953)
She Wore a Yellow Ribbon (John Ford, 1949)
The Sheik (George Melford, 1921)
Shoah (Claude Lanzmann, 1985)
Sitting Bull (Sidney Salkow, 1954)
Skyjacked (John Guillermin, 1972)
Song of Russia (Gregory Ratoff, 1944)
The Son of the Sheik (George Fitzmaurice, 1926)
Spartacus (Stanley Kubrick, 1960)
Stagecoach (John Ford, 1939)
Star Wars: Episode IV – A New Hope (George Lucas, 1977)
The Sting (George Roy Hill, 1973)
The Story of Ruth (Henry Koster, 1960)
A Streetcar Named Desire (Elia Kazan, 1951)
Sudden Impact (Clint Eastwood, 1983)
Sword of Gideon (Michael Anderson, 1986)
Syriana (Stephen Gaghan, 2005)
The Tall T (Budd Boetticher, 1957)
Taxi Driver (Martin Scorsese, 1976)
Taza, Son of Cochise (Douglas Sirk, 1954)
The Ten Commandments (Cecil B. DeMille, 1923)
The Ten Commandments (Cecil B. DeMille, 1956)
They Died with Their Boots On (Raoul Walsh, 1941)
The Thief of Baghdad (Raoul Walsh, 1924)
Three Russian Girls (Henry S. Kesler and Fedor Ozep, 1943)
The Towering Inferno (John Guillermin, 1974)
Triumph of the Will (Leni Riefenstahl, 1935)
Troy (Wolfgang Peterson, 2003)
True Lies (James Cameron, 1994)

Two-Minute Warning (Larry Peerce, 1976)
Unconquered (Cecil B. DeMille, 1947)
United 93 (Paul Greengrass, 2006)
Victory at Entebbe (Marvin J. Chomsky, 1976)
War of the Worlds (Steven Spielberg, 2005)
The War Wagon (Burt Kennedy, 1967)
White Feather (Robert D. Webb, 1955)

Television series cited

24 (Fox, 2001–2014)
Homeland (Showtime, 2011–2020)
Sleeper Cell (Showtime, 2005–2006)
That's My Bush! (Comedy Central, 2001)

DVD bonus material

Orrison, Katherine. 'Commentary'. *The Ten Commandments*. Special collector's ed., DVD. Directed by Cecil B. DeMille. Paramount, 2004.

Index

Abrams, Nathan 6
action film genre 127–8
Adler, Les K. 19
Adler, Renata 94–5
A.I. Artificial Intelligence 158
Airport 101, 127, 191 n.3, 205 n.39
The Alamo 9, 49, 77, 91–5, 97–8
Alford, Matthew 161
al-Husseini, Haj Amin 83, 167
All Fall Down 195 n.82
Altman, Rick 15
American Sniper 198 n.5
Amistad 139, 158
Anastasia 178 n.31
Apache 56
Arab-Israeli conflict 96, 105–6, 117,
    144–52, 155–6, 162–72, 200 n.43
  Entebbe 10, 111–12, 134–5
  hijacking of TWA Flight 847 126, 130,
    134
  King David Hotel bombing 169–70
  Munich Olympics massacre 10, 123,
    138, 140, 146, 154, 162
  Operation Wrath of God 138–9,
    146–51, 155–6, 201 n.48
  Six Day War 6, 10, 62, 99, 109–11,
    163
  Suez crisis 5, 165–6
Arabs as demonological Other 2, 12, 153,
    164–8, 171–3; *see also* Orientalism
  Arabs as Indians 9, 55, 67–71, 73–4,
    95–7, 122–3, 167–8, 171–2, 187
    n.87
Arendt, Hannah 141

Babington, Bruce 23
The Bad Man 129
Bakhtin, Mikhail 73, 96
Balsam, Martin 112, 127, 198 n.129
Bana, Eric 153, 201 n.55
Bartov, Omer 6, 51–2, 62–3
Bataan 55

Bazin, André 67
Beattie, Keith 109
Beit-Hallahmi, Benjamin 167
Bell, Daniel 108
Bell-Metereau, Rebecca 118–19
Belton, John 94
Ben-Gurion, David 50, 85, 168, 171
Ben-Hur 7–8, 11, 13–15, 45, 47–8, 51, 58,
    88–9, 153, 159, 161–2, 165, 176–7
    n.5
  Christianization of the Jews 27–30, 39
  as Cold War allegory 7, 14–15, 26–7,
    47, 51
  masculinity 38–44, 47–8, 64
  Nazism 30–3
  Orientalism 171–2
Ben-Hur: A Tale of the Christ (film) 38
Ben-Hur: A Tale of the Christ (novel) 8,
    26, 38
Bentley, Eric 10, 78, 95
Berger, Senta 9, 76
Berkman, Ted; *see Cast a Giant Shadow*
    book
Bernstein, Matthew 165
The Big Country 59
The Birth of a Nation 2, 70–2, 96
Bishop, Joey 127
Biskind, Peter 43
Black Hawk Down 198 n.5, 201 n.55
Black Sunday (film) 10, 102–6, 109, 126–7,
    135–6, 156, 159, 161–3
  Arabs as demonological Other 137,
    153, 172
  captivity narrative 123
  Israel as model of action 109, 119–25,
    134, 136, 161–2, 173
  masculinity 109, 115, 117–20, 123–5,
    133
  as post-Vietnam film 113–15, 117–19,
    122, 125, 129, 162, 173
Black Sunday (novel) 10, 103, 105, 117,
    123, 196 n.190

Bluhdorn, Charles 103
Bly, Robert 108
Body of Lies 198 n.5
Bonnie and Clyde 99
Boone, Daniel 60, 97, 122
Bowling for Columbine 46–7
Boyd, Stephen 41–4, 185 n.68
Brando, Marlon 42–3, 64
Braudy, Leo 37, 88
Breines, Paul 34, 38, 62, 112
Britton, Andrew 128, 133, 157–8
Brooks, David 145, 148
Broken Arrow 56
Bronson, Charles 81, 112, 127
Brown, Hannah 145
Brynner, Yul 9, 19, 76, 89, 97, 178 n.31
  star image 37, 43, 181 n.89
Buntline, Ned 70
Burgoyne, Robert 1–2, 143
Buscombe, Edward 56
Bush, George 46
Bush, George W. 46, 154–5
Butch Cassidy and the Sundance Kid 64

Canby, Vincent 34, 104
Carter, Jimmy 113, 128–9, 131, 172
Cast a Giant Shadow (book) 76, 83, 86, 95–6
Cast a Giant Shadow (film) 9–10, 74, 75, 77–8, 103, 156, 159
  Arabs as demonological Other 95–8, 137, 153, 171–3
  captivity narrative 96–8, 123
  masculinity 88–9, 97
  pro-interventionism 82–99, 106–7, 125, 161–3
Cawelti, John G. 56–7
Champion 88
Chandler, Jeff 56
Cheyenne Autumn 56, 167, 204 n.21
Churchill, Winston 20
Cleopatra 98
Clift, Montgomery 42–3, 64
Cobb, Lee J. 8, 50
Coburn, James 81
Code of Silence 127
Cody, William 'Buffalo Bill' 70, 97, 122
Cohan, Steven 13, 19, 35, 37–8, 42–3, 49, 181 n.89, 182 n. 112

Cold War 56, 81, 92–3, 166, 168
  Communists as demonological Other 2, 137, 164
  Hollywood's engagement in 17–21
  masculinity 41–4
  religiosity 16–17, 20, 23, 26, 30
  Truman Doctrine 15–16
Coming Home 113
Condon, Richard 120
Cool Hand Luke 64
Cooper, Gary 43, 64
Cooper, James Fenimore 70
Corkin, Stanley 19, 81, 84
Cosell, Howard 140
Countryman, Edward 53
The Cowboys 120
Coyne, Michael 81
Craig, Daniel 153, 201 n.55
Creekmur, Corey K. 104
Crenna, Richard 197 n.123
Cripps, Thomas 56
Crockett, Davy 91–2, 97, 122
Crowther, Bosley 166
The Crusades 204 n.18

Danoch, Ehud 145–6
Dean, James 42–3, 64
The Deer Hunter 113–14, 135
The Delta Force 10–12, 102–3, 125–7, 159, 161–2, 164
  Arabs as demonological Other 137, 153, 172
  Israel as model of action 10, 103, 134–6, 161–2
  masculinity 132–3, 136
  as post-Vietnam film 10, 103, 131–3, 135
  as Reaganite Entertainment 130–4, 136
D'Emilio, John 41–2
DeMille, Cecil B. 13, 17–19, 21–2, 26, 32, 35
Derek, John 50, 68
Dern, Bruce 113–14, 120, 127
Devil's Doorway 56
Dickinson, Angie 9, 76
Dirty Harry 196 n.90
'Dirty Harry' Callahan 124, 130, 196 n.90
disaster film genre 102–3, 172
Doane, Mary Ann 63

Double Indemnity 117
Douglas, Kirk 9, 76, 91, 98, 111, 153, 185 n.68, 190 n.48
  star image 43, 64, 88–9, 125
Downs, Cathy 67
Dreyfuss, Richard 111
Drums along the Mohawk 68
Dulles, John Foster 16
Dunne, Philip 180 n.68
Dyer, Richard 44–6

Earthquake 101
East of Eden 43
Eastwood, Clint 120, 127, 130
Easy Rider 99
Ebert, Roger 152
Eichmann, Adolf 141, 156
Eisenhower, Dwight D. 5, 16, 79, 166
El Cid 45
Emerson, Jim 146
The Enforcer 196 n.90
epic films 49–50, 65, 101
  as Cold War allegory 7, 14–15, 163
Erens, Patricia 6, 86
E.T. the Extra-Terrestrial 145, 157
Evans, Peter William 23
Evans, Robert 103, 105–6
Executive Decision 138
Exodus (film) 8–9, 13, 48, 49–52, 57, 78, 83, 121, 153, 156, 159, 161–3
  Arabs as demonological Other 55, 67–71, 73–4, 96–7, 123, 137, 166–68, 172–3
  captivity narrative 70–1, 73–4, 96–7, 123
  glorification of Israeli militant groups 168–171
  masculinity 62–5
  Western film tropes 8–9, 51–2, 58–61, 65–71, 73–4, 75–6, 87, 96–8, 122–3
Exodus (novel) 8, 34, 49–50, 62

Fail-Safe 120
Fargo, James 196 n.90
feminism 10, 102, 108–9, 115, 117, 119, 133, 135
Finch, Peter 112
First Blood 132
Fonda, Henry 55, 67

Ford, Gerald 111
Ford, John 22, 49, 55–8, 68, 71–2, 77, 96, 167, 186 n.78, 187 n.102, 205 n.26
Fort Apache 55, 72, 186 n.78
Frankenheimer, John 102–3, 105–6, 117–21, 172, 195 n.82
Friedman, Lester D. 6, 22, 51–2, 65
Frost/Nixon 176–7 n.5
Fury at Showdown 189–90 n.43

Giant 49
Gilboa, Eytan 5, 110
The Godfather Part II 142
Golan, Menahem 10, 126, 134
Goldberg, Michelle 148
Goldwater, Barry 77
Gone with the Wind (book) 7
Gone with the Wind (film) 13–14
The Graduate 99
The Great Train Robbery 54
The Greatest Story Ever Told 45, 77
The Green Berets 9–10, 77–8, 91, 93–5, 97–8, 107, 112, 191 n.79
Griffith, D.W. 70–1
Griffith, Hugh 50
Guinness, Alec 185 n.68
Gun for a Coward 189–90 n.43
Gun Glory 189–90 n.43
Gunfight at the O.K. Corral 88, 185 n.72
The Gunfighter 56, 189 n.43
At Gunpoint 189–90 n. 43

Hang 'Em High 120
Hansen, Miriam 38, 70, 152–3, 158
Harris, Thomas; *see Black Sunday* (novel)
Hawks, Howard 22, 55
Hearts and Minds 82
Heflin, Van 101, 205 n.39
Hell Night 128
Herberg, Will 5
From Here to Eternity 43, 89
Heston, Charlton 25–6, 34–5, 38, 41, 62, 89, 101, 153, 185 n.68
  star image 44–7, 64, 125
Higashi, Sumiko 7, 14
High Noon 56, 67, 189 n.43
Hilliard, Charles 36
Hinds, Ciarán 153
Hoberman, J. 158

Hoffman, Dustin 125
Homans, Peter 60–1, 86, 170
Homeland 198 n.5
Hoover, J. Edgar 17, 19
Hopkins, Anthony 111
The Horse Soldiers 186 n.78
How the West Was Won 49, 77
Hud 57, 64
The Hurt Locker 198 n.5
The Hustler 64
Huston, John 180 n.68

Intolerance 98
Invasion U.S.A. 127
Iran hostage crisis 103, 131
Iron Man 198 n.5
Israel; *see also* Arab-Israeli conflict
    as military power 109–12

Jabotinsky, Vladimir 170
James Bond film series 172
Jaws 103, 120, 126, 145, 157
Jeffords, Susan 112, 130, 133
Jennings, Peter 140
Jews
    Christianization of the Jews 22–30, 33, 39
    tough Jews 34, 38–40, 62, 112
Johnny Concho 189–90 n.43
Johnson, Lyndon 5–6, 80, 90, 93, 106–7
Johnston, Eric 17
Jonas, George; *see* Vengeance
Judgment at Nuremberg 52

Kaplan, Amy 51
Karnow, Stanley 106
Kassovitz, Mathieu 153
Kazan, Lainie 127
Keller, Marthe 104–5
Kennedy, George 127
Kennedy, John F. 45, 78–81, 92, 107
Khalidi, Rashid 96, 148–9
Khartoum 45
Khatib, Lina 2
The Killers 197–8 n.123
Kimmel, Michael 108, 118–19
The King and I 37
The Kingdom 198 n.5
Kissinger, Henry 106

Klein, Aaron J. 147, 149
Kolker, Robert 128–30, 132–4, 137, 157
Kozloff, Sarah 32
Kracauer, Siegfried 20
Krauthammer, Charles 145
Kundnani, Arun 164–5

Ladd, Alan 125
Lancaster, Burt 43, 101, 111
Lanzmann, Claude 158
The Last of the Fast Guns 189–90 n.43
The Last Outpost 129
Last Train from Gun Hill 88
Law and Order 129
Lawford, Peter 50, 63
Leffler, Melvyn P. 16
The Left Handed Gun 64
Lehman, Peter 72
Leigh, Janet 119
Lenihan, John H. 56
Levy, Emanuel 77
Lincoln 158, 198–9 n.8
Little Big Man 122
Little, Douglas 5
Lonely Are the Brave 57, 88
The Longest Day 49, 77
Loshitzky, Yosefa 63, 68, 158
Lucas, George 126

The Magnificent Seven 81–4, 87, 91–2
Magnum Force 196 n.90
The Manchurian Candidate 102, 117–20
Man from Del Rio 189–90 n.43
The Man Who Shot Liberty Valance 56–7, 59, 205 n.26
Man without a Star 189–90 n. 43
Marathon Man 105
Mart, Michelle 23–5, 34, 36, 166
Martin, Dean 101
Marvin, Lee 127, 130, 134–5, 196 n.97, 197–8 n.123
McAlister, Melani 102, 110
McCarthy, Joe 32, 118
McCormick, Thomas J. 163
McKay, Jim 140
McPherson, Harry 110
McQueen, Steve 81
Medved, Michael 145, 148

Meir, Golda 141–2, 146, 148, 152, 154–5, 202 n.62
Midnight Cowboy 99
Mihalic, John 128
Miller, Douglas T. 16
Mineo, Sal 8, 50
The Misfits 57
Missing in Action 127
Missing in Action 2: The Beginning 127
Mission to Moscow 20
Miss V. from Moscow 20
Mivtsa Yonatan 134–5, 198 n.129
Monti-Belkaoui, Janice 110
Moore, Michael 46–7
Moore, Robin 93
Morin, Edgar 46
Mourlet, Michel 45
Munich 10–11, 136, 138–59, 161–2
   critical response 144–8
   as 'War on Terror' allegory 139–40, 152–9, 164
Mustazza, Leonard 89
My Darling Clementine 55, 67
My Son John 2

Nadel, Alan 26
Nasser, Gamal Abdel 5, 110, 204 n.18
Native Americans 1, 12, 56, 59, 67–74, 75, 94–6, 167; see also Arabs as Indians
Netanyahu, Yonatan 111, 135
Newman, Paul 8–9, 50, 62, 121, 153, 168
   star image 63–5
Nixon, Richard 77, 107, 114, 129, 176–7 n.5
Nordau, Max 33
Norris, Chuck 127–8, 130, 135
The North Star 20
Northwest Passage 71
Novarro, Ramon 38
Nowak, Marion 16

Olivier, Laurence 105, 185 n.68
Operation Burma 55
Operation Eagle Claw 131
Oren, Michael B. 3, 6, 109–11
Orientalism 2, 38, 104, 137, 165, 171–2
The Outlaw Josey Wales 122

Pacino, Al 125
Pappé, Ilan 163
The Passion of the Christ 145
Paterson, Thomas G. 19
Paths of Glory 88
The Pawnbroker 52
A Place in the Sun 43
Planet of the Apes 45
Plummer, Christopher 185 n.68
The Poseidon Adventure 101, 127
The Postman Always Rings Twice 117
Preminger, Otto 8, 13, 34, 50–1, 58
Prince, Stephen 104, 172
The Prodigal 24
The Proud Rebel 189–90 n.43
Pye, Douglas 60, 67, 72, 187 n.102

Quo Vadis 31

Rabin, Yitzhak 109–11
Raid on Entebbe 111–12
Raiders of the Lost Ark 128
Rambo (character) 99, 130–2
Rambo: First Blood Part II 2, 10, 103, 130–4
Raymond, Emilie 44, 46
Reagan, Ronald 46, 99, 126, 128–33
Reaganite Entertainment 127–30, 132–6, 157
Rebel without a Cause 43
Red River 55
Redacted 156
Rendition 156
Reservoir Dogs 196 n.97
Reston, James 80
Rio Grande 55, 72, 186 n.78
Rogin, Michael 2, 70, 118–19, 130, 137, 164
Rolling Thunder 113–14
Rosenstone, Robert A. 163
Rumsfeld, Donald 155
Rush, Geoffrey 156
Russo, Vito 41

Safty, Adel 4, 63, 170
Said, Edward 2, 38, 96; see also Orientalism
Saint, Eva Marie 8, 9, 50, 67
Samson & Delilah 24

Saud, Ibn 83
Saving Private Ryan 139, 158
Schatz, Thomas 57, 60
Scheider, Roy 126
Schindler's List 139, 143–4, 158–9
Schoenfeld, Gabriel 144–5
Schwarzenegger, Arnold 128, 138
Scranton, William 111
The Searchers 56–7, 71–4, 186 n.78
Semmerling, Tim Jon 2, 104, 114, 116, 196 n.87
September 11, 2001 11, 104, 138–9, 148, 152–7, 162, 164, 173, 192 n.13
Seven Samurai 81
Shaheen, Jack 166
Shalev, Eran 3
Shane 56, 61, 87, 125, 189 n.43
Shavelson, Melville 9, 76, 85, 89–91, 176 n.43
Shaw, Robert 120, 172
Shaw, Tony 2, 17, 22, 61, 102–3, 127, 168–9
Shazar, Zalman 6
She Wore a Yellow Ribbon 55, 72, 186 n.78
The Sheik 165
Shoah 158
Shohat, Ella 57–9, 68–9, 73, 98, 168, 170
Sidney, Sylvia 112
The Siege 138
Siegel, Don 196 n.90, 197–8 n.123
Silver, Matthew M. 50–1
Sinatra, Frank 9, 76, 89, 119–20
Sitting Bull 56
Skyjacked 101
Sleeper Cell 198 n.5
Slotkin, Richard 1–2, 54–6, 60, 69–70, 73, 75, 77, 81–2, 87, 96–7, 122
Smith, Henry Nash 70
The Son of the Sheik 165
Song of Russia 20
Spartacus 88
Spielberg, Steven 11, 138–9, 144–8, 151–3, 156–9, 162, 198–9 n.8
Stagecoach 72, 96
Stallone, Sylvester 128, 130
Stam, Robert 57–9, 68–9, 73, 168, 170
Stanwyck, Barbara 117
Star Wars: Episode IV – A New Hope 126
Stephanson, Anders 52

Stewart, James 56
The Sting 120
The Story of Ruth 24
A Streetcar Named Desire 43
Sudden Impact 130
Suid, Lawrence 76
Sword of Gideon 202 n.65
Syriana 156

The Tall T 189–90 n.43
Tasker, Yvonne 128, 130
Taxi Driver 113
Taylor, Elizabeth 111
Taylor, Maxwell D. 80
Taylor, Robert 56, 185 n.68
Taza, Son of Cochise 56, 68–9
The Ten Commandments (1923) 13
The Ten Commandments (1956) 7–8, 11, 13–14, 44–5, 47–8, 51, 58, 64, 68, 88, 153, 159, 161–2
  Christianization of the Jews 22–27, 30, 39
  as Cold War allegory 7, 14–15, 18–22, 26, 47, 51, 161, 165–6
  masculinity 34–8, 41–4, 47–8, 64, 89, 97
  Nazism 19, 30
  Orientalism 38, 165, 171–2
That's My Bush! 46–7
On the Waterfront 67
They Died with Their Boots On 186 n.78
The Thief of Baghdad 165
Three Russian Girls 20
Tivnan, Edward 8
Tobin, Jonathan 145
The Towering Inferno 101
Triumph of the Will 31
Troy 201 n.55
True Lies 138
Truman, Harry 4–5, 15–16, 20, 23
Trumbo, Dalton 8, 50, 88
Turner, Frederick Jackson 53, 73
Turner, Lana 117
24 198 n.5
Two-Minute Warning 101

Unconquered 71
United 93 198 n.5

United States
   benevolent supremacy 36, 66
   'chosenness' 3, 7, 15, 24, 52, 57–8
   frontier mythology 1, 34, 53, 60, 69–71, 75, 96–7, 122–3
   Judeo-Christian identity 5–7, 23–4, 66
   Manifest Destiny 52–3, 57–8, 70
   religious heritage 3–4
   Special relationship' with Israel 6–7, 15, 30, 111, 162–3
Uris, Leon; *see Exodus* novel
Ustinov, Peter 185 n.68

Valenti, Jack 93
Valentino, Rudolph 37–8
Vengeance 10, 138, 147–51, 155
Vernet, Marc 22
Victory at Entebbe 111
Vidal, Gore 41
Vidor, King 71, 189–90 n.43
Vietnam War 78–80, 82, 84–5, 90–1, 93–5, 106–8

Wallace, Lew; *see Ben-Hur: A Tale of the Christ* (novel)
War of the Worlds 158
'War on Terror' 11, 104, 136, 138–9, 153, 155–7, 162, 164
The War Wagon 88
Warden, Jack 112
Warshow, Robert 67
Wayne, John 9–10, 72, 76–8, 88–98, 120, 122, 171, 191 n.86

Batjac 9, 76–7, 88, 91, 93
   star image 43, 64–5, 72, 76–7, 125, 127
Wayne, Michael 91, 93–4
Weaver, Fritz 120, 127, 172
Weizmann, Chaim 171
western film genre 1–2, 22, 51–60, 66–7, 81, 86–7, 101, 122, 189 n.43, 205 n.26
Westmoreland, William 82
White, Hayden 162–3
White, Patricia 44
White Feather 56
Wieseltier, Leon 144, 148
Wilkinson, Rupert 33–5, 39–40, 63, 85, 89, 119
Williams, Linda 140, 149–50
Wills, Gary 77
Winkler, Martin 7, 14, 31–3
Winters, Shelley 127
Winthrop, Joh 3
Wisse, Ruth R. 109
Wood, Michael 22, 40, 185 n.68
Wood, Robin 158
Wright, Melanie 25
Wyke, Maria 7, 14
Wyler, William 7, 13, 26, 31–2, 38, 40–1, 180 n.68
Wylie, Philip 118–19

Xavier, Ismail 78

Yadin, Yigael 170

Zischler, Hanns 153

www.ingramcontent.com/pod-product-compliance
Lightning Source LLC
Chambersburg PA
CBHW072107010526
44111CB00037B/2021